PATHWAYS TO TEACHING SERIES

Practical Strategies for the Inclusive Classroom

JUDY W. WOOD

Virginia Commonwealth University

NATIONAL CENTER FOR EDUCATION INFORMATION

Merrill
is an imprint of

Upper Saddle River, New Jersey
Columbus, Ohio

Library of Congress Cataloging-in-Publication Data
Wood, Judy W.
Practical strategies for the inclusive classroom/Judy Wood.
p. cm. — (Pathways to teaching series)
ISBN-13: 978-0-13-513058-2
ISBN-10: 0-13-513058-1
1. Inclusive education—United States. 2. Classroom management—United States.
3. Teachers—In-service training—United States. I. Title.
LC1201.W667 2009
371.9'046—dc22

2007052421

Vice President and Executive Publisher: Jeffery W. Johnston
Executive Editor: Darcy Betts Prybella
Editorial Assistant: Nancy J. Holstein
Project Manager: Sarah N. Kenoyer
Production Coordinator: Sarvesh Mehrotra/Aptara, Inc.
Design Coordinator: Diane C. Lorenzo
Photo Coordinator: Valeric Schultz
Cover Design: Jeff Vanik
Cover Image: Jupiter Images
Operations Specialist: Susan W. Hannahs
Director of Marketing: Quinn Perkson
Marketing Coordinator: Brian Mounts

The book was set in 10/12 Palatino by Aptara, Inc. The book and cover were printed and bound by Courier Stoughton, Inc.

Photo Credits: Chapter 1: Valerie Schultz/Merrill, Chapter 2: Laura Bolesta/Merrill, Chapter 3: Hope Madden/Merrill, Chapter 4: Laima Druskis/PH College, Chapter 5: Anthony Magnacca/Merrill, Chapter 6: Patrick White/Merrill, Chapter 7: Hope Madden/Merrill, Chapter 8: Barbara Schwartz/Merrill

---

Pearson Education Ltd.
Pearson Education Singapore Pte. Ltd.
Pearson Education Canada, Ltd.
Pearson Education–Japan
Pearson Education Australia Pty. Limited
Pearson Education North Asia Ltd.
Pearson Educación de Mexico, S.A. de C.V.
Pearson Education Malaysia Pte. Ltd.

Merrill
is an imprint of

10 9 8 7 6 5 4 3 2 1
ISBN-13: 978-0-13-513058-2
ISBN-10: 0-13-513058-1

Brief Contents

This text presents practical, research-based interventions to be used so that students are provided access to the curriculum. Information will be presented for providing appropriate interventions during lesson planning (instruction and assessment) and during lesson implementation.

Teacher Resources

The end of each chapter includes resources for teacher use. Specific to each chapter, websites, and resources are provided.

Inside Text Cover

The inside cover of the text provides a matrix for Interstate New Teacher Assessment and Support Consortium (INTASC) Standards for Beginning Teachers. The alignment of the text's chapters to the standards will be presented.

ACKNOWLEDGEMENTS

A book is never an individual effort. Many members were on my team to see this project to fruition. My appreciation is expressed to Darcy Betts Prybella, editor; Sarah Kenoyer, project manager; Diane Lorenzo, design coordinator; and Jeff Vanik, cover designer.

Many reviewers assisted with the long process of reading chapters, reviewing outlines, reading more chapters, and so on. For their valuable comments and vision for this mission, I am indebted to Chris Burkett, Columbia College; Pamela D. Parkinson, Western Governors University; Marlene A. Sassaman, Brevard Community College; and Jayna Snyder, Brevard College.

The first string on the team worked endlessly typing, researching, outlining, seeking permissions, and seeing that all the endless tasks finally came to an end. I humbly thank Paula Friedrich, my administrative assistant, and David A. Duncan, my husband, for their contribution to this work.

CHAPTER FORMAT

All chapters have the same format, one that aligns with effective teaching and presents a model for all educators.

- **Chapter-at-a-Glance.** Each chapter has a Chapter-at-a-Glance illustration to help the reader see the complete structure of the chapter and how all sections of the chapter are connected.
- **Learner Objectives.** All chapters begin with learner objectives that explain what each learner will accomplish upon completion of the chapter.
- **Vignettes.** Each chapter will have a vignette and real-life examples sprinkled throughout the chapter.
- **Summary.** At the conclusion of each chapter, a brief summary is provided. This serves to help students reflect on the information covered.
- **Resources and Suggested Readings.** Each chapter concludes with a list of resources and suggested readings that the reader may find helpful.

INFORMATION FOR SPECIAL EDUCATION AND GENERAL EDUCATION TEACHERS

To better serve all students and our readers, each chapter includes information on diversity, technology, classroom collaboration, and standards-based education. A matrix for Interstate New Teacher Assessment and Support Consortium (INTASC) Standards for Beginning Teachers seeking national board certification is included in the text's inside cover.

Classroom Collaboration

Professionals must work together to provide quality education for all students. Strategies for professionals to use when co-teaching or collaborating are included.

Standards-Based Education

The year 2006 marked a decade of standards-based educational reform. With the development of standards, alignment of curriculum to the standards, and accountability, a transformation in our nation's educational systems began. High-stakes assessment also marked this decade. As the decade moved forward, systems were being held accountable not only for the general education student, but focus began to shift to students with special needs. No longer would this population be exempt from state testing. Educators now must provide access to the general curriculum for all students, and the students with special needs will be included in state testing.

PREFACE

INTRODUCTION

The expanding student population and fewer teachers selecting education as a profession have produced national teacher shortages. The demand from the No Child Left Behind Act to have "highly qualified" educators in all classrooms has added to school systems' ever growing teacher training issues. Teachers with degrees are now seeking alternate areas of certification. This text, *Practical Strategies for the Inclusive Classroom*, is part of the *Pathways to Teaching Series,* which includes five texts that address teacher shortage and professional development issues. Additional topics in this series include English Language Learners, teaching methods, classroom management, and assessment. This text complements the other texts designed for teacher certification by presenting a two-tiered research-based process. The first tier is a problem solving approach for identifying if a problem exists or could exist, what hypothesis should be made, and why the problem is occurring. The second tier provides a framework for selecting and employing research-based strategies/interventions for the identified problem. The text focuses on quality classroom instruction. Practical, seamless interventions will be provided for classroom instruction. The interventions may be used across ability levels and grade levels, and require little or no resources. The interventions are seamless or universal in that they may be used in an on going manner in the classroom and used for all students.

ORGANIZATION OF THE TEXT

Chapter 1 presents the big picture of inclusion and critical terms. Chapter 2 presents the "process" of inclusion, collaboration, and co-teaching. Chapter 3 continues with the second component of inclusion, the content, where we intervene. The remaining chapters focus on what teachers do to include all students. Specifically, Chapter 3 introduces the SAALE Model (a Systematic Approach for Assessing/Accessing the Learning Environment). This model is a problem-solving approach for identifying student problems so appropriate interventions may be selected and implemented. This process assists in preventing any child from being left behind. The process also answers the call for the Response-to-Intervention (RTI) language in IDEA 2004. The remaining chapters 4 through 8 provide extensive information on interventions to be used in instructional planning and implementation in inclusive settings.

This book is lovingly dedicated to the following persons who continuously support and encourage me on my journey.

Aunt Janet Nutter, my friend and later-life mom.

Paula Friedrich, my friend and administrative assistant. Paula has blessed me with two granddaughters-of-choice, Alaina, Emma, and one grandson, Clay.

David A. Duncan, my friend and husband.

Eddie Wood, Scott Wood, and Jason Wood, my sons, who have provided me inspiration for life, and have walked with me through good times and bad, always cheering me along. My sons have also gifted me with two wonderful daughters-in-law, Ashley and Melissa. And they have blessed me with four beautiful "grands": Clay, the twins Tanner and Camden, and Rylan. All have made contributions by coloring on the manuscript, cutting finished products, sitting in my lap, giving me hugs when I was tired, singing and dancing for my entertainment, and helping at the keyboard. Who couldn't author a book with all of this assistance!

CONTENTS

Chapter 1

SETTING THE STAGE: THE BIG PICTURE

Key Terms

Interventions *(page 6)*
Preplanned Interventions *(page 6)*
Spontaneous Interventions *(page 6)*

CHAPTER-AT-A-GLANCE

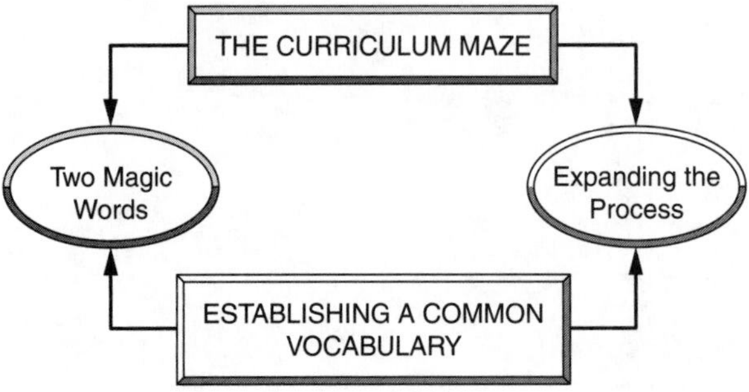

LEARNER OBJECTIVES

After you read this chapter, you will be able to

- *Discuss the big picture of curriculum.*
- *Discuss the importance of the words* assess *and* access.
- *Define interventions and the two types.*

VIGNETTE

In the third grade, I was issued a third-grade math book. As a third-grade student, I thought each day brought a new lesson. I never thought that Monday's lesson had anything to do with Tuesday's. On Monday all I had to do was simply finish the lesson. On Tuesday, simply finish the lesson. On Wednesday, my "third-grade mind" knew that I only had to survive Wednesday's math lesson, which had nothing to do with Monday's or Tuesday's lessons. Of course my mind-set was incorrect. In math, Monday's lesson prepared me for Tuesday's, and Monday's and Tuesday's lessons were the foundation for Wednesday's. My point is that as a young child, I only saw math lessons as "lessons," not as building blocks for future lessons. Of course math lessons build each day.

Note: From Reaching the Hard to Teach *by J. W. Wood, 2008, Richmond, VA: Judy Wood, Inc. Reprinted with permission.*

To children, education and the many "lessons" students experience appear to be separate entities. Even to professional educators, all the extensive information received runs together and nothing appears to fit. Setting the Stage for this text will assist the reader in seeing how all parts of the text "fit," that is, support one another. Let's start with the "Curriculum Maze."

THE CURRICULUM MAZE

In America, educators for many years have frantically raced to establish standards, align the curriculum to the standards, teach the students, and hope that everyone will do well when testing time arrives. This hope is only 50% correct. Figure 1.1 displays this "maze."

Figure 1.1 The curriculum maze.

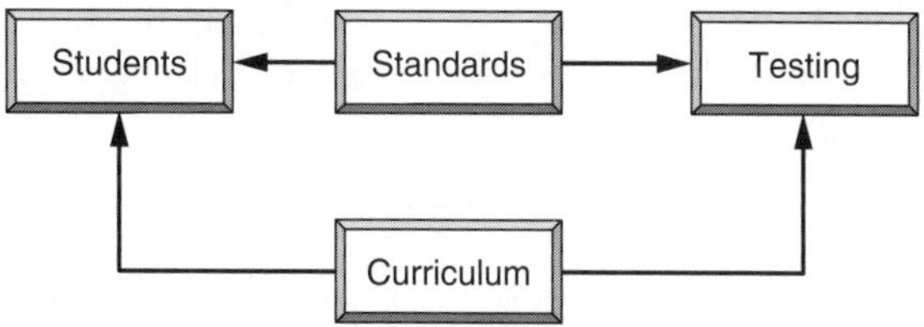

Note: From *Reaching the Hard to Teach* by J. W. Wood, 2008, Richmond, VA: Judy Wood, Inc. Reprinted with permission.

Educators can align the curriculum to the standards as much as they wish, but this alignment is only 50% of the process. The curriculum must also be aligned to the students. Now this is where this text fits.

Two Magic Words

Two magic words make possible the second 50% of the Curriculum Maze. The words are *access* and *interventions*. (See Figure 1.2.) Students must be able to access the curriculum, and providing interventions assists with this access. Included in

Figure 1.2 The curriculum maze and two magic words.

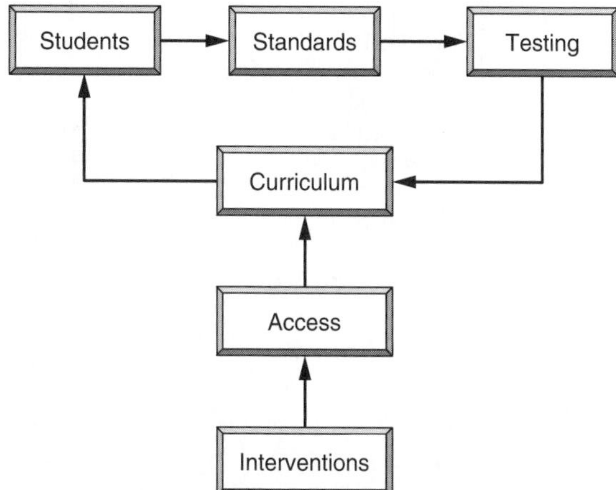

Note: From *Reaching the Hard to Teach* by J. W. Wood, 2008, Richmond, VA: Judy Wood, Inc. Reprinted with permission.

this second 50% of the Maze is that the curriculum must be aligned with the students. That is, we can align curriculum to standards, but to ensure that the curriculum reaches students, they must have access, or the curriculum must be taught to students in a manner in which they "get" the curriculum. Interventions provide this access. Let's expand the picture.

Expanding the Process

For students to be able to access the curriculum, however, they must be included, thus the term *inclusion* in Figure 1.3. However, inclusion is a general term, not an

Figure 1.3 The SAALE model process in the big picture.

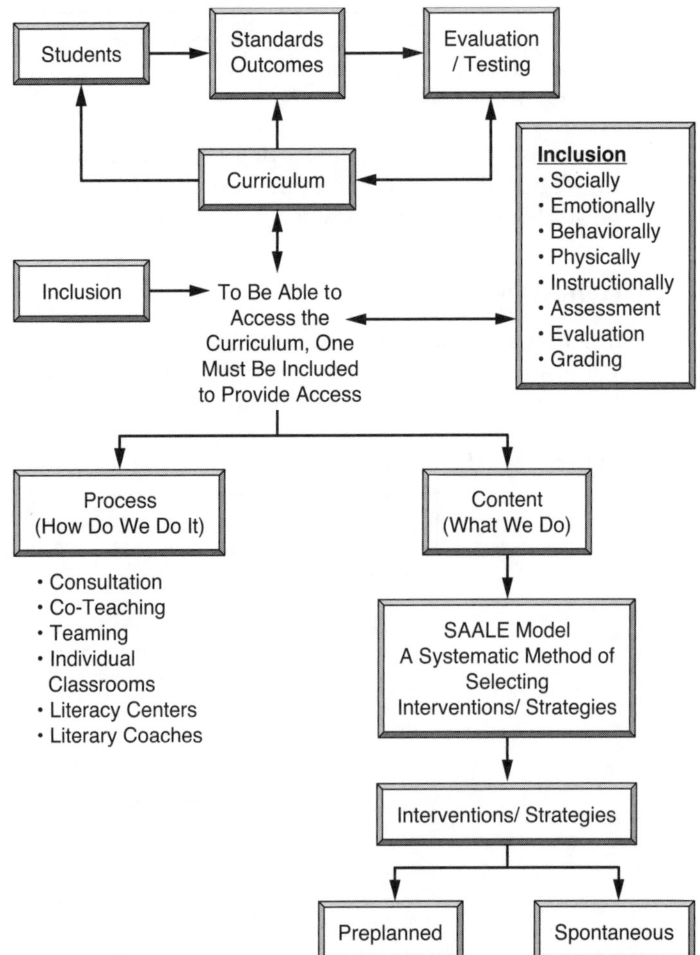

Note: From *Reaching the Hard to Teach* by J. W. Wood, 2008, Richmond, VA: Judy Wood, Inc. Reprinted with permission.

educational one. We are either included or excluded in life. These inclusion or exclusion measures may be social, emotional, behavioral, physical, instructional, or through evaluation and grading. Students must be included in the curriculum to have access to it. They cannot move on to standards (or outcomes) or evaluation if they do not first have access to the curriculum.

The word *inclusion* has become attached educationally to the regular education classroom. Initially, inclusion referred to students who were placed in regular education classrooms for part or all of the day. Depending on district philosophy, students of all disability areas were totally or partially included. In some districts perhaps only the student with mild disabilities were included. The range of disability and duration of time in the general education classroom varies. However, this writer sees inclusion as a "life word." A student may or may not have a disability and be included or excluded.

Access is provided in two ways: *the process* (how we do it) and *the content* (what we do). The process of inclusion is displayed in Figure 1.3 and discussed in Chapter 2. The content of inclusion (Figure 1.3) is what we do to get the curriculum to students. This is where the magic word *intervention* comes into play. The SAALE Model provides this access. Chapters 3–8 will discuss the "what to do" to get the curriculum to the students. The Model uses interventions for reaching each student.

ESTABLISHING A COMMON VOCABULARY

Figure 1.3, The SAALE Model Process in the Big Picture, presents the relationship among the student, standards, evaluation, and curriculum. The curriculum must be accessible to all students. The SAALE Model provides this access. We have two ways to access: the process (collaboration) and the content (the Model). Intervention is the secret to accessing or getting curriculum to students. Many terms surface when we speak of doing something differently: *accommodations, strategies, modifications, adaptations,* or *supports.* I like to use the term *intervention* (Wood, 2006).

The term *intervention* has another use in the schools because of the Response to Intervention (RTI) process. RTI will be discussed in detail in Chapter 2. According to RTI, if students are not at benchmark, we provide systematic interventions, monitor the progress, adjust instruction, and provide intensive intervention as needed. Chapter 5 discusses adapting lesson plans, standards, benchmarks, and so on, and these are visually displayed in Figure 5.1. Therefore, some educators prefer to use the term *intervention* only when referring to the RTI process. This writer likes to keep education simple! So, *interventions* may be used at any time during the educational process. For example, Johnny is having difficulty reading. However, he will be held accountable for his social studies lesson. The teacher simply provides Johnny with the social studies book chapter on CD, Johnny listens to the lesson, and now he has been provided *access* to the social studies chapter. Johnny may or may not be referred to the RTI committee for suggested interventions. His teacher handled the issue within the classroom.

Research Notes for Classroom Application

Diversity in language, culture, and ability is increasing in classrooms across the nation, creating a need for teachers to understand how they can most effectively meet the needs of all learners. Several interventions have been shown through research to be especially successful in helping students at risk of falling behind access the curriculum (Snow, 2003). These include

- Whole-class instruction: the teacher working with the entire class simultaneously. A combination of approaches that help students come to their own understanding of a concept and practices that recognize the teacher as an expert passing along information to students is best.
- Cognitively oriented instruction: strategies that help students think about how they learn and how to better plan and reflect. The most effective interventions help students become better learners in a wide variety of contexts and content areas.
- Small groups: instruction in both like-ability and mixed-ability small groups. The peer interaction that occurs in cooperative learning can help low-achieving students if the activity is carefully planned and implemented.
- Tutoring: using a wide variety of individuals, with the proper training, to tutor at-risk students. The basis of a good tutoring program should be a strong theoretical approach or a step-by-step structure.
- Peer tutoring: pairs students with each other in the classroom. Highly structured sessions in which students are instructed in their roles and carefully monitored can effectively meet the needs of diverse students.
- Computer-assisted instruction: using a computer to present concepts or topics, monitor student growth, and appropriately adjust to needed advancements. Teacher or tutor training may make this intervention even more effective.

Including these interventions in the instruction of a diverse student body can help level the playing field for struggling learners and give them the best opportunity for succeeding in the classroom.

Source: Snow, D. (2003). *Noteworthy perspectives: Classroom strategies for helping at-risk students.* Retrieved December 28, 2006 from http://www.mcrel.org/PDF/Noteworthy/5032TG_NW2003_ClassroomStrategies.pdf.

Note: From *Reaching the Hard to Teach* by J. W. Wood, 2008, Richmond, VA: Judy Wood, Inc. Reprinted with permission.

Interventions: Trying what we have not tried. There are two types of interventions: **preplanned interventions** and **spontaneous interventions**.

1. **Preplanned**—Interventions preplanned by the teacher during the lesson planning stage.

Example: Intervention required by IEP or 504. Teacher establishes choices within the lesson based on ability levels, learning styles, interest, and so on. Teacher establishes choices for assignments, projects, products, assessment measures, and the like.

2. **Spontaneous**—Interventions implemented by an educator when a student's need for options occur during instruction implementation. This is an "on-your-feet" change in what you are doing so that students' needs are met.
   Example: You are giving oral directions (several at one time). A student only needs one direction at a time. During a class discussion you realize a student is lost. You quickly write the main points on an overhead or chalkboard.
   You will be referred back to preplanned and spontaneous interventions as we travel through the text. Using these two terms, *preplanned* and *spontaneous*, prepares us for differentiating instruction. Remember these terms!

Now that we have a basic understanding of the puzzle and how the pieces fit, let's begin taking a closer look at the *process* or how the student accesses the curriculum.

SUMMARY

Chapter 1 sets the stage for the remainder of the text. Understanding how the puzzle pieces fit helps provide a mental visual of where the text is going and how each chapter builds on the previous one. We must know where we are going before our journey begins. Our journey begins with Chapter 2, which discusses the process of how educators work together (collaboration) and how two educators may teach together (co-teaching).

RESOURCES

Council for Exceptional Children (CEC)
1110 West Glebe Road
Suite 300
Arlington, VA 22201-5704
703-620-3660
www.cec.sped.org

SUGGESTED READING

Wood, J. W. (2006). *Teaching students in inclusive settings: Adapting and accommodating instruction*. Upper Saddle River, NJ: Merrill/Prentice Hall.

Chapter 2

THE PROCESS: COLLABORATION AND CO-TEACHING

Key Terms

Collaboration *(page 15)*
Co-Teaching *(page 17)*

CHAPTER-AT-A-GLANCE

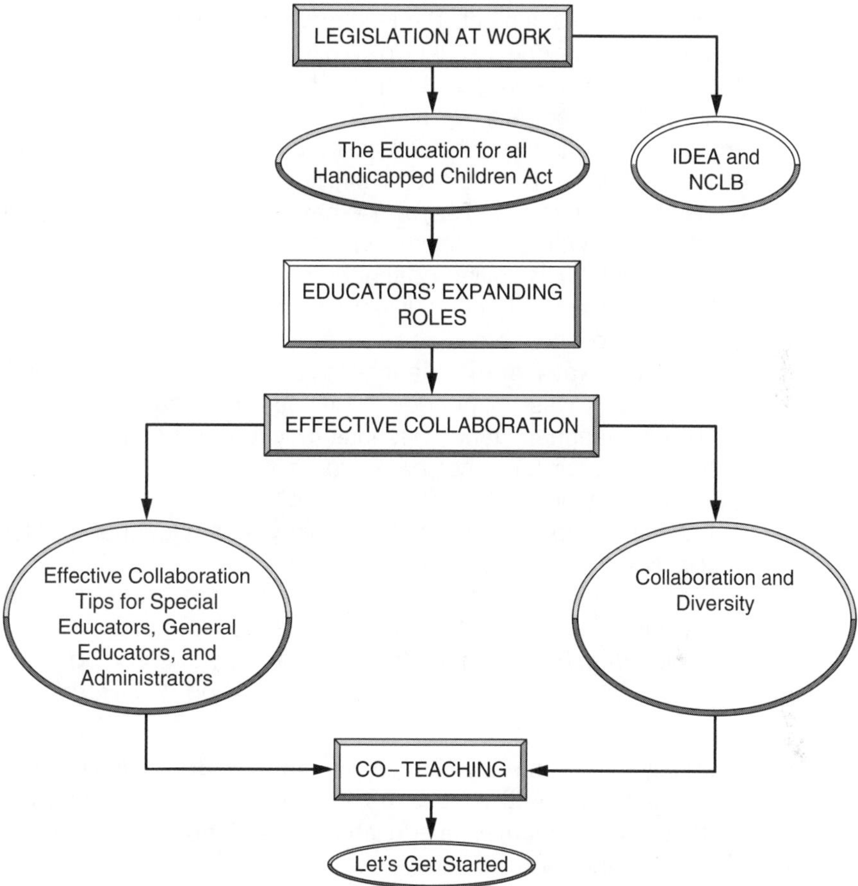

LEARNER OBJECTIVES

After you read this chapter, you will be able to

- *Define collaboration and explain how collaboration differs from co-teaching.*
- *Discuss the skills necessary for an effective collaboration process.*
- *Explain the three tiers of the Response to Intervention (RTI) Model.*
- *List those responsible for educating all students and their roles.*
- *Explain how collaboration and multicultural education are similar.*
- *List the various models used to provide effective co-teaching.*
- *List the three stages of the co-teaching process and explain how the eight components of each stage contribute to a successful collaborative learning environment.*
- *Explain how scheduling affects co-teaching.*

VIGNETTE

Observing a co-taught classroom, I saw that every student was on task and engaged in the assignment. The teachers were busy moving from student to student. From time to time one teacher would direct teach a skill as the second walked around the classroom checking on learning. The class was running so smoothly. Of course, both teachers had been expecting my visit. Finally, I asked the teachers if they would mind if I spoke to the class and asked a few questions. Both teachers were secure in their abilities or I would not have felt comfortable asking my questions.

I asked the students, "Do you like having two teachers?" I received an extremely loud, "Yes!" "Would you tell me why?" I asked. The answers were interesting and certainly validated having co-teachers in the classroom. Responses follow:

"When I attend this class I feel like a 'someone.' The class is small and the teachers know my name."

"There is always an extra teacher to answer a question when I am confused."

"Last year I was suspended 10 times—this year only twice." (A smile came across the teachers' faces because they realized that this was an improvement.)

"If one teacher turns her back, you better watch out. There is always another teacher on the loose!"

"I receive more help in this class. Last year the teacher was too busy with other students to help me."

"We have a phone in the room. Last year when it rang, I would get into trouble. This year when it rings, I know that one teacher answers and one watches me!"

Note: From Reaching the Hard to Teach *by J. W. Wood, 2008, Richmond, VA: Judy Wood, Inc. Reprinted with permission.*

The stage has been set for looking at "how we do" inclusion. That is, what service delivery models will we use to facilitate student movement into more inclusive settings? Many changes in educational legislation have pushed Americans to see the importance of inclusion.

The past four decades have witnessed the greatest changes in our educational system. Merely 40 years ago, students with disabilities and students at risk of not achieving school success rarely crossed the stages at high school graduation. These students dropped out or were pushed out as they traveled their educational pathway. Legislation began to flow, though slowly, and students with special needs and their families began to see hope, however dim.

LEGISLATION AT WORK

The Education for All Handicapped Children Act

The Education for All Handicapped Children Act (EAHCA, P.L. 94-142) mandated that children with disabilities have access to public schools, and provided several safeguards and minimum standards for their participation. States were required to follow those minimum standards in order to receive federal financial assistance. Congress defined the purposes of the act as follows:

- "To assure that all children with disabilities have available to them… a free appropriate public education which emphasizes special education and related services designed to meet their unique needs"
- "To assure that the rights of children with disabilities and their parents… are protected"
- "To assist States and localities to provide for the education of all children with disabilities"
- "To assess and assure the effectiveness of efforts to educate all children with disabilities"

IDEA and NCLB

Public Law 94-142 has undergone many changes. In the 2004 update, the Individuals with Disabilities Act (IDEA), the language of the law was aligned with the language of the No Child Left Behind (NCLB) Act of 2001. This law included new requirements for states to develop standards for grades 3 through 8 and in high school in key academic areas—reading/language arts, science, and mathematics. Annual assessments related to those standards were implemented.

IDEA 2004 refers to the use of scientific, research-based interventions to become part of the eligibility for learning disabilities. Local Educational Agencies (LEA) were provided with the option of using Response to Interventions (RTI) as one approach when determining a student's educational needs. RTI provides that,

> …when determining whether a child has a specific learning disability… a local education agency shall not be required to take into consideration whether the child has a severe discrepancy between achievement and intellectual ability in oral expression, listening comprehension, written expression, basic reading skill, reading comprehension, mathematical calculation, or mathematical reasoning. (20 U.S.C. 1414 (b)(6)(A))

The RTI movement is new for tenured teachers as well as for beginning teachers. The process of determining if a student has a learning disability has been under discussion for many years. The federal legal framework now allows states to use the Response to Intervention (RTI) model instead of the other methods states selected to determine if a student has a learning disability. Section 300.307, Specific Learning Disabilities of IDEA 2004 states:

1. *General.* A State must adopt criteria for determining whether a child has a specific learning disability… the criteria adopted by the State –
2. May not require the use of a severe discrepancy between intellectual ability and achievement for determining whether a child has a specific learning disability as defined in § 300.8; ["Discrepancy" model]

3. Must permit the use of a process that determines if the child responds to scientific, research-based intervention...[RTI model]

Therefore, states may choose to use the Response to Intervention approach for determining if a student has a learning disability. Each state selects the details of what their RTI model will include. Traditionally, a simple triangle represents the RTI process (Figure 2.1). This process replaces the traditional referral to placement process. This process is discussed in any text that presents the traditional service delivery model. In brief, the RTI triangle/model has three tiers.

Tier 1 is implemented within the general education classroom. Any student may be in need of academic or behavioral assistance to succeed in the classroom. The RTI hope is that 80% to 90% of students can be helped by implementing interventions and measuring the progress of the interventions. Ongoing professional development will be made available to give educators the necessary tools to provide quality education for all students. The team, using a problem-solving approach, will identify the necessary interventions to be used in Tier 1. If the student's progress in Tier 1 is insufficient, the teacher will refer the student back to the school support team. This team is comprised of teachers from the building and, on occasion, a specialist from the district.

Figure 2.1 Response to intervention.

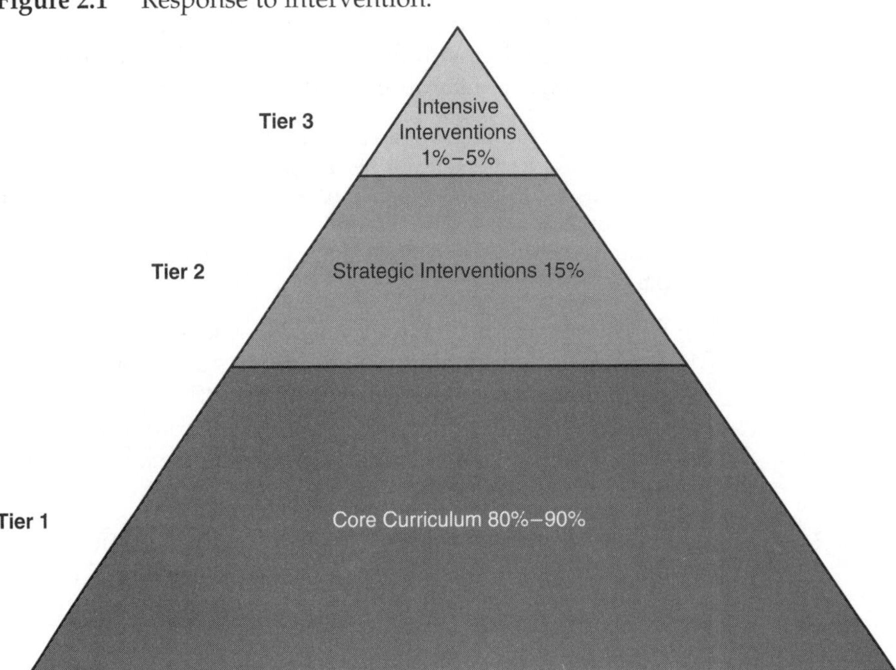

Research Notes for Classroom Application

While the Response to Intervention (RTI) approach has been used in education for years, it has recently received much more attention as its potential for helping all students who struggle with learning has been explored. The benefits of using the RTI approach include (National Joint Committee on Learning Disabilities, 2005) the following:

- Identification of students with learning disabilities early in their academic lives.
- Reduction in the number of students referred for special education.
- Reduction in the overidentification of minority students.
- Data more relevant to instruction.
- Promotion of collaboration between general and special educators, other school professionals, and parents.

The ability-achievement discrepancy method of identifying students with learning disabilities is increasingly criticized because it requires students to fall behind for a substantial period of time before they are eligible for special education assistance. Under the RTI model, students receive well-designed instruction and intensified interventions as early as kindergarten or first grade (National Center for Learning Disabilities, 2006). This increases the likelihood that many struggling students will succeed without the need for special education (Cortiella, 2004). Those that do not respond to these interventions are evaluated by a multidisciplinary team to determine eligibility for special education services.

Additional research is necessary to refine the RTI process, and the U.S. Department of Education is funding several research initiatives (Samuels, 2006). Among these studies, researchers are trying to determine valid ways of monitoring a student's "responsiveness" to an intervention, define "nonresponsiveness," and also determine how accurately RTI can be used to predict a student's learning disability. This continuing research further strengthens the promise a well-implemented RTI system holds for struggling students with or without learning disabilities.

Sources: Cortiella, C. (2004). *Responsiveness-to-Intervention—an Overview.* Retrieved December 30, 2006 from http://www.schwablearning.org/articles.asp?r=840.

National Center for Learning Disabilities. (2006). Response to intervention. In *New roles in Response to Intervention: Creating success for schools and children* (pp. 35–40). Retrieved December 30, 2006 from http://www.ncld.org/images/stories/downloads/ldnews/Rti/new%20roles%20in%20rti-november%202006.pdf.

National Joint Committee on Learning Disabilities. (2005). *Responsiveness to Intervention and learning disabilities.* Retrieved December 30, 2006 from http://www.ldonline.org/?module=uploads&func=download&fileId=461.

Samuels, C. A. (2006, November 6). Ed. Dept. backs research plans for RTI method. *Education Week.* Retrieved December 30, 2006 from http://www.edweek.org/ew/articles/2006/11/08/11rti.h26.html?qs=rti.©

Note: From *Reaching the Hard to Teach* by J. W. Wood, 2008, Richmond, VA: Judy Wood, Inc. Reprinted with permission.

Tier 2 begins. The team will recommend protocol interventions to be used during Tier 2. These are more intensive interventions and frequently ones designated by the district. Typically, instruction and interventions are delivered in small groups, and data are collected more frequently. Student response to previous teaching and interventions is measured. Assessments are administered to pinpoint areas of difficulty among students who continue to struggle. Based on measured results, interventions become more intense. Progress monitoring continues. It is hoped that 5% to 10% of students will respond to Tier 2.

Tier 3 begins. This is the most intensive level. It is where interventions are delivered individually and student progress is monitored frequently. Tier 3 interventions may take place in regular or special education. At this level, a problem-solving team typically monitors the effectiveness of the individualized interventions and adapts them as needed. If needed, an evaluation for special education usually takes place while the student is at Tier 3. It is hoped that 1% to 5% of the students will meet success in Tier 3.

EDUCATORS' EXPANDING ROLES

Calls for sharing the responsibility in educating all students echo across America. Legislation has personified the echoes. To provide equal educational opportunities for students with disabilities and those at risk, those in the education field must alter traditional roles and responsibilities. No longer can general educators direct their teaching efforts to the middle level of the class, using standardized teaching techniques, curricula, testing procedures, and grading systems. Special educators must also modify their views of themselves, particularly their role as entities separate from the rest of the school. Their new roles (Bauwens & Hourcade, 1995) require that they consult with general educators about strategies to use with students with special needs within the context of the general education classroom (Gersten, Darch, Davis, & George, 1991). The pull-out program models of the past have not been found to benefit children (Walther-Thomas, Korinek, McLaughlin, & Williams, 2000). Building administrators can no longer follow traditional grouping, placement, and scheduling practices, nor can they expect to meet students' needs using the lockstep sequence of the traditional curriculum within the structure of a graded system. District administrators must realize that maintaining separate budgets for general and special education is not cost efficient and therefore not fiscally defensible. Increasingly, parents are realizing that they can no longer leave their children's education in the hands of the experts; they, too, are now considered expert members of their children's educational teams. Finally, students with disabilities and those at risk must assume some responsibility for their own educational outcomes, as much as their abilities allow. They must let their teachers and parents know when they need modifications in the general environment, which modifications are successful, and which ones are not.

The reality of education is that no individual can or should assume full responsibility for a student's success in inclusive settings. Teachers, parents, administrators, related services personnel, counselors, students, and the general school community must accept and share responsibility to provide equal educational opportunities to all students, regardless of the diversity of the population.

EFFECTIVE COLLABORATION

Collaboration is an ongoing interaction that occurs when stakeholders are planning for students, solving student-related problems, or making student-related or school decisions. When educators are sharing responsibilities for students, effective collaboration is crucial. The concept of inclusion, a special philosophy defined by school districts, is the core of collaboration and school-based delivery systems. Inclusion is a commitment to educate each student with disabilities with their peers without disabilities. Educational services are brought to the student in the general education classroom. Inclusion is a process or a delivery system that involves collaboration, which is "how people work together, not what they do" (Friend & Bursuck, 2002, p. 77).

Effective Collaboration Tips for Special Educators, General Educators, and Administrators

Special educators and general educators must strive to acknowledge that they both have specialized skills, but that their experiences, values, and knowledge bases are different. Both are stakeholders in a student's educational process and both will share a place on the student's team. As the team begins to develop, both educators take on new roles, and the ability to communicate becomes more important.

Special Educators. Special educators should recognize that the techniques of instructional and behavioral management used by general educators can be effective means of working with students with special needs. For instance, teachers in regular classrooms must respond rapidly to the needs of many students every day. The special education teacher should acknowledge that placing a student with special needs in a general classroom does not relieve the teacher of his or her responsibilities to the other students. The special educator must realize that no classroom teacher can devote the majority of time to any one student. Finally, the special education teacher must strive to recognize that teaching techniques or programs that may be successful in a separate special education class may not be appropriate for the general classroom environment.

General Educators. General educators must strive to understand that special educators may be responsible for a large number of students in a variety of settings and therefore have a limited amount of time to devote to each student. General educators should accept that a new intervention strategy or instructional approach may not have an immediate effect and that a fair trial must be given before a technique is judged ineffective. Finally, general educators should be familiar with each student's IEP, sharing responsibility with special educators for determining how goals and objectives can be reinforced during the course of the general education activities.

Administrators. Administrators are in a unique position to promote successful collaboration between special and general educators. Because of their dual roles of instructional leader and building administrator, principals are central to the implementation and maintenance of effective collaborative arrangements. Not only can they enact the necessary administrative procedures to accommodate students with special needs in inclusive settings, but they can also provide access to necessary training opportunities for staff members who are implementing classroom adaptations. District-level administrators, who play more central roles in the allocation of resources and development of district-wide policies, can also have a direct influence on the implementation of integrated programming at the building level.

Collaboration and Diversity

As the inclusive movement and the emphasis on collaboration grow, educators can work together on blending multicultural education within our schools. Perhaps this emphasis could become a planning format for inclusive educators. Educators have progressively learned how one concept can spread throughout different content subjects. Just as educators strive to integrate standards into the curriculum and students with disabilities into general education classrooms, so must they make multicultural education a central part of the school's curriculum. No longer can schools offer multicultural education as a separate entity such as in articles, units, or separate lessons. "Multicultural education is more than content; it includes policy, learning climate, instructional delivery, leadership, and evaluation" (see Banks, 1994; Bennett, 2003; Grant & Gomez, 2000).

When integrating multicultural content within the decision-making process in the class, teachers might do the following:

- Create learning goals and objectives that incorporate multicultural aspects, such as "developing students' ability to write persuasively about social justice concerns."
- Use a frequency matrix to ensure that the teacher includes a wide variety of ethnic groups in a variety of ways in curriculum materials and instructional activities.

- Introduce different ethnic groups and their contributions on a rotating basis.
- Include several examples from different ethnic experiences to explain subject matter concepts, facts, and skills.
- Show how multicultural content, goals, and activities intersect with subject-specific curricular standards. (Gay, 2004, p. 32)

CO-TEACHING

Co-teaching, also known as cooperative teaching, is another model for integrating students with special needs into the general education classroom. The special educator participates in instruction in the general classroom. In co-teaching, however, the special educator has increased responsibility for classroom instruction. In most co-teaching situations, special educators continue to take the lead in activities such as child study, consulting with parents, and offering individual, intense instruction to students in need. Co-teaching means that both teachers share equal responsibility for planning, instructing, evaluating, and monitoring all members of the class. A distinct advantage is the opportunity for co-teachers to combine their individual strengths and expertise to address particular student needs. Co-teaching is "two or more professionals delivering substantive instruction to a diverse or blended group of students in a single space" (Cook & Friend, 1995, p. 2). Co-teaching is like having two cooks in one kitchen, each measuring, observing, adapting, sharing ideas, taking turns, and sometimes doing tasks on their own.

Typically, minimal standards are set for co-taught programs; these limit the number of students in a class and prescribe an allowable ratio among teachers, general education students, and special education students. For example, a program might specify that two full-time teachers will be assigned to the class and that no more than one-quarter of the class may be comprised of special needs students or identified high-risk students. Students also may need to meet certain standards, such as the ability to read content-area materials, before being placed in co-taught classes. Co-taught classes offer the obvious advantage of enabling students with disabilities to receive instruction in inclusive environments with necessary support without being singled out as the targets of special instruction.

Although co-teaching is a popular model for inclusion, research supporting it is scarce. Murawski and Swanson (2001) provided excellent research on the concept of co-teaching. The overall effect size of their study suggested "that co-teaching is a moderately effective procedure for influencing student outcomes" (p. 264). They stated:

> The fact that the research on co-teaching is lacking does not mean that co-teaching in schools should be eliminated altogether. In fact, for researchers to collect the needed data, teachers who are employing co-teaching as a service delivery option at all grade levels should open their classrooms for study. (p. 266)

Let's Get Started

When preparing for a co-teaching situation, the following factors should be addressed: the three stages of co-teaching and the relationship of the eight co-teaching components to each stage; issues related to co-teaching; and scheduling concerns and models to implement the process.

Stages of the Co-Teaching Process. Like most relationships, co-teaching has stages: The "honeymoon" or *beginning stage* moves into a *compromise stage* and then settles into a *collaborative stage* (Gately & Frank, 1997). Table 2.1 presents each stage and the transition continuum for each of the eight components of co-teaching that contribute to a successful collaborative learning environment.

As educators progress through each of the three stages, changes in their behaviors are reflected across the eight components. *Interpersonal communication* moves from guarded to open and finally into a stage in which educators respond to each other's nonverbal behavior. *Physical arrangement* in materials and space develop. Initially, educators keep materials and students separate. Slowly, sharing begins. At the collaborative stage, both educators feel more comfortable during the co-teaching process and materials are used for all students. The students with disabilities are integrated within the general class seating and more whole-group instruction occurs.

During the third component, *familiarity with the curriculum*, the special educator becomes comfortable with the general education content and both educators begin to appreciate their own competencies. The *curriculum goals and modifications* component moves from the issue of "no planning time" and a textbook, standards-driven program to both educators viewing the co-teaching process with a "bigger idea" of concepts taught. The fifth component, *instructional planning*, initially begins with the teaching of very separate curricula. As educators "give and take," a continual planning inside and outside the classroom begins to transpire. As the sixth component, *instructional presentation*, develops, the process progresses to both teachers presenting, instructing, and structuring lesson activities.

Classroom management is an ongoing issue. During the development of the co-teaching process, one educator surfaces as the enforcer and the other as the teacher. At the end of this progression, both educators equally become involved in the development and implementation of classroom management. The last issue, *assessment*, begins with two different plans and develops into the exploration of a variety of assessment plans.

Co-Teaching Issues. Argüelles, Hughes, and Schumn (2002) list seven factors that must be in place for a successful co-teaching process: a common planning time, flexibility among both teachers and administrators, risk-taking, clarity of roles and responsibilities, compatibility, effective communication skills, and administrative support.

Bauwens & Hourcade (1995) listed eight issues expressed by educators as necessary when co-teaching. Six of these issues were reflected in Argüelles and

Table 2.1 The three stages and the components for each stage of the co-teaching relationship.

	Components of the Co-Teaching Classroom that Contribute to a Successful/Collaborative Learning Environment	1 Beginning Stage	2 Compromise Stage	3 Collaborative Stage
1	Interpersonal Communication	Guarded communication.	Open and interactive.	Use more nonverbal communication and development of nonverbal signals.
2	Physical Arrangement	Separateness of students & materials.	More sharing of space and materials.	Student seating more integrated. More whole-group lessons.
3	Familiarity with the Curriculum	Special education teacher is unfamiliar with content or methodology in general education.	Curriculum confidence of both teachers grows.	Both educators begin to appreciate their competencies they bring to the content.
4	Curriculum Goals and Modifications	"No planning time" an issue. Programs driven by textbooks, standards, tests. Special education teacher is viewed as a "helper."	Both teachers begin to see more ways to modify.	General educator may view modifications as "giving-up" or "watering down." Both educators begin to see the "big idea" of concepts taught.
5	Instructional Planning	District and separate curriculum taught.	Educators begin to show a more "give and take" in planning.	Continuous planning inside and outside the classrooms begins to transpire.
6	Instructional Presentation	One educator is the "boss" and one is perceived as the child.	Movement to mini-lessons or clarification of strategies.	Both teachers present, instruct, and structure learning activities.
7	Classroom Management	One teacher surfaces as the behavior enforcer and one as the teacher.	Mutual rule development. Discussion on behavior plans.	Both educators involved in rules and routines.
8	Assessment	Usually two assessment plans.	Exploration of various assessment measures.	A variety of assessments emerge.

Note: From "Understanding Co-teaching Components," by S.E. Gately & F.J. Frank, Jr., *Teaching Exceptional Children*, 29(6), (1997) p. 40-47, Copyright (1997) by The Council for Exceptional Children. Reprinted with permission.

colleagues' (2000) list of seven. Bauwens & Hourcade added meeting individual student needs and measuring the effects of the co-teaching programs. See Figure 2.2 for suggestions for establishing successful co-teaching and collaboration.

Co-Teaching and Scheduling. The nature of elementary schools, middle schools, and high schools varies according to teacher training, physical building structure, and time frames of classes. Scheduling of co-taught classes also varies. The elementary school has extended time for language arts and math. Classes for other areas may be limited to 25- to 30-minute segments. Students enjoy specialties such as physical education, music, art, and drama. Many students with disabilities are removed from the classroom for speech and language, occupational therapy, physical therapy, or counseling. Scheduling becomes a "juggling act." However, bringing services inside the classroom benefits all students. Miss Robin, an occupational therapist from Ohio, visits lower elementary classes each week to assist the classroom teacher with correct positioning for student handwriting. This in-room consulting benefits all students, not only the student who has had occupational therapy prescribed on the IEP. Mrs. Oats, a speech and language specialist, works daily with language in the elementary classes. Both educators provide enriching experiences for all students. When educators work within one room, scheduling issues diminish.

Middle schools report fewer scheduling problems than elementary schools (Walter-Thomas, 1997). Middle schools frequently have one special educator shared by one team. A team planning time and a common planning period are frequently allowed. Unlike elementary schools, where special education teachers have large caseloads, middle schools find scheduling more manageable.

In high schools curricular materials are complex, the ability gap among students widens, and the teachers' attitudes change from "what will I give up?" to "what will I learn?" and "how many more will I help?".

Secondary educators are trained to be content centered. As students move into the secondary level, the disability is often perceived as gone when, in fact, it is still present. What has to change is service delivery. Helpful options include hand scheduling students with disabilities instead of computer scheduling, and changing the schedule from the traditional six or seven blocks to a flexible system in which subjects are offered on a rotating schedule. For instance, students attend language classes on Monday and Wednesday and math and science classes on Tuesday and Thursday. Friday provides extra study or support time for all classes. When co-teaching at any level, specifically the secondary level, educators must also be sensitive to identifying students with disabilities. No one wants to be labeled.

Educators must be careful not to resort to segregated practices in the guise of co-teaching. An eighth-grade science class was reported to have an excellent co-teaching model with the scheduling running smoothly. On closer look the special educator teacher appeared with 10 students with disabilities at the beginning of the class, marched them in, and then moved up and down the aisle observing only those students. This is an example of physical inclusion that is not full inclusion. It resulted in separating the students and emphasizing the students with disabilities.

Figure 2.2 Co-teaching/collaboration issues.

1 Finding Planning Time:
- Arrange for shared planning periods.
- Schedule teacher cores/share students.
- Develop shared team.
- Share lesson plans with suggested "Help Me Here" tips.

2 Using Planning Time Effectively:
- Develop objectives for each planning time.
- Keep notes on who will develop/implement ideas.
- Develop a follow-up plan for ideas suggested.
- Make a brief list, before meeting ends, of objectives not completed or needed to be added for next meeting.

3 Meeting Individual Student Needs During Co-Teaching/Collaboration:
- Acquire a knowledge base of curriculum alignment.
- Decide the priority of skills to be taught.
- List any prerequisite skills needed for present skill base.
- Develop accommodations for teaching skills.

4 Balancing Time Across a Variety of Different Educational Activities:
- Get organized.
- Set priority of activities.
- Before you become too stressed out, share concerns with supervisor (if possible).
- Consult with the teacher who seems to balance everything well.

5 Communicating About Co-Teaching Activities:
- Have more daily communication.
- Have personal meetings/written communication.
- Clarify role of teachers to each other, parents, and students.
- Identify who will be primarily responsible for parent communications and who students should approach for adaptations, etc.

6 Resolving Conflicts with Co-Teaching Partners:
- Be open to other points of view and ideas.
- Have an agreed upon third party sit with you during discussions.

7 Obtaining Support for Co-Teaching Programs:
- Find successful models to observe.
- List when you would like to begin your program.
- Develop an outline of how your program will look.
- Present your proposal to the administration. Be sure you have general educators and special educators involved.

8 Measuring the Effects of Co-Teaching Efforts:
- Keep data on pre-referral rate and pre/post co-teaching/collaborative efforts.
- Have parents complete a "Parent Pleased" inventory.
- Have other teachers complete a student progress report.
- Evaluate your administration's reactions.
- Don't forget to ask your students (pre/post).

Note: From *Reaching the Hard to Teach* by J. W. Wood, 2008, Richmond, VA: Judy Wood, Inc. Reprinted with permission.

Issues from: Bauwens, J. & Hourcade, J. J. (1995). *Cooperative teaching: Rebuilding teaching: Rebuilding the schoolhouse for all students.* Austin, TX: Pro-Ed.

Co-Teaching Models. What does the concept of co-teaching physically look like? Frequently, educators do not know where to go or what to do within the class. The following models (see Figure 2.3) may be used in any co-taught class. They include ideas for large groups and small groups. Each day or during the week's planning, co-teachers should decide which model best fits the lesson. Naturally, more than one alternative can be used.

Large-group models include tag teaching and direct teaching/support teaching. With tag teaching both educators deliver subject content. This requires that the special educator knows the content and that both educators are comfortable with sharing the content. Tagging is excellent when combining different content classes. For example, a literature lesson might coincide with a certain historical era. The class meets jointly and the class information is delivered by both teachers.

Direct teaching/support teaching requires that one teacher provides direct teaching of content and the second teacher provides student support. Support could include employing classroom-embedded assessment, checking classroom assessments, answering questions one on one, recording questions for class discussion, observing students for needed preplanned interventions or spontaneous interventions, and managing student behavior. In this model, teachers can trade roles.

An important benefit of a large-group model is that it provides time for the special education teacher to become more comfortable with the content. Students benefit from having an "extra" teacher and behavior issues may be handled without class or task interruption.

Small group models of co-teaching include academic stations/shared teaching and academic stations/support teaching. The first small group model, academic stations/shared teaching, has three variations. In split groups/same content, the group is split into two sections and each teacher teaches one group. With split groups/flip groups, the group is split into two sections and the subject matter is divided in half. Each teacher teaches one half of the lesson and then "flips" the groups to teach the content to the other group. Splitting groups based on students' styles of learning or abilities allow one teacher to teach to most of the class while the second teacher teaches the same lesson focusing on learning modalities or material that may be at a different instructional level.

With academic stations/support teaching the class is divided into groups or stations with one teacher direct teaching and the second supporting. The support station could include test review, homework, projects, or reteaching what was learned during direct teaching.

Benefits of the small group models include smaller class size, immediate support for student needs, and providing new co-teachers time to adjust to the general education curriculum. Working with small groups allows students to move around to prevent too much "seat time." With small groups, student problems may be more readily seen, and the student-teacher ratio is reduced.

Here are some additional co-teaching tips:

1. During inclusionary procedures, one teacher can position him- or herself in the corner of the room. If that teacher cannot hear a question or an answer,

Figure 2.3 Co-teaching models.

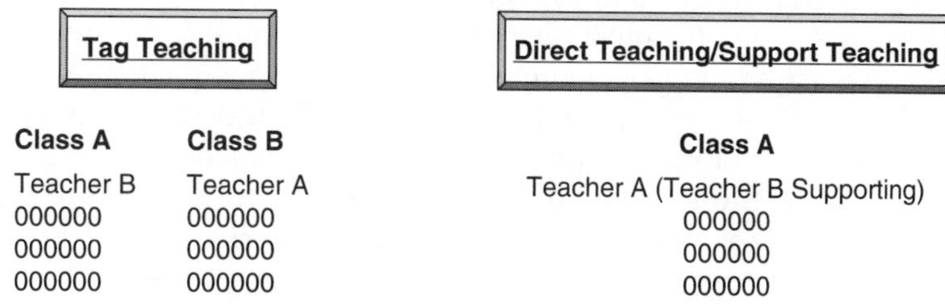

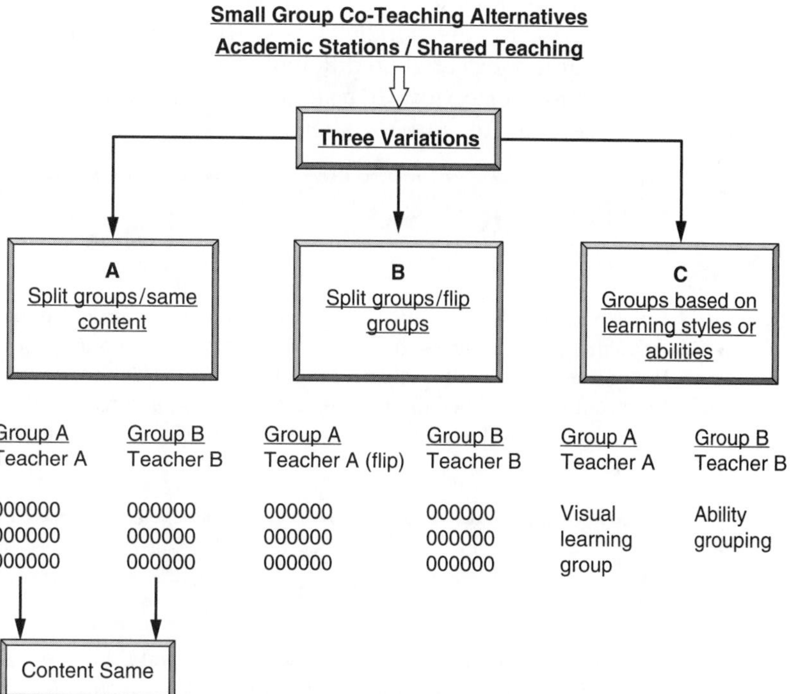

Academic Stations/Support Teaching

Group A
Homework/Review

000
000

Group B
Test Review

000
000

Group C
Reteaching Skills

000
000

Group D
Direct Teaching

000
000

Teachers A and B move from group to group

he or she may raise a hand for a repeat. It is quite possible that students also did not hear.

2. Students can suggest strategies that work best for them. Sometimes we forget the most important player in the IEP, the student.
3. Support personnel can provide a one-page handout listing their students' strengths, needs, successful techniques, and so on. This will be extremely helpful for the general classroom teacher.
4. Students who are auditorily distracted in a large classroom can use earphones when they do their work. Older students like the smaller earphones younger students like the big ones.
5. For parallel programming, teachers who are particularly good at this type of assignment can lead. A peer helper also may be assigned to the student receiving the parallel lesson. (*Parallel programming* means teaching the same subject but on different levels.)
6. A major step toward a successful co-teaching program is the ability of team teachers to work together.

SUMMARY

Roles and responsibilities are in constant change. General educators are developing and implementing new strategies. Special educators are moving from separation to inclusion in the general education classroom. To implement the new movement, Response to Intervention, all educators will share the educational responsibilities for all students.

Chapter 2 reflected on the process (how we do it) of inclusion. Chapters 3–8 will focus on the content of inclusion (what we do).

RESOURCES

National Clearinghouse for Professions in Special Education. The website contains information on the nature of paraeducator work, education required, personal qualities, job outlook and advancement, preparation, and additional resources. www.special-ed-careers.org.

SUGGESTED READINGS

Pickett, A. (1969). *Restructuring the schools: The role of paraprofessionals.* Washington, DC: Center for Policy Research, National Governor's Association.

Rainforth, B., & Kugelmass, J. W. (Eds.). (2004). *Curriculum and instruction for all learners: Blending systematic and contructivist approaches in inclusive elementary schools.* Baltimore: Brookes.

Riggs, C., & Mueller, P. (2001). Employment of and utilization of paraeducators in inclusive settings. *Journal of Exceptional Children, 35*(1), 54–62.

WEBSITES

Council for Exceptional Children IDEA Practices Website. A site designed to answer questions and provide information about the Individuals with Disabilities Education Act, and to support efforts to help all children learn. *www.ideapractices.org.*

National Clearinghouse for Professions in Special Education. The website contains information on the nature of paraeducator work, education required, personal qualities, job outlook and advancement, preparation, and additional resources. *www.Special-ed-careers.org.*

Congress on the Implementation of the Individuals with Disabilities Education Act. This website is a link to this report and provides current information on new data on statistics describing students with disabilities served by school districts. *www.ed.gov/about/reports/annual/osep/2003/25th-vol-2-front.doc.*

Individuals with Disabilities Act (IDEA). This site provides information on IDEA 2004. *www.wrightslaw.com/idea/index.htm.*

REFERENCES

Argüelles, M. E., Hughes, M. T., & Schumm, J. S. (2000). Co-teaching: A different approach to inclusion. *Principal,* 48–51.

Banks, J. A. (1994). *Multiethnic education: Theory and practice* (3rd ed.). Boston: Allyn & Bacon.

Bauwens, J., & Houreade, J. J. (1995). *Cooperative teaching: Rebuilding teaching: Rebuilding the schoolhouse for all students.* Austin, TX: Pro-Ed.

Bennett, C. I. (2003). *Comprehensive multicultural education: Theory and practice.* Boston: Allyn & Bacon.

Cook, L., & Friend, M. (1995). Co-teaching: Guidelines for creating effective practices. *Focus on Exceptional Children, 28*(3), 1–6.

Friend, M., & Bursuck, W. D. (2002). *Including students with special needs: A practical guide for classroom teachers.* Boston: Allyn & Bacon.

Gately, S. E., & Frank, F. J., Jr. (1997). Understanding co-teaching components. *Teaching Exceptional Children, 29*(6), 40–47.

Gay, G. (2004). The importance of multicultural education. *Educational Leadership, 61*(4), 30–34.

Gersten, R., Darch, C., Davis, G., & George, N. (1991). Apprenticeship and intensive training of consulting teachers: A naturalistic study. *Exceptional Children, 57*(3), 226–236.

Grant, C. H., & Gomez, M. I. (2000). (Eds.). *Making school multicultural: Campus and classroom* (2nd ed.). Upper Saddle River, N J: Merrill/Prentice Hall.

Murawski, W. W., & Swanson, H. L. (2001). A meta-analysis of co-teaching research: Where are the data? *Remedial and Special Education, 22*(5), 258–267.

Walther-Thomas, C. S. (1997). Co-teaching experiences: The benefits and problems that teachers and principals report over time. *Journal of Learning Disabilities, 30,* 395–407.

Walther-Thomas, C., Korinek, L., McLaughlin, V. L., & Williams, B. T. (2000). *Collaboration for inclusive education: Developing successful programs.* Boston: Allyn & Bacon.

Chapter **3**

SYSTEMATIC ASSESSMENT FOR INCLUSION: THE SAALE MODEL

Key Terms

SAALE Model *(page 29)*
Mismatch *(page 32)*
Intervention/Transition Checklist *(page 35)*

CHAPTER-AT-A-GLANCE

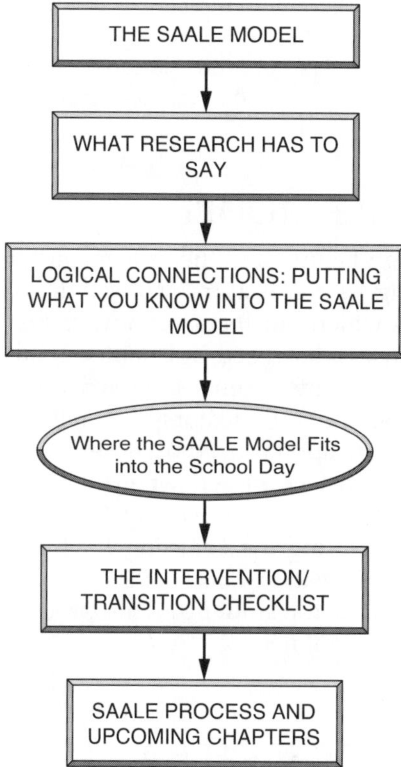

LEARNER OBJECTIVES

After you read this chapter, you will be able to

- *Explain the use of the SAALE Model.*
- *Explain how the SAALE Model fits into the big picture of education.*
- *Explain how to use the intervention/transition checklist.*
- *Define interventions.*

VIGNETTE

Sara has been in a resource room for three years. The IEP committee decided that Sara will do well in general education classes. Sara's resource teacher sends the classroom checklist to the general education teacher, who completes her section. From data that the resource teacher has on Sara, Mrs. Hamada completes the student section of the checklist. The two teachers compare both checklists and plan the classroom interventions to ensure Sara's success. The SAALE Model and Intervention Checklist in this chapter will also assist you in planning for student success.

Note: From Reaching the Hard to Teach *by J. W. Wood, 2008, Richmond, VA: Judy Wood, Inc. Reprinted with permission.*

THE SAALE MODEL

No Child Left Behind and the movement for Response to Interventions present new challenges for educators. More students with disabilities and those with diverse needs widen our focus on how to teach all students. Access requires not only the process discussed in Chapter 2, but the content, what educators do to ensure that students receive the curriculum in a manner appropriate to meet their learning needs. Educators must begin to provide interventions for all students with educational needs. These interventions cannot occur in a random fashion, but must be placed where the educational need manifests, or at the point of what I call the *mismatch*. The SAALE (Systematic Approach for Assessing/Accessing the Learning Environment) Model and its accompanying Intervention/Transition Checklist is a systematic method for providing appropriate interventions for students. This process is a problem-solving method for identifying student needs.

WHAT RESEARCH HAS TO SAY

Problem solving in regard to children with special needs has been defined as "a systematic process that includes the assessment of children and their environments, identification of needs, development and implementation of supports to meet needs, and the monitoring and evaluation of outcomes" (Thomas & Grimes, 1995, p. V). The process generally progresses through four basic stages: (a) problem identification, (b) problem analysis, (c) plan implementation, and (d) problem evaluation (Bergan, 1995). Problem solving does not need to be a formal process; classroom teachers can informally identify a student's struggles and try out various interventions throughout the instructional day until one successfully addresses the problem. Problem solving, in part, is designed to "reduce the need for special education services by providing assistance to students in the general education classroom… [and] increase the abilities of teachers to educate students who are experiencing difficulties" (Nelson & Smith, 1991, p. 243).

Adopting a problem-solving approach such as the SAALE Model described in this chapter can have several benefits. When educators intervene within general education classrooms, the stigmatization of a separate special education placement can often be avoided (McNamara & Hollinger, 2003). Additionally, a problem-solving model tends to focus on specific obstacles of immediate concern, which often reduces the length of time spent addressing a particular student's difficulties and helps contain costs (Bergan, 1995). Problem solving also fits well with recommendations made by the President's Commission on Excellence in Special Education in its 2002 report. The commission recommended implementing identification and intervention plans early, incorporating responses to interventions in planning and evaluation, and including a student's response to research-based instruction as part of the criteria for diagnosing a learning disability (President's Commission, 2002). The SAALE or a similar model would fulfill these recommendations.

Since the 1980s, a majority of states have required or recommended implementing interventions before referring students to special education services (Sindelar, Griffin, Smith, & Watanabe, 1992). Decades of research support this approach. Bergan stated, "An impressive body of evidence indicates that [a problem-solving model] is effective in promoting the learning and adjustment of children and youth" (1995, p. 121). The President's Commission refers to a National Research Council report that showed that early screening and effective interventions in the classroom actually prevented many disabilities (2002). Studies of early intervention programs found reduced special education referral rates; high satisfaction among teachers, parents, and students; and positive student behavior change (Sindelar et al., 1992). Another analysis found that "such interventions can increase the abilities of teachers to educate students who are experiencing difficulty and improve the attitudes of teachers toward such students" (Nelson & Smith, 1991, p. 243). Such results indicate the positive outcomes that are possible with the adoption of a problem-solving process like the SAALE Model.

Research on the SAALE Model (Wood, 1989) has repeatedly shown that the use of the SAALE process provides significant educational gains in diverse populations. The SAALE Model is a growing concept, and any best practice fits somewhere within the model's pattern. Now let's take a look at this model, prepare a foundation for effective teaching, and get ready for the remainder of the text.

The **SAALE Model** is a framework for making decisions on how to teach students with special needs and all students served in an inclusive setting. This is the cornerstone for creating an inclusive classroom. The SAALE Model is a process for differentiating instruction to ensure students' success.

Proponents of the SAALE Model conceptualize the school day not as a whole but as several environments that interact continuously. The model provides a framework to help educators decide where in the instructional day (or in which environment) a student is having or will have a mismatch. Figure 3.1 demonstrates the components of the model.

Research Notes for Classroom Application

A problem-solving model can address the needs of a diverse student population, including those struggling with learning, those receiving special education services, and those with behavioral challenges. Positive outcomes include fewer referrals for specialized testing, fewer special education placements, improved learning and behavior, and promotion of school-based collaboration (Telzrow, McNamara, & Hollinger, 2000). While these results have led to its wide use, the way a problem-solving approach is implemented and practiced can have a great impact on its effectiveness.

A collaborative team approach is critical to a problem-solving method, but also requires a wider variety and more advanced skills among the participating practitioners. They must have expertise in assessment and intervention, clinical judgment and experience to know which assessments and interventions to apply, and the knowledge to accurately measure the effectiveness of a given intervention (Fuchs & Fuchs, 2006). Staff must be well trained and have ample resources available to optimize the problem-solving process. Parents are also key members of the problem-solving team and must be well informed and trained in the methods used so they can be an effective support for the student.

The implementation of a problem-solving approach can have a great impact on student outcomes. Telzrow et al. (2000) write that "a clearly conceptualized, well-articulated problem-solving model, and sufficient training and technical assistance for those who will implement it, are essential for facilitating reliable implementation" (p. 457). Additionally, those implementing such an approach must decide how much rigidity or flexibility to build into the system (National Joint Committee on Learning Disabilities, 2005). A relatively stable, consistent framework increases the opportunity and likelihood that successful models can be researched and replicated, but a more flexible structure can be more responsive to each student and can maximize problem-solving opportunities. To reap the greatest benefits from a problem-solving process, educators and officials must carefully consider these issues as they adopt and implement their chosen model.

Sources: Fuchs, D., & Fuchs, L. S. (2006). Introduction to Response to Intervention: What, why, and how valid is it? *Reading Research Quarterly, January/February/March 2006*, 93–99. Retrieved January 1, 2007 from http://www.reading.org/Library/Retrieve.cfm?D=10.1598/RRQ.41.1.4& F=RRQ-41-1-Fuchs.pdf.

National Joint Committee on Learning Disabilities. (2005). *Responsiveness to Intervention and learning disabilities*. Retrieved December 30, 2006 from http://www.ldonline.org/?module=uploads&func=download&fileId=461.

Telzrow, C. F., McNamara, K., & Hollinger, C. L. (2000). Fidelity of problem-solving implementation and relationship to student performance. *School Psychology Review, 29*, 443–461.©

Note: From *Reaching the Hard to Teach* by J. W. Wood, 2008, Richmond, VA: Judy Wood, Inc. Reprinted with permission.

Figure 3.1 The SAALE model process.

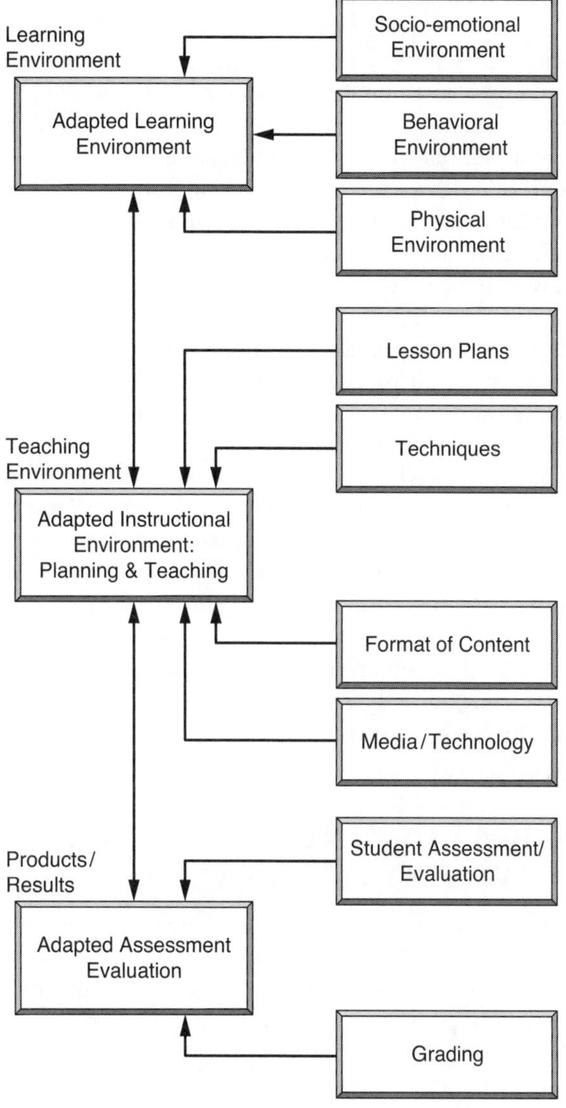

Note: From *Reaching the Hard to Teach* by J. W. Wood, 2008, Richmond, VA: Judy Wood, Inc. Reprinted with permission.

According to the SAALE Model, content and students interact in three major environments: the *learning environment,* which includes socio-emotional, behavioral, and physical aspects; the *teaching environment,* in which educators plan, deliver, and assess instruction (teaching techniques and content); and the *evaluation and grading environment*. Each of the three environments are ongoing and include technology. At any point a student may experience a mismatch. When a mismatch occurs and is identified (using the checklist), the *point of intervention* is identified and the appropriate research-based strategy is implemented. Educators must identify mismatches and employ effective strategies based on the identified match. For example, if a student does not copy or cannot copy from a chalkboard, the educator must ensure that information written on the chalkboard is provided to the student. What is important in a classroom is that students *receive* the content and be *assessed* for content knowledge in a manner in which they learn. In the above example it is important for the student to *learn,* not *copy,* the material on the chalkboard.

Understanding the concept of *mismatch* is crucial when using the SAALE Model. Mismatches are not caused by child or teacher. A **mismatch** is simply a point where the child cannot succeed because the teacher has expectations that are not compatible with the student's abilities. In the example of the student who cannot copy from the chalkboard, the teacher must understand that there is nothing wrong with requiring copying from the chalkboard or not being able to copy; the point is simply that a mismatch has occurred. No one is at fault. The teacher has identified a point of intervention.

I have changed my stand on who has the mismatch from the view previously expressed. With maturity I have grown to understand that what happens, happens. No one is ever too old to learn. Teachers do the best they can; even if they are not doing their best for a student, it is usually because they simply do not know what to do. If they did, they would do it. However, because we are professionals, we must (a) find the mismatch and (b) develop and implement the appropriate intervention. Children are not going to adjust to the environment; the environment must be adjusted to the student. For too long we have tried to make students fit our molds, but we can no longer follow this reasoning.

LOGICAL CONNECTIONS: PUTTING WHAT YOU KNOW INTO THE SAALE MODEL

To demonstrate how to place everything you know into the SAALE model, I would like to teach you the concept of *logical connections*. Let's pretend that I'm giving you one of my business cards. Now, what might be the purpose of your having one of my cards? Well, you can write to me, fax me, or perhaps e-mail me. But if I return in three months and ask if you still have my card, odds are that you will have lost it or at least left it at home.

Now let's pretend that I'm giving you one of my business cards and telling you that I'll return in three months. If you can produce my card at that time, you'll receive $10,000. Will you have the card when I return? You bet! You now have a logical connection between my card and a special reward.

When you are given something with no meaning (or logical connection), it has no value. However, if you have something and someone teaches you *why* it is important to learn, keep, or know, it has value. We often forget to provide logical connections for our students. For example, we issue textbooks and assume that the students realize that the text has a connection with a specific course. But we must teach students what the text is for and how to use it. Throughout the year we should make those logical connections for the students.

Now that you understand what a logical connection is, let me use the term in reference to you. Figure 3.2 presents the SAALE model (see also Figure 3.1) in a filing cabinet format. Visualize the model as a large filing cabinet with nine drawers. Each drawer represents one of the blocks in the model. Everything you know and everything you will know can be filed away in a drawer. Can you remember some of the college courses you took although you simply did not understand why? Now you have a place (a mental drawer) to file away the information learned. For example, did you take a course about teaching reading? Well, what you learned fits neatly into the content drawer. You will begin to see how all the information you learn can

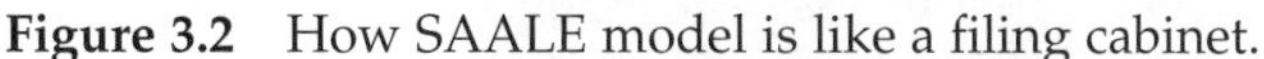

Figure 3.2 How SAALE model is like a filing cabinet.

Note: From *Reaching the Hard to Teach* by J. W. Wood, 2008, Richmond, VA: Judy Wood, Inc. Reprinted with permission.

be filed away. When a student has a mismatch, you can identify where within the model the mismatch is occurring, mentally pull out the drawer, and select an intervention for the mismatch. You see, an intervention is simply doing something that you have not tried. If one idea does not work, then try another. The remaining chapters in this book correspond with each block in the model. In this way, I will help you fill up the file drawers. Now let's draw some logical connections between the SAALE Model and your own knowledge.

Where the SAALE Model Fits into the School Day

Many things go on during a school day. For our purposes, however, we are going to simplify the school day into four blocks: student outcomes/standards (what we want the students to learn); assessment/evaluation, the tests (where we hope students exhibit success); the curriculum (what we will teach the students, based on student outcomes/standards); and the students themselves. In Chapter 1 this was called the Curriculum Maze. (Refer to page 3, Figure 1.1.)

For students to reach selected or established outcomes, they must learn the curriculum. Therefore, teachers must teach the curriculum (which will be based on student outcomes and should be student appropriate) effectively to their students. The SAALE Model provides a framework that helps teachers continually watch for mismatches so that they can more effectively deliver the curriculum to the students and thus reach the established outcomes. In this way they align the curriculum to the students.

The curriculum has been thought of as what we teach and interventions as "those things" that are too much trouble to do. Often the curriculum takes so much time that no time is left for preparing and implementing interventions.

By reconsidering how we think, we can make the intervention process an integral part of the curriculum. One does not function without the other. From now on let's become a new generation of teachers—ones who see curriculum and intervention as equal. However, remember that the interventions must be applied in an organized manner. The SAALE Model provides the organization of identifying the mismatch, finding the correct intervention, and applying it as we teach the curriculum.

I would like to show you how the SAALE Model fits into educational history. In the early years of education, only privileged males received an education. Women cooked, spun yarn, sewed, and did other household tasks. But as time passed, our country began to develop a two-track educational system: general education and special education. The systems were extremely separate, including facilities and curriculum. By the 1970s special education slowly began to move into general education buildings. However, the curriculum remained separate.

In the late 1970s I taught a special education class that met in the basement of the school, even though there were empty rooms on the first and second floors. My students were as far removed from the other students as possible. We had to eat lunch and go out to recess at times separate from the general education students. We have really come a long way since then.

In the 1980s students with special needs were gradually moved or integrated into general education classes. Mostly you would see these students in art, music, and physical education classes. Resource or self-contained classes for students with disabilities were still major models for placement. Nonetheless, interventions for general class curriculum were slowly surfacing. In the 1990s, we moved toward an inclusive environment in our schools.

Inclusion is our goal. But for our students to become included with general education, doors need to open and stay open. The 2000s are seeing a movement to serve all students, not only those with special needs. Students with special needs need to fit in socially, behaviorally, physically, and academically in order to be successful in general education classes. Imagine coming home late one evening and discovering you have the wrong door key in your hand. Will you remain outside all night or try another key? The logical answer is to try another key. This is exactly what we must do for students: try another key or intervention to unlock the door and keep it open.

I want you to think *SAALE Model* when you see that a student is having difficulty with instruction. In other words, I want you to think about where the mismatch might be occurring. Then you will be on the right path toward identifying the problem.

For students to be able to access the curriculum, however, they must be included, thus the term *inclusion*. However, inclusion is a general term, not an educational one. We are either included or excluded in life. These inclusion or exclusion measures may be social, emotional, behavioral, physical, instructional, or through evaluation and grading. Students must be included in the curriculum to have access to it. They cannot move on to standards (or outcomes) or evaluation if they do not first have access to the curriculum.

Remember in Chapter 2, we discussed access as "the process" (how we do it) and "the content." The big picture is displayed in Figure 1.3. The content of inclusion is what we do to get the curriculum to students. The SAALE process provided this access. The remaining parts of the chapter and of this text explain in detail how we get content (subject matter) to students.

If your school does not use the SAALE Model, you still may use the checklist to follow and certainly you may use all of the interventions presented in the remaining chapters of the text. The SAALE Model is simply a process for organizing interventions.

THE INTERVENTION/TRANSITION CHECKLIST

The key to success in any inclusive placement is applying the appropriate intervention to the learning environment. A major function of the school-based team that is guiding the student's learning outcomes is the identification of needed areas of interventions in the inclusive environment. The **Intervention/Transition Checklist** is a helpful and practical method of identifying where adaptations or interventions in the learning environment may be needed. This simple device enables teachers and other team members to compare characteristics of the general class setting with the performance levels of the student in that setting. The entire checklist appears in Appendix A. However, the checklist, and how to use it, will be discussed here.

The Intervention/Transition Checklist is divided into two parts, a checklist for the classroom and a checklist for the student. I encourage all classroom educators to complete the classroom checklist. This has to be done only once. When you review how you have responded to the checklist (rarely, sometimes, or most of the time), you will discover that you have *normed* yourself; that is, you have documented what you usually do or require in your classroom, and how often you require a skill will be documented. This is your norm or standard. Perhaps you realize that when you give a test, you always use multiple-choice items. What about the student who does not respond well to multiple-choice questions? Do you have an accurate measure of this student's learning? When you have completed the classroom checklist, compare your responses on the student checklist. Remember, your answers are not right or wrong. If I completed the classroom checklist for a university class and then completed another for an in-service program, my norm would be different. Nothing would be wrong. I would simply know more about my "style" (norm).

Without comparing the classroom with the student, we *cannot* find mismatches. Identifying possible mismatches between a student's performance and the classroom learning environment is the first step to developing prereferral or postplacement interventions. For example, if the checklist reveals that a history teacher requires students to copy extensive notes from the board, and the student has difficulty copying, then a mismatch has occurred. The general and special education teachers can now work cooperatively to develop necessary accommodations for the student, perhaps by providing a graphic organizer for note taking. General educators can use this procedure for all students. The remaining chapters in this book provide numerous suggestions for ways to adapt each learning environment.

The checklist also assesses related environments. Completing this section of the checklist helps team members assess the student's performance during other nonacademic portions of the school day.

Many times the high-risk student has difficulty in one or more of the related environments, resulting in his or her removal from the regular class. Although learning is going on in the classroom, the high-risk student is no longer participating. Therefore, the area of *related environments* becomes extremely important.

Figure 3.3 displays the sections of the checklist that assess the skill of following directions. In this classroom students are expected to understand and follow oral directions. According to the notation on the student's checklist, the student is unable to understand and follow oral directions. For this skill area, there is a mismatch between the inclusive environment and the student's present skill level. The special and general educators and the student can now work together to develop interventions that will enable the student to be successful in completing assignments that require following oral directions.

Figure 3.3 Sample from intervention/transition checklist.

SECTION OF CLASSROOM CHECKLIST	
R (required **R**arely) **S** (required **S**ome of the time) **M** (required **M**ost of the time)	
Format of Content	
Directions	R S M
oral directions	o o ⊗
written directions	o o o
Vocabulary Study	
understanding/learning vocabulary	o o o
Homework	
homework listed on chalkboard	o o o
homework shown on overhead projector	o o o
homework listed on calendar/checklist	o o o
homework assigned orally	o o o
homework filed in notebook	o o o
independent work required	o o o
homework turned in	o o o

SECTION OF STUDENT CHECKLIST	
R (**R**arely demonstrates) **S** (demonstrates **S**ome of the time) **M** (demonstrates **M**ost of the time)	
Format of Content	
Directions	R S M
understands and follows oral directions	⊗ o o
understands and follows written directions	o o o
Vocabulary Study	
Understands/learns vocabulary	o o o
Homework	
copies accurately from chalkboard	o o o
copies accurately from overhead projector	o o o
follows calendar/checklist	o o o
understands and retains oral directions	o o o
accurately files homework in notebook	o o o
completes homework independently	o o o
locates and turns in homework	o o o

Note: From *Reaching the Hard to Teach* by J. W. Wood, 2008, Richmond, VA: Judy Wood, Inc. Reprinted with permission.

Beyond identifying needed areas for interventions, the checklist can be used in several other ways. For students receiving instruction in a variety of classrooms, the checklist or appropriate subsections can be used to compare students' performances across educational settings. Each of the student's teachers may complete a copy of the checklist, or the special education teacher consultant may complete copies of the checklist while observing each classroom. This enables team members to compare observations about the student's learning environments and needs throughout the school day and develop consistent interventions.

The checklist can also be effective for students who are making a transition into the general education setting from a self-contained or resource placement. The special education teacher fills out the "student's present performance level" column and reviews the checklist with the general education teacher before the student joins the general classroom. This gives the general education teacher insight into the student's learning characteristics and special needs, enabling him or her to make accommodations in the learning environment to facilitate a smoother transition. For transitioning students who continue to be identified as students with special needs, the checklist can be used to generate objectives for the IEP.

Teachers can also make valuable use of the checklist in conferences with the parents. Too often, teachers present the parents with test scores or grade reports that provide information about achievement and failure but offer no reasons for them. Using the checklist as a before-and-after comparison of the student's current level of performance (for example, at the beginning and midpoint of the school year), teachers can give parents concrete information about how the educational environment may be contributing to performance and which interventions have proven successful. Parents, in turn, can use the information to help structure an appropriate learning environment for the student at home. This will help prevent the frustration that often results when parents attempt to help students with homework but use inappropriate pacing, methods, or materials.

The following list summarizes nine ways to use the checklist:

1. A special education teacher who is considering placing a student in an inclusive environment sends copies of the checklist to several general teachers and asks them to fill out the "characteristics of setting" column. The special education teacher fills out the "student's present performance level" column. The results of the checklist are used to make the best possible match between the general classroom and the student to be included. For example, if the science teacher uses small-group instruction almost exclusively in her class, and the student works best in a small-group setting, a possible match has been made. On the other hand, if assessment reveals that the history teacher requires students to copy extensive notes from the chalkboard, and the student has difficulty copying, educators will question the wisdom of placing the student in that class or consider interventions for copying. Remember, the history teacher is still doing an excellent job; teachers are simply matching the student to an appropriate environment.

2. The special education teacher fills out the "student's present performance level" column and sends it to the general teacher either before or after a child has been placed in the general classroom. This gives the general classroom teacher information about the student's learning characteristics and facilitates a closer match between teaching procedures and student learning style. For example, if the teacher uses the lecture approach, and the included student has listening problems, a good match has not been made. However, if the teacher makes some simple adaptations to the lectures (such as using the overhead projector as a visual aid or providing a printed lecture outline), then the student's placement in the class may be appropriate.
3. The special education teacher observes the inclusive setting and fills out the checklist independently or together with the general teacher. Results are then compiled by the special education teacher and shared with the general education teacher, helping to determine the appropriateness of the inclusive placement.
4. The special education teacher uses the checklist to identify skills that the student needs to master before entering an inclusive setting and includes these skills in the student's IEP. For example, if the teacher discovers that a student cannot accurately copy notes from the chalkboard, the IEP should include note-taking skills as an objective. However, note-taking interventions may still be necessary.
5. Multidisciplinary teams use the checklist to help them determine a student's readiness for inclusion.
6. The child study committee, teacher assistance team, and others use the checklist to assess a student before deciding on a special education evaluation or planning an IEP.
7. The classroom teacher completes the "student's present performance level" and places it in the student's folder for next year's teacher to review.
8. The checklist can be used to document appropriate prereferral interventions or interventions to be used for the Response to Intervention (RTI) process.
9. The checklist can be used for the Response to Intervention movement. The RTI movement requires a problem-solving process for identifying student problems. The checklist does this.

SAALE PROCESS AND UPCOMING CHAPTERS

The SAALE model will be expanded throughout the remaining chapters of this text. "Adapting the Learning Environment," Chapter 4, addresses student attitudes and ways of improving these attitudes as well as helping students develop appropriate social skills. How to work with mild to severe behavior problems and how to schedule and group students are covered in that chapter. The learning environment sets the stage for the teaching environment. Chapter 5 looks at lesson planning in the teaching process. Chapter 6, "Adapting Teaching Techniques," discusses the process for delivering instruction. Chapter 7, "Adapting the Format of Content," looks at ways to organize instruction and ideas for teaching subject matter. Chapter 8, "Adapting Assessment, Evaluation, and Grading," looks at how to provide classroom-embedded assessment, how to adapt tests, and numerous alternatives to assessment and grading.

SUMMARY

Making the transition from one educational setting to another can be either a positive experience or a frustrating one for a student with special needs or one who is at risk for school failure. By assessing the setting and determining whether the student has the skills needed to enter the environment, educators can enhance the student's chances for successful learning.

Now that we have learned about two parts (the model and the checklist) of the three-step process and are using the same vocabulary, we will move ahead to step 3: strategies or interventions. Remember that everything you already know, and will learn, can be placed into your filing cabinet (our model). The rest of this book will suggest hundreds of ideas for you to consider.

RESOURCES

ERIC Clearinghouse on Handicapped and Gifted Children
1110 West Glebe Road Suite 300
Arlington, VA 22201-5704
(703) 620-3660
www.cec.sped.org

SUGGESTED READING

McNamara, K., & Hollinger, C. (2003). Intervention-based assessment: Evaluation rates and eligibility findings. *Exceptional Children, 69,* 181–193.

REFERENCES

Bergan, J. R. (1995). Evolution of a problem-solving model of consultation. *Journal of Educational and Psychological Consultation, 6*(2), 111–123.

Nelson, J. R., & Smith, D. J. (1991). Prereferral intervention: A review of the research. *Education & Treatment of Children, 14*(3), 243–254.

President's Commission on Excellence in Special Education. (2002). *A new era: Revitalizing special education for children and their families.* Jessup, MD: U.S. Department of Education.

Sindelar, P. T., Griffin, C. C., Smith, S. W., & Watanabe, A. K. (1992). Prereferral intervention: Encouraging notes on preliminary findings. *The Elementary School Journal, 92*(3), 245–259.

Thomas, A., & Grimes, J. (Eds). (1995). *Best practices in school psychology, III.* Washington, DC: National Association of School Psychologists.

Wood, J. W. (1989). *Mainstreaming: A practical approach for teachers.* Upper Saddle River, NJ: Merrill/Prentice Hall.

Chapter **4**

ADAPTING THE LEARNING ENVIRONMENT

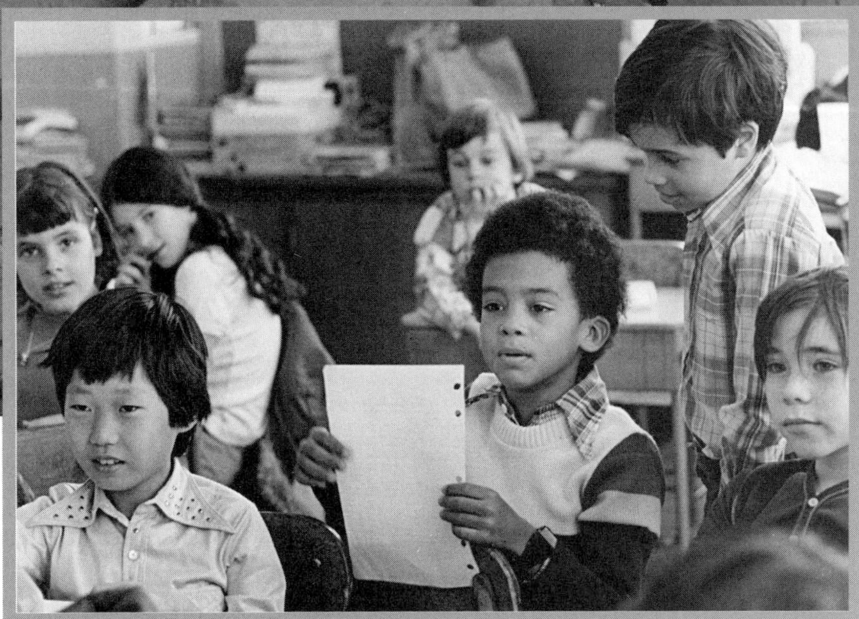

Key Terms

Risk-Free Environment
(page 45)
Communication
(page 47)

CHAPTER-AT-A-GLANCE

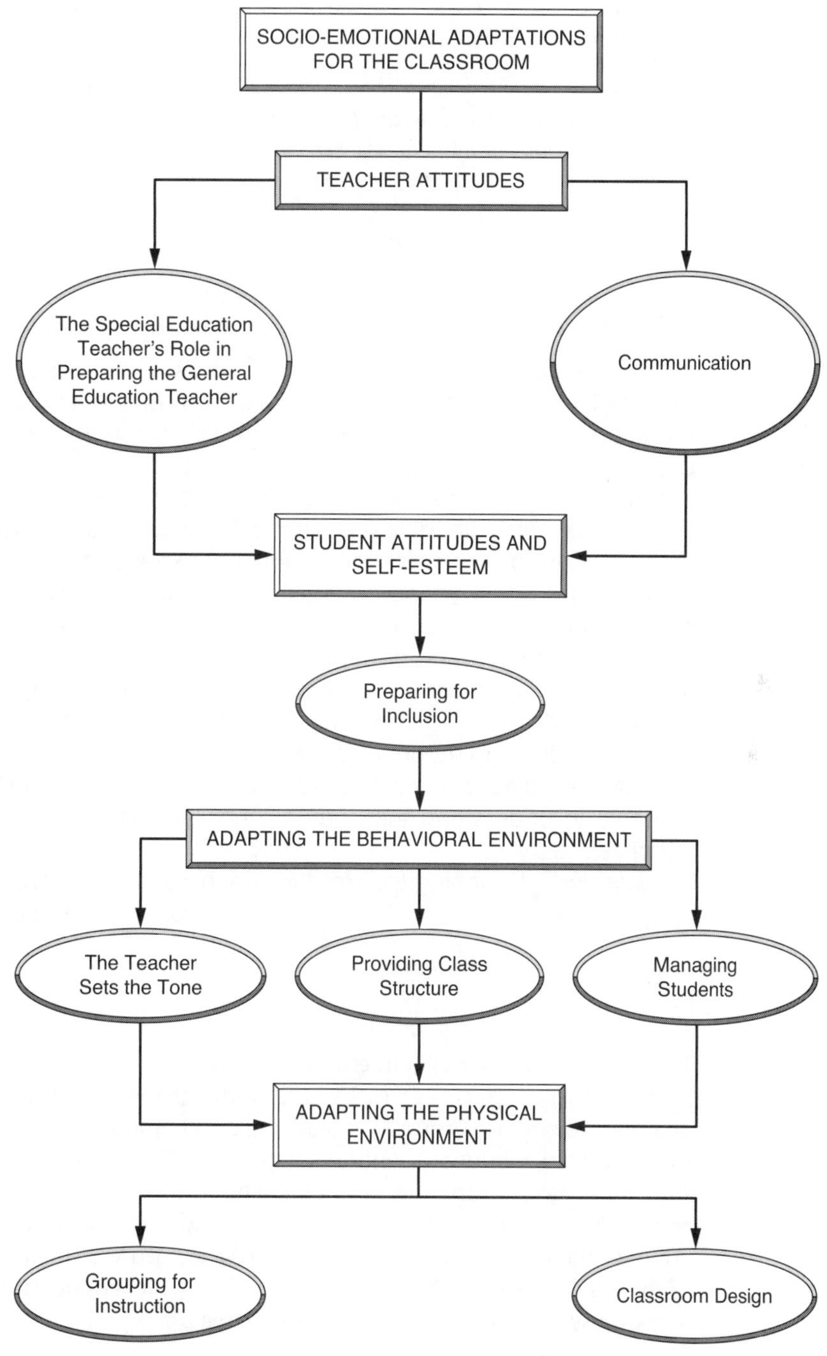

LEARNER OBJECTIVES

After you read this chapter, you will be able to

- *Discuss how teacher attitudes affect student learning.*
- *Explain various grouping techniques.*
- *List various designs for the classroom.*

VIGNETTE

Mr. James has taught reading for 21 years. During these years many young readers have passed through his classroom and benefited from his skills as a reading specialist. Dan has been a struggling reader for three years. Dan was placed in Mr. James's third-grade remedial program. After implementing numerous reading programs, Mr. James decided to use the technique of realness. *Realness* is a strategy of teacher behavior in which the teacher decides to relate to the student by sharing similar personal experiences. Mr. James said to Dan, "Dan, when I was a young boy I also had a difficult time reading." A huge smile passed across Dan's face. "Mr. James, you make me so happy." Mr. James was thrilled to see this burst of happiness. "Mr. James," Dan continued, "you make me so happy because I now know that you are dumb, too!" Mr. James was shocked but also delighted. Now he had a new opportunity to speak with Dan about his slow reading development. Dan was not dumb, but educators had not yet discovered the appropriate reading strategies to meet Dan's needs. Helping students to understand that they are not inadequate is a step toward student success.

Note: From Reaching the Hard to Teach *by J. W. Wood, 2008, Richmond, VA: Judy Wood, Inc. Reprinted with permission.*

The class learning environment is vast. Here educators set the stage for learning. Think of these aspects of the SAALE model as the soil of the classroom where educators prepare the ground for learning and begin to sow the seeds of instruction. Just like Dan, many students need preparation for learning. Many mismatches start with the learning environment. The three components of the learning environment are socio-emotional, behavioral, and physical. After reading this chapter, you will have a deeper understanding of the nature of the child as well as the role of the teacher. You will be given many ideas (interventions) that will assist you in working with students in these critical areas.

SOCIO-EMOTIONAL ADAPTATIONS FOR THE CLASSROOM

Our children come to school with much more than the latest tennis shoes, lunch money, and backpacks. Because many come from homes where the climate is much different from the classroom, entering the classroom can be an emotional-social adjustment. Educators need to establish a warm and accepting environment for all children so they feel more comfortable and have a greater opportunity to learn. This is what we call a risk-free environment. Let's think first about *risk-filled* environments.

Recall a teacher you had in high school or perhaps a professor you had in college. Have you ever waited with breathless anticipation for that person to ask you a question, not knowing which question you would be expected to respond to or when you would be called on? Perhaps the teacher called on students randomly to read aloud. In such cases, your anticipation might have become almost too great.

During my undergraduate studies I had a professor who was unpredictable in this way. I never knew when I would be called on, what types of items were going to be on the tests, or how my papers or projects would be graded. I also had a teacher who took great pleasure in pointing out how wrong I was when I answered. In elementary school my class would take turns reading aloud. Because I was an extremely poor reader, I almost had a nervous breakdown before my turn arrived.

These were certainly not risk-free environments. An environment that is risk-free is one in which students are not afraid to take chances. A **risk-free environment** is a safe place for students where mistakes are seen as stepping-stones to success. Before everyone runs to the playground, the teams are established. No one must stand anxiously waiting to be picked. When an answer is incorrect, the student is praised for trying. Everyone's efforts are appreciated. A risk-free environment is safe, relaxed, and nonthreatening to students.

A risk-free environment has many components. Two of the most important are positive teacher attitudes and honoring students' self-esteem.

TEACHER ATTITUDES

The classroom teacher plays an important role in the success of an included child. Establishing a warm socio-emotional climate helps teachers to maximize student achievement. The teacher's attitude toward students is the major catalyst that affects interaction and achievement. "Whether in special or general education, there is growing evidence that the single most important school influence in a student's education is a well-prepared, caring, and qualified teacher" (Council for Exceptional Children, 2000).

When inclusion first became a reality, teachers generally expressed reservations about accepting students with special needs into the general classroom setting. Teachers were concerned about what might have been perceived as dumping students with special needs back into general classrooms. Teachers felt unprepared

Research Notes for Classroom Application

Both special and general education teachers have great responsibility for the success of all students in their class, both those of high ability and particularly those with low ability. A teacher's attitude toward his or her position and responsibilities, the class as a whole, and each individual student play a powerful role in student success.

Research has shown that teachers tend to respond to a negative outcome like test failure differently for students with and without disabilities (Clark, 1997). They are more likely to reward rather than punish, feel more pity and less anger toward, and have higher expectations of future failure for students with learning disabilities. These students often interpret this response pattern to mean that they have low ability, thus affecting their self-esteem, sense of competency, and motivation. They may think they have little control over their success and failure.

Because a student's daily interactions with his or her teacher play such a strong role in building the student's sense of personal competence, teachers must be conscious of the messages they intentionally and unintentionally send to their students. Simply being aware of the tendency to expect less from struggling students may help a teacher develop and convey more positive expectations. Even a small change in the interaction pattern of a student and teacher can have a significant effect on students' learning identities (Dudley-Marling, 2004, as cited in Berry, 2006).

A teacher's attitude toward a particular student also affects how that student will be treated by other students. "Teachers need to keep in mind that children mirror the attitudes and behaviors of the adults around them. If the teacher hounds and scolds a child constantly, the students in the class tend to do the same. If the teacher shows a lack of patience, understanding, or respect for a student, the other children follow her example" (Adjustments in classroom management, 1997, Avoiding social problems section, para. 5). Thus, the power of a teacher's attitude cannot be underestimated in the success of diverse students.

Sources: Adjustments in classroom management. (1997). Retrieved January 6, 2007 from http://www.ldonline.org/article/5924.

Berry, R. A. W. (2006, Fall). Inclusion, power, and community: Teachers and students interpret the language of community in an inclusion classroom. *American Educational Research Journal, 43*(3), 489–529.

Clark, M. D. (1997). Teacher response to learning disability: A test of attributional principles. Retrieved January 6, 2007 from http://www.ldonline.org/article/6162.©

Note: From *Reaching the Hard to Teach* by J. W. Wood, 2008, Richmond, VA: Judy Wood, Inc. Reprinted with permission.

to work with diverse special populations and feared these students would demand too much of their time in classes that were already full. Teachers were also concerned about their roles, increased paperwork, possible conflict with special education teachers and related service providers, and fulfilling parent's expectations. The results of a study by Michele Wood, University of California, Santa Barbara, indicated that "in the initial stages of inclusion, teachers maintained discreet role boundaries through a relatively clear, albeit division of labor. As the school year progressed, role perceptions became less rigid as the teaming became more cooperative" (Wood, 1998).

Many teachers who once felt isolated and alone in their classroom now see a network of resources if they are willing to be open to suggestions and to risk changing their presentation of material or how they might review or design a test. Many of the suggestions help not only the student with special needs in the classroom, but the student at risk as well.

For inclusion to be successful, positive teacher attitudes are essential. Equally important, teachers need appropriate support and training. Meyen, Vergason, and Whelan (1993) suggested that teacher attitudes should be continually reassessed. Areas of assessment may include "opinions of perceived success or failure in providing curriculum content, increased learning for all students involved, student discipline, team efforts, and grading procedures" (p. 101).

More needs to be done to provide training for teachers and school staff on attitudes toward and acceptance of, not only students with special needs, but the increasing number of students from diverse populations. Teachers need information on supports for maximizing student success and providing appropriate interventions and accommodations when necessary.

The Special Education Teacher's Role in Preparing the General Education Teacher

Special educators are in a unique position to promote positive inclusive experiences as well as to offer support and expertise to their general education peers. General educators, in turn, have special expertise that will benefit special educators. Special personnel and general teachers of students with special needs need to work together to plan and implement inclusion. Table 4.1 presents issues and suggestions for the special education teacher's role in preparing the general class teacher.

Communication

Communication—the exchange of ideas, information, and suggestions—is crucial to establishing a good working relationship between special and general education teachers.

Because the general educator faces the task of accommodating instruction in inclusive classrooms, the special educator bears more, although not all, of the responsibility for making the communication process easier. To communicate better,

Table 4.1 The special education teacher's role in preparing the general class teacher.

ISSUE	SUGGESTIONS
The student with special needs may not fit into the regular class setting.	1. Prepare the student with special needs as to class expectations prior to entry. 2. Arrange for the student with special needs to have short visits in the general education class prior to entry. 3. If the disability is severe, have someone explain to the class what is involved for the student.
The teacher is reluctant to have a student with special needs in her class.	1. Although today all children belong to all educators, some educators are still reluctant to serve students with special needs. This works both ways. Special educators resist "giving up" their students, and general educators resist "receiving" students with special needs. 2. Begin by seeing the advantages for all students and teachers when students are combined. 3. Start sharing materials, supplies, etc. Everyone benefits from this. 4. Discuss how having an extra teacher in the class will be a support for all students.
The teacher does not believe his training includes working with students with special needs or with general education students.	1. Begin cross training. Be sure that in-service programs serve all educators. 2. Teachers can begin to model skills and strategies for each other. 3. Involve literacy centers and coaches.
The teacher does not know how to develop and implement instruction to a diverse population.	1. Classrooms have always been diverse. Remember the one-room schoolhouse? Teaching to diverse populations requires organization and planning. When two work as one, this planning is possible. 2. Remember that when you teach a class or subject, everyone benefits. Learn to differentiate the subject. Not everyone will learn all. Some will learn more than others, but all will learn according to his or her abilities. 3. Draw on all of the school resources. Many times resources are untapped (for example, the literacy coach).

Note: From *Reaching the Hard to Teach* by J.W. Wood, 2008, Richmond, VA: Judy Wood, Inc. Reprinted with permission.

special education teachers must understand themselves, realize that others see and respond to them as they project themselves, be able to listen, demonstrate an understanding of others' concerns by acting in positive ways, respect the problems and concerns of their colleagues, and respond quickly to the needs of others.

Understanding oneself leads to good communication. In addition, knowing and internalizing the role of special educator and then projecting that role in a positive way gives others guidelines for communication. If special educators project confidence in their abilities, others trust that competence. However, the reverse is also true. If special educators project a lack of confidence in their abilities, others may view them as incompetent.

Listening is the basis of all communication. Often we listen to others without actually hearing what they are saying. Special educators must not only listen but also hear the concerns of general educators. Then they can show evidence of hearing those concerns by reacting to their colleagues' needs in a positive manner. For example, special education teachers who quickly provide the appropriate instructional material, suggest an alternative teaching technique, or assist in designing a behavior management plan for an inclusive student show that the problems of others are important. Once general educators believe that the door of communication is open, effective inclusion becomes a reality.

STUDENT ATTITUDES AND SELF-ESTEEM

Like adults, students develop a set of attitudes about themselves and their peers. Students who have been found eligible for special education services or who are at risk for school failure usually have experienced learning difficulty for a long time. Often educators wonder why students have low self-esteem or why they seem unmotivated. Failure is a cumulative process. It does not occur overnight, and the damage it causes cannot be repaired overnight. Students with disabilities often have lower positions of class status than their nondisabled peers do, and this pattern of rejection holds true in both general and special classrooms.

Following is an excerpt from a wonderful work by Anne F. Parkinson, Isabel Dulfano, and Carl E. Nink (2003) on student self-esteem:

> Self-esteem is increased when individuals are involved in activities they enjoy and at which they excel. "Students having trouble in the classroom need to be involved in something they do well, whether painting, baseball, or dancing. Otherwise, they may experience chronic success deprivation" (Levine, 1990). "When a student is experiencing academic stress and failure, art, music, mechanical pursuits, or sports may serve as venues in which he feels successful and can obtain longed-for positive recognition" (Levine, 2002, p. 186). Some students are better creators than learners; for these, opportunities to be creative and brainstorm enhance self-esteem and motivation. (p. 14)

Quotes from Levine are also included in this wonderful work and certainly address the issue of self-esteem:

> Most kids simply lack the insulation to handle repeated frustration and personal failure. Some simply surrender. Some become permanently anxious or depressed. Others act out, cause trouble, get themselves pregnant, or take drugs. Still others become transformed into conservative nonrisktakers, shutting down and decisively writing themselves off at an early age. Or else they keep criticizing and putting down whatever it is they can't succeed at. (Levine, 2002, p. 246)
>
> A student's enhanced insight into his or her learning disorders (and strengths) will engender hopefulness and ambition. (Levine, 1990, p. xi)
>
> Expertise kindles intellectual self-esteem. (Levine, 2002, p. 323)

Preparing for Inclusion

Even though we consider the general classroom to be the home base for the student with a disability, we need to make preparations to provide a smooth transition for all concerned. Some special students may spend a large portion of their day receiving services in alternative settings. Students with mild disabilities will spend most of their day within the general classroom in multiage or multi-ability groupings. In either case, students as well as teachers need support.

Special students need many skills to function within the general class environment. Whether a student is new to the general class or has previously spent a large portion of time there, he or she needs skills to help smooth the transition.

The structure of the class can present major problems for students with special needs who must be taught the rules and routines. Even if teachers post and review rules, the students may not truly understand them. After reviewing the rules and routines, teachers should encourage students to discuss them and ask questions if a rule is unclear. To avoid embarrassment, older students can ask such questions after school or during a study break.

Figure 4.1 presents a checklist of rules and routines. The teacher may complete the checklist and give it to the students, who can keep it in a notebook for reference. This checklist is also excellent for substitute teachers because it helps them clearly understand classroom expectations.

For younger children, you may want to videotape last year's students modeling the rules. When fall arrives, and as you discuss each rule, you can show the rule modeled on the videotape. Tell the children that if they work very hard, they will be the movie stars for next year's children. However, be sure that you have administrative permission to videotape students. You may need written permission. Also, remember to show the modeled rules one at a time with practice sessions. Showing all the rules at one sitting may overwhelm young children.

Figure 4.1 Checklist for rules and routines.

Class____________ **Teacher** ____________ **Period** ______

1. Seating arrangement:
   ___ Open seating
   ___ Assigned seating
2. Behavior for entering the class:
   ___ Visiting with friends allowed
   ___ Visiting with friends not allowed
   ___ Place personal belongings in desk, locker, or bookshelf, etc.
   ___ Place class materials on desk
   ___ Copy class work from board
   ___ Copy homework assignment from behind
   ___ Other
3. Behavior when leaving the class:
   ___ Leave when the bell is sounded
   ___ Leave only when dismissed by teacher
4. Format for heading papers
   Model of format ____________
   ___ Location on paper
5. Procedure for turning in completed work:
   ___ Will be discussed with each assignment
   ___ At beginning of each class
   ___ At end of each class
   ___ Only when requested by teacher
6. How to request a drink of water:
7. Procedure for going to the restroom:
8. Procedure for going to the clinic:
9. Procedure for going to the office:
10. Procedure for sharpening pencils and requesting supplies:
11. What to do when tardy for class:
12. Procedure for going to the locker:
13. Policy regarding book covers and jackets:
14. Policy on care of texts:
15. Materials needed for class:
16. Procedure if you do not have class materials:
17. What to do when you need to leave class or cannot cope:
18. Class policy for making up work:
19. Penalty for late work:
20. Grading policy:
21. Testing schedule:
22. Structure of class procedures:
23. Where to put trash:
24. Can I chew gum or have snacks?
25. How to ask for assistance:
26. When is talking allowed?
27. Procedure for asking questions:
28. Procedure for responding to questions:
29. Procedure if you are unsure about asking a question in front of peers:
30. Rules of attire–hats:
31. Rule of clothes which advertise:
32. Rules on cigarettes and alcohol:

Note: From *Reaching the Hard to Teach* by J.W. Wood, 2008, Richmond, VA: Judy Wood, Inc. Reprinted with permission.

ADAPTING THE BEHAVIORAL ENVIRONMENT

Ongoing educators manage student behavior and teaching. No system is foolproof; sometimes problem behaviors distract from the positive instructional atmosphere that teachers have so carefully built. In preparing the behavior environment, educators must consider class structure, how to provide a risk-free environment, and how the teacher's behavior affects the classroom.

The Teacher Sets the Tone

The teacher sets the tone in the classroom. He or she adjusts the lighting, controls the temperature, arranges the seating, decides how to present lessons, elects when to give tests, and chooses what types of tests to administer. The teacher sets the affective atmosphere of the classroom and the stage for learning. The teacher alone has the power to invite or not invite each student to learn. The teacher's attentiveness, expectations, encouragement, attitudes, and evaluations strongly influence students' perceptions of themselves as learners. Thus, the teacher's behavior influences the students' behavior. To assess their potential influence on student behavior, teachers should ask themselves the following questions:

- Do I leave my personal problems at home?
- Am I in good physical and emotional health?
- Am I happy with my role in life?
- Does my voice convey confidence?
- Does my walk convey confidence?
- Do I have a positive self-concept?
- What is my attitude toward my peer group?
- What is my attitude toward children?
- Do I accept the responsibility of students at risk?
- Do I feel comfortable about admitting mistakes?
- Will I change my opinion when someone presents a valid reason for doing so?
- Do I have a sense of humor?
- Can I laugh at myself?
- Am I an attentive listener?
- Do I teach subjects or children?

Figure 4.2 offers eight behavior suggestions for the teacher.

Providing Class Structure

When trouble occurs in the classroom, teachers should first assess themselves and the environment. If they are still having difficulty managing student behaviors, they should look at class structure.

Frequently, mild misbehaviors will disappear when the student is given structure within the class environment. Providing boundaries for students facilitates a

Figure 4.2 Behavior suggestions for the teacher.

Fairness: Teachers must demonstrate fairness in assisgnments, giving help, etc., or they cannot expect students to begin to like them.

Appearance: Appearance is often mentioned by students when they describe teachers for whom they have high regard. Good grooming and a pleasant appearance are interpreted as a sign of respect.

Humor: William Glasser says humor is a form of caring. Teachers need not be joke tellers, but those who respond openly to humorous moments or who can kid lightheartedly with students seem to strike particularly responsive chords.

Courtesy: Courtesy in the classroom helps build personal relationships and is frequently responded to in kind.

Respect: Teachers show respect by encouraging students to express ideas without criticism, by valuing student products, or by not "putting down" a student. When respect is extended, it is usually returned.

Realness: Students see teachers as "real" only when the teacher allows them to do so. Teachers share anecdotes with students from their own lives, integrating personal experiences into explanation and presentations.

Reestablishing Contact: After a student has been reprimanded, reestablishing contact by showing that a grudge is not held helps the student reenter the emotional flow of the classroom.

Active Listening: Teachers listen carefully to the content, reflect back the message, and do so with feeling.

Note: Adapted from *The Skillful Teacher: Building Your Teaching Skills,* 5th ed. (pp. 347–349), by J. Saphier and R. Gower, 1997, Carlisle, MA: Research for Better Teaching. Adapted with permission.

risk-free environment and allows students the freedom to relax in the class, knowing what is and is not expected. Not knowing how to behave or being unclear about the teacher's expectations creates a confusing situation for many students.

By effectively introducing structured rules, teachers can control the environment of the class and prevent inappropriate behaviors. For example, the teacher should let all students, especially those with special needs, know what behaviors are permitted. Inappropriate behavior will often disappear when students know their limits. For teachers, setting rules for behavior establishes a structure for managing the classroom environment. For students, working within the boundaries of the rules establishes a structure for being responsible. Teachers can use the following guidelines when setting rules:

1. Involve students in formulating the rules.
2. Keep the list of rules short.
3. Keep the rules short and to the point.
4. Phrase the rules positively.

5. Don't just mention the rules when someone misbehaves; remind students about them at other times.
6. Post rules in a conspicuous place and review them regularly.
7. Record the number of times that rules have been reviewed with the class.
8. Make different sets of rules for different activities. Let students know when those different rules apply.
9. Only make rules that can be enforced.
10. When a student first breaks a rule, review the rule together one on one.

Managing Students

Students are motivated when they "buy into" what is being presented. This is intertwined with who you are as a teacher. If you're fair, empathetic, and willing to modify when appropriate, you will gain an incredible edge with your students. They will respect you and want to do well. Moreover, they will be more receptive to redirection or private discussions about problems when that becomes necessary. The foremost characteristic they intuit is, are you *really* interested in them? Treating them with respect lays the foundation for motivation. As with all students, respecting the dignity of "reluctant learners" and students with behavioral challenges is still the cornerstone for developing rapport and the effective use of most strategies.

Following are good motivating actions teachers can use inside or outside the classroom:

1. Try not to react to the behavior of children at risk, but try to understand what they want to gain. Is it attention, power, or revenge?
2. Speak quietly while in a stressful situation with a student. Try not to yell—it doesn't help.
3. Send positive notes to parents.
4. Discipline with dignity.
5. Talk with students about the problem and ask how you might work together to solve it.
6. Treat all children the way you want to be treated.
7. Touch children on the elbows. This is the least intrusive part of a person.
8. Practice being a listener to problems.
9. Allow students to choose a "time-out" place or time if they feel the need for one.
10. Develop a behavior analysis/intervention:

Behaviors	Situation
Feelings	Thoughts

- Outline what happened in sequence, in the appropriate boxes.
- Determine what (in what area and in what specifics) would result in different outcomes.

ADAPTING THE PHYSICAL ENVIRONMENT

Teachers instruct students within the tightly woven framework of the school day. For harmonious and structured management, schools design the day around various schedules and physical arrangements. This framework affects students and teachers because it affects the types of subjects taught, class size, resources, students' choice of subjects, and educational philosophy. Regardless of the framework used, however, educators want to be able to adapt it to make instruction easy and productive. The following sections consider grouping for instruction and classroom design.

Grouping for Instruction

Grouping procedures vary from school to school and from teacher to teacher. Many teachers feel that grouping within classrooms creates an even heavier workload. However, children do learn at different rates and in different ways and therefore do not always learn best in one large group.

In 2003 Smith, Moiner, and Zahorik conducted a study of the effects of class size on student achievement. Reducing the K–3 class size to 15 students (with one teacher), they found that by the end of the third grade, students entering the study at grade 1 increased in achievement at a level of one-third to one-half year ahead of the students in larger classes.

Regretfully, schools across the nation are increasing class size due to financial cutbacks and teacher shortages. These increases in class size usually dictate whole-group instruction. But whole-group instruction does not provide the best benefits to students academically: Questions go unattended, easily distracted students remain off task, and students become lost in the masses. Instruction continues to move along, leaving students with special needs and those at risk lost and confused, which in turn means that many of these students drop out of school.

Fortunately, there are a variety of ways to group students that will help teachers individualize within whole-group situations. Here are some examples.

Creative Grouping. When teachers group students, students become labeled. This can present a problem: No matter what the teacher calls the group, all children know which ones are bright, average, and slow. Creative grouping, however, allows for a diversity of academic skills, thus eliminating labels and giving students the freedom to move among groups.

Creative grouping may be used at either the secondary or elementary level. Teachers set up the groups according to academic subject and then break the subject into specific objectives or skills. They assign a student to a creative group based on the specific skill that the student needs to work on. No one is locked into a group because each student moves into another group after mastering the skill. Figure 4.3 shows a chart for a creative mathematics group that allows a student to complete a skill, keep a personal record, and then move on.

Figure 4.3 Chart for a creative mathematics group.

	Tanner	Camden	Clay	Nora	Emma
Identifies penny, nickel, and dime by name.					
Identifies penny, nickel, and dime by value.					
Identifies quarter, half-dollar, and dollar by name.					
Identifies quarter, half-dollar, and dollar by value.					

Note: From *Reaching the Hard to Teach* by J. W. Wood, 2008, Richmond, VA: Judy Wood, Inc. Reprinted with permission.

Creative grouping may include at least three variations, all of them working simultaneously: a learning station, a seatwork station, and a small-group instructional station. When class begins, the teacher color codes or numbers the stations and gives each student a direction card or uses a list on the board to indicate the station the student should use first. Remember, a student who masters a given skill can enter a new creative group.

Interest Grouping. Interest grouping is a method of grouping students based on their specific interests. For example, in reading, students may select the same types of books to read. In social studies, students may be interested in the same period of history. These students may be grouped by interest and develop a series of questions, review a specific book, or research a certain period.

Research Grouping. Research groups can be established by giving each group a specific problem to research. Each group then reports back to the class with the results of the research. Teachers may give groups lists of specific research questions to be answered and possible sources to investigate.

Cooperative Learning. Cooperative learning, a worthwhile grouping strategy for heterogeneous student populations, is a method of class structure in which students work together to achieve a shared academic goal. Students are held accountable for their own academic behaviors as well as for those of their peers. Students with disabilities work well in cooperative settings and develop class behaviors such as asking questions. Additionally, they learn from their nondisabled peers. Groups are assigned a group task with individual duties. Grades may be given for individual task completion and group completion. The beginning teacher can use four basic formats to implement cooperative learning: peer teaching, group projects, the jigsaw, and the shield.

Teachers should not overlook one of a school's most valuable resources—its students. Within class groups, teachers can assign peer tutors to assist students who are having difficulty with the content of a lesson. For example, peer tutors may record assignments so that the student with mild disabilities can listen to the tape for extra reinforcement. Peer tutors can also work one on one using a flannel board, manipulating real or paper money, and helping a student with special needs at the computer. At the secondary level, peer tutors can help small groups of students with disabilities look up their chapter study questions, work on class work or homework assignments, and participate in study or review sessions. A peer can also call out words during group or individual spelling tests. Using peers and grouping for spelling tests helps students with disabilities who may need to have their spelling words called out more slowly.

Peer tutoring has numerous advantages: facilitating the interaction between students without disabilities and students with disabilities; making use of children's insights about how to teach recently learned or newly presented content to other students; making learning more cooperative and less competitive; and providing experiences related to living in a democracy, to caring, and to being cared for.

In project groups, students share knowledge and skills to complete a task. All students are included in the process, and motivation is heightened. Each student contributes to the group project based on his or her skill level. But if the group project is not structured, the burden of task completion may be shouldered by only one or a few students.

Classroom Design

The physical environment of a classroom should stimulate students if effective learning is to occur. Before developing a classroom design, teachers may use the checklist in Table 4.2 to evaluate the effectiveness of the classroom's physical environment. The physical environment includes all physical aspects of the room: wall areas, lighting, floors, and room area. Being aware of the classroom's physical organization can help teachers prevent classroom problems.

Class designs should be developed around the type of grouping strategies the teacher has selected. At both the secondary and elementary levels, classroom designs are important because they dictate whether a teacher uses small-group instruction, one-on-one instruction, or whole-class instruction. Once teachers decide which type of instructional design to use during a lesson, they can alter room arrangements to meet their needs. Because no one design works best for every student, teachers need to change from time to time. Students can often help to choose a viable design for the day's lesson.

Table 4.2 Checklist for creating an effective classroom environment.

	YES	NO
Wall areas		
• Walls clean to prevent distractions.	___	___
• Bulletin boards neatly designed and seasonally up-to-date.	___	___
• Bulletin boards available for students' use and display.	___	___
• Windows clean or neatly covered.	___	___
• Blackboards in view of all students, clean and undamaged.	___	___
Lighting		
• Proper window lighting.	___	___
• Ceiling lighting sufficient.	___	___
Floors		
• Clean.	___	___
• Obstructive objects removed.	___	___
• Barrier-free for wheelchairs, etc.	___	___
Room area		
• Appropriate chair sizes for age levels.	___	___
• Arrangements for left– as well as right-handed students.	___	___
• Areas provided for small-group instruction.	___	___
• Areas provided for independent instruction.	___	___
• Areas in room designated for specific behaviors, such as quiet time, reading in twos, game areas, motor areas, art areas.	___	___
• Learning centers provided.	___	___
• Study carrels provided.	___	___
• Areas designated for listening to tapes, such as recordings of lessons or chapters in books.	___	___

Note: From *Reaching the Hard to Teach* by J.W. Wood, 2008, Richmond, VA: Judy Wood, Inc. Reprinted with permission.

Learning Centers. A learning station or learning center is a selected space in the classroom where students may go to work on a new assignment or on a skill or concept they have recently learned. The learning station approach to teaching or reinforcing skills saves the classroom teacher's time and energy. At the same time, it allows student freedom of choice in activities, successful completion of tasks, and immediate feedback for correct or incorrect responses. The learning center gives the teacher a way to individualize instruction and work with specific educational objectives. Common in elementary schools, learning stations are rarely used in secondary classrooms. Nevertheless, they can give the secondary teacher a desirable instructional alternative.

Advantages of Learning Centers for Inclusion. Learning centers serve multiple purposes in instructing students. For one thing, the teacher saves time during the day because a group or an individual can work alone at the center. In addition, learning centers in inclusive classrooms have the following specific advantages:

- Many students prefer to work alone, and the learning center gives them this option.
- Self-correcting learning centers provide immediate feedback about correct or incorrect responses without embarrassment.
- Students with special needs can work at their own pace without pressure.
- From a variety of activities, students can select the most appropriate.
- Because students with special needs in inclusive environments may work below the level of other students in the general classroom, learning centers provide them with appropriate activities at their own levels.
- Activities at the learning center can reinforce the objectives specified on the student's IEP.
- Learning centers reinforce the mode of learning best suited to the student with a mild disability. For example, if the student learns better visually, the teacher can present more activities in a visual manner. If the student learns better auditorily, the teacher can put activities on tape recorders.

Learning Centers and Standards. With the emphasis on standards-driven curricula, learning centers may be developed to reteach standard strands. One elementary school in Ohio established an excellent procedure for doing so. The 10 strands for standards in math/language arts were reviewed for each student. Each student's strand with an 80 percent or lower score was identified, and then the three lowest strands were selected for reteaching in a learning center. Learning centers for each of the 10 strands were developed. One teacher was assigned three strands, one teacher was assigned four, and the third teacher three strands for center development. Activities were developed to reteach or reinforce the specific strands. During one 90-minute block each week, the students floated to the classroom that housed the center for the strand on which the student scored 80% or lower. Each student worked at three centers during the 90-minute block.

A Few Last Tips for Learning Centers. Seats from an old SUV and a table on which to store records or tapes and headphones can make a great listening center. Floating centers, consisting of materials in boxes that can be moved to various locations, can be useful when room space and class size become issues. To start a learning center, the teacher should survey the materials available and ask peers for additional materials. Because centers are always a work in progress, teachers should add to centers as students' needs change.

Bulletin Boards. Most classrooms have at least one bulletin board. Teachers usually design bulletin boards as seasonal decorations or as special places to display work. However, bulletin boards can also reflect a specific learning purpose. Bulletin boards designed for incidental learning are simply placed around the room with the hope that students will pick up a little extra learning. For example, in one school, the halls are painted to look like highways, street signs hang over classroom doors, and the ABCs run around the walls. It is hard to get a drink of water without learning a little multiplication. As children line the halls, incidental learning takes place in every direction they look. Many books have ideas that teachers can use to design bulletin boards for incidental learning.

Figure 4.4 Types of bulletin boards.

Language involvement bulletin board	This bulletin board is designed with round rotating disks that are used interchangeably for any subject or content.
Slide-study bulletin board	This bulletin board can be used for any subject area. Slides are taken related to the desired subject matter and stored in compartments attached to the bulletin board.
Auditory-action bulletin board	This bulletin board contains an activity mounted beneath the display on the bulletin board. A cassette is prepared by the teacher, which guides the students through the required lessons.
Lift panel bulletin board	These bulletin boards are made with pieces of construction paper folded in half. The outer flap of the panel contains a question or idea. The inner flap is secured to the bulletin board and contains the answer or solution.
Sentence strips bulletin board	Strips are attached to the bulletin board and may convey relevant printed information or questions. They may be changed frequently to maintain interest.

Note: From "Instructional Games" by J. G. Greer, I. Friedman, and V. Laycock, 1978. In R. M. Anderson, J. G. Greer, & S. Odle (Eds.) *Individualizing Education for Special Children in the Mainstream* (pp. 267–293). Baltimore: University Park Press. Copyright 1978 by PRO-ED, Inc. Adapted by permission.

In contrast, intentional learning is planned learning. Teachers can design bulletin boards based on a lesson or current events. One school has a "good morning news" bulletin board for the class. The teacher broadcasts the news, and each student brings an item for the bulletin board or the announcements. This method uses intentional learning effectively.

Figure 4.4 presents different types of bulletin boards with a brief description of each. Teachers may adapt the content format to match the individual needs of students.

SUMMARY

Establishing an effective learning environment requires a careful look at the socio-emotional, behavioral, and physical aspects of the classroom. When this foundation is laid, it is time to plan for the teaching environment, which includes lesson planning, incorporating teaching techniques, content, and evaluation.

RESOURCES

Council for Children with Behavioral Disorders,
c/o Council for Exceptional Children (CEC)
1110 W. Glebe Road Suite 300
Arlington, VA 22201-5704
www.cec.sped.org

American Academy of Child and Adolescent Psychiatry Public Information Office
1615 Wisconsin Avenue NW
Washington, DC 20016
(202) 966-7300
www.aacap.org

SUGGESTED READINGS

Lewis, C., Schaps, E., & Watson, M. (1996). The caring classroom's academic edge. *Educational Leadership,* 54(1), 15–21.

Zins, J. E., Travis, L. F., & Freppon, P. A. (1997). Linking research and educational programming to promote social and emotional learning. In P. Salovery & D. Syulter (Eds.), *Emotional development and emotional intelligence: Implications for educators.* New York: Basic Books.

WEBSITES

Coalition of Essential Schools. A website of the organization directed at improving schools and school systems. *www.essentialschools.org*

National Center for Children in Poverty home site. *www.nccp.org*

REFERENCES

Meyen, D., Vergason, H., & Whelan, C. (1993). "In my dreams": A second look at inclusion and programming. *Journal of the Association for Persons with Severe Handicaps, 18,* 296–298.

Levine, M. (1990). *Keeping a head in school: A student's book about learning abilities and learning disorders.* Cambridge, MA: Educators Publishing Service.

Smith, P., Molnar, A., & Zahorik, J. September 2003. "Class size reduction in Wisconsin: A fresh look at the data," Education Policy Research Unit (EPRU), Arizona State University.

Levine, M. (2002). *A mind at a time.* New York: Simon & Schuster.

Parkinson, A. F., Dulfano, I., & Nink, C. E. (2003). *Removing barriers: Research-based strategies for teaching those who learn differently.* Centerville, UT: MTC Institute.

Wood, M. (1998). Whose job is it anyway? Educational roles in inclusion. *Exceptional Children, 64,* 181–195.

Chapter 5

ADAPTING LESSON PLANS

Key Terms

Acquisition *(page 71)*
Benchmarks *(page 66)*
Generalization (or Transfer) *(page 71)*
Indicators *(page 66)*
Retention *(page 71)*
Standards *(page 65)*

CHAPTER-AT-A-GLANCE

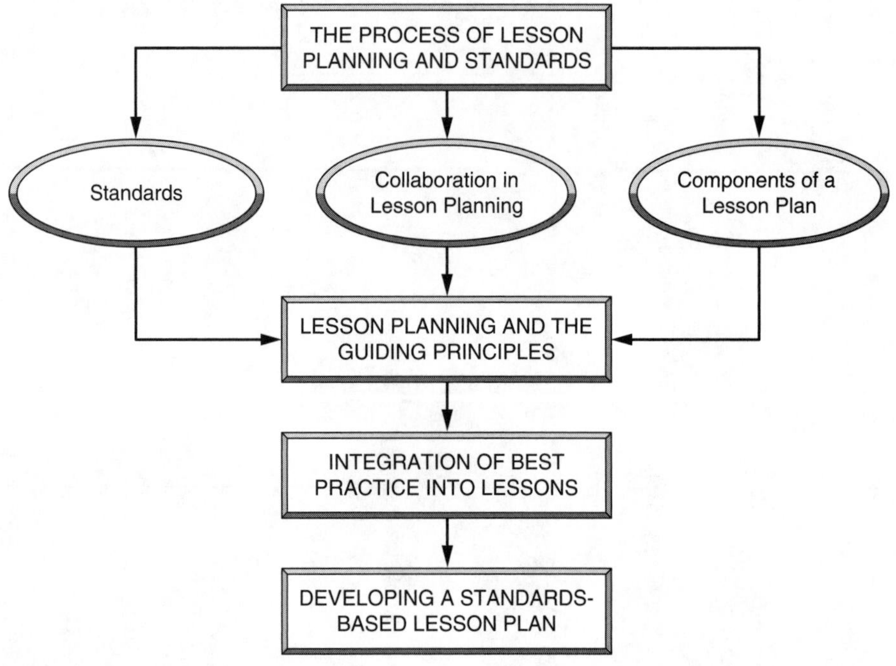

LEARNER OBJECTIVES

After you read this chapter, you will be able to

- *Explain how lesson planning and standards go together.*
- *Provide collaboration tips for lesson planning.*
- *Discuss how the principles of learning are ongoing interventions during the implementation of the lesson plan.*
- *Discuss research-based strategies, lesson planning, and student achievement.*
- *Plan for interventions during lesson planning.*

VIGNETTE

Mr. Suri began his third year of teaching. His first two years had been extremely difficult. His students' behaviors were unmanageable, and parents complained that their children were not learning up to capacity. Mr. Suri's supervisor was greatly disturbed with students' test scores. Finally, the supervisor asked Mr. Suri to discuss these issues with his mentor teacher, Mrs. Hayes. The first step for Mrs. Hayes was to review Mr. Suri's lesson plans. To her amazement, he had not developed any lesson plans for three years. Mrs. Hayes told Mr. Suri that the lesson plan is the beginning and end of the instructional process. She provided Mr. Suri with sample lesson plans and explained that teaching from day to day without seeing the big picture makes lesson planning a piecemeal process. One of the first tips Mrs. Hayes gave Mr. Suri was to create a yearly, monthly, weekly, and daily plan. She also explained the importance of incorporating interventions into lesson plans.

Note: From Reaching the Hard to Teach *by J. W. Wood, 2008, Richmond, VA: Judy Wood, Inc. Reprinted with permission.*

This chapter offers simple techniques that both general and special education teachers can use when developing interventions for lesson plans. The following topics will be discussed: the lesson planning process as it relates to standards; lesson planning collaboration; components of the lesson plan; principles of learning; and the SAALE model and lesson planning.

This chapter also introduces a broad framework for managing transitions during the instructional process. As such, it has a direct bearing on the issues addressed in the remaining chapters of the text. Try to keep this chapter in mind as you continue reading the remainder of the text.

THE PROCESS OF LESSON PLANNING AND STANDARDS

The nation and states have been busy developing guidelines for curricula selection for school districts. From the curricula educators begin to develop their units and resulting lessons before lesson planning begins. Let's back up and take a look at national and state preparation for curricula development.

Standards

National statements or standards include what all students should learn in schools. From these statements or standards, each state develops a list of what its students should learn from kindergarten to twelfth grade. These statements are completed for math, language arts, and other subjects. After completion of the broad categories, states develop lists of what students should learn by grade level.

Traditionally, educators within school districts were free to select what to teach and what materials to use. Across the nation attention was drawn to the diversity in the skills students were taught. Many felt that our students were capable of learning more. As a result, states began to develop **standards** for school districts to follow when developing curricula. These standards were further broken into small steps, or **benchmarks,** and **indicators** were inserted into the benchmarks to establish a measuring point for educators. Figure 5.1 provides an overview of the relationship of standards to lesson planning.

Collaboration in Lesson Planning

Most often, the special education teacher becomes actively involved in the lesson planning process only when the general education teacher is in the last stage of planning: developing a daily lesson plan. However, it is more beneficial to the student with special needs if the special education teacher becomes involved in the first phase of planning: the yearly plan. A year's worth of learning outcomes as set forth in daily plans might be attainable for students without disabilities, but difficult for a student with special needs. It's a losing battle to try to keep a student in a general education class where the skills being taught are instructionally too advanced. A balance must be maintained between skills taught and those that are reasonably attainable.

Many students with special needs and those at risk can achieve success during general lesson plan activities when intervention points are identified and appropriate accommodations or modifications are provided. This process depends on careful, well-planned collaboration between the general and special education teachers. As teachers work together, they should follow several guidelines:

1. Realize that interventions may be necessary in the general class lesson.
2. Be specific in listing what will occur during each component of the lesson plan. Include an objective, strategies, resources, and evaluation.
3. Allow time for both teachers to review the lesson plan and develop appropriate interventions.
4. Be flexible when an adaptation or intervention does not work.
5. Be prepared to develop an alternate intervention.
6. Realize that when an intervention is made to the lesson plan, the plan is still valid and not watered down.

Components of a Lesson Plan

All lesson plans have several essential parts, although various authors may give these parts different names.

1. The *purpose* states instructional objectives, including what students should learn from the lesson based on the stated standard or benchmark.
2. The sequence of lesson *strategies,* or learning experiences, describes the work-study activities that will occur during the lesson.
3. The *learning process* lists the resources (learning materials, media, or technology) needed to teach the lesson.
4. The *evaluation* describes the activities designed to measure the lesson process. Evaluation is also an ongoing process.

Figure 5.1 An overview of the relationship of standards to lesson planning.

Standards
What students should know and do
Sample Standard
Students define and investigate self-selected or assigned issues, topics, and problems. They locate, select, and make use of relevant information from a variety of media, reference, and technological sources. Students use an appropriate form to communicate their findings.
Benchmarks
Standards are grouped by scope and sequences, what needs to be taught in each grade, and what will be taught first, second, etc.
Sample Benchmark
Identify important information and write brief notes about the information. (This is one of several benchmarks established to meet the above standard.)
Indicators
Established to measure outcomes:
• How will students be involved to show achievement?
• Steps established for students to meet standards.
• Indicators act as a "stop sign." When students exhibit indicated behavior (identify and write), they have demonstrated ability to meet benchmark.
Simple Indicator
Identify and write indicator for the above benchmark.
Curricula
Established based on what standards indicate will be taught.
Curricula
Curriculum is developed for all subjects.
Unit Lesson Planning
Educators develop units and resulting lesson plans that include activities to teach each benchmark or standard.
See Table 5.6 for lesson plan developed for the above standard/benchmark.

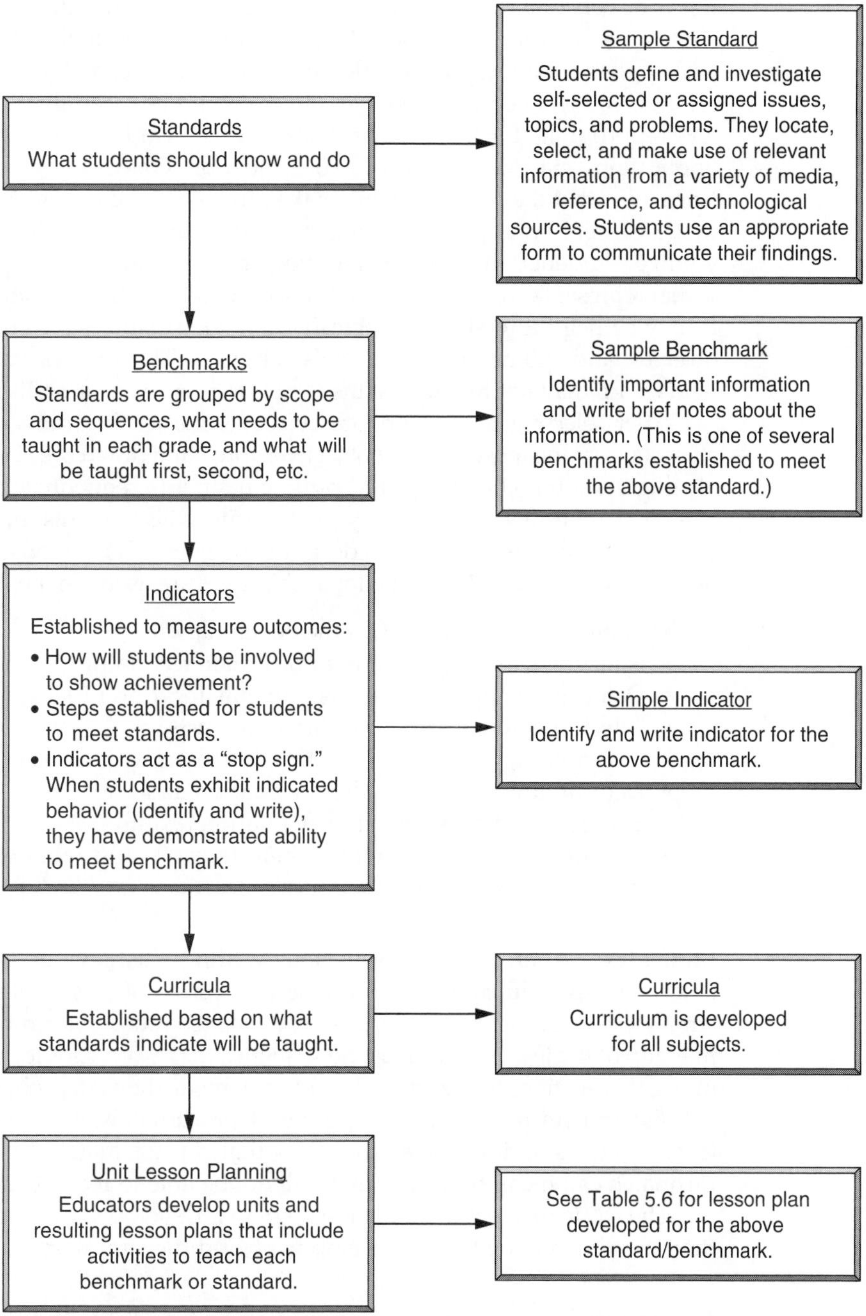

Note: From *Reaching the Hard to Teach* by J. W. Wood, 2008, Richmond, VA: Judy Wood, Inc. Reprinted with permission.

Instructional Objectives. The instructional objective, which is based on the standards or benchmarks of the lesson, is a statement of specific learner outcomes that should result from the lesson. Objectives should be focused on the student, be clearly stated, express the intended behavior outcome, and identify how the behavior outcome will be measured. Objectives should be carefully written in the domain level appropriate for the student. These levels include knowledge, comprehension, application, analysis, synthesis, and evaluation. Objectives should be shared with learners so that they will be aware of the purpose of the lesson. A teacher can explain to the learner how objectives spring from established standards and benchmarks. For younger students, the teacher may need to paraphrase the objective or provide a visual representation of the desired outcome to help them understand the objective. It may be helpful to show graphically how today's objective continues yesterday's objective and will tie into tomorrow's objectives. This provides a connection for students, who may not readily see the logical sequence of the skills being taught.

After selecting an appropriate objective, the teacher moves ahead to the next steps: (a) making a list of all subobjectives (breaking down the class objective), (b) analyzing the subobjectives by task (putting them into sequential order from simple to complex), (c) listing the necessary prerequisite skills students must have before they can master the objective, and (d) deciding the point of entry for students with special needs or who are at risk. Instructional objectives are useful in the following situations:

- Planning lessons based on the benchmarks.
- Selecting learning aids and appropriate technology.
- Determining appropriate assignments for individual students.
- Selecting and constructing classroom tests.
- Determining classroom embedded-assessment measures.
- Determining when to gather evaluation data.
- Summarizing and reporting evaluation results.
- Helping learners determine where they are and where they need to go as they strive to become independent learners.

Strategies. After carefully selecting, writing, displaying, and explaining the objectives, the educator begins the second phase of lesson planning: developing strategies or learning experiences. The teacher must determine the instructional makeup of the lesson as well as the sequence the lesson should follow. While developing this section, the teacher should remember the stated objectives and carefully build strategies around the objectives. Unfortunately, it is common to find excellent objectives and excellent strategies that do not match. Such an instructional mismatch can mean that a student will not be able to reach the objectives.

The strategies section of the lesson plan is developed around three major parts: the introduction, the lesson development, and the summary or closing activity.

Lesson introduction. In the lesson plan introduction, the teacher should state and/or demonstrate what students should learn; use a provocative question, artifact, or hands-on activity to stimulate student interest in the lesson; or link the present lesson to past lessons or student experiences. The teacher should follow these six steps during the introduction:

1. Review the relationship of the objective, or lesson purpose, to the standard or benchmark.
2. Review what is to be learned, including the major instructional objective and all subobjectives. Think in terms of preparing the student for the lesson itself, and make sure that instructional objectives are on the student's instructional level and are in sequential order. Also include an assessment of the students' prerequisite skills.
3. Demonstrate what the student should learn. This might include a whole-part-whole method using a lecture outline or organizer, or providing sequential written directions.
4. Use a mind capturer or activator such as a manipulative or hands-on activity to boost interest.
5. Link past lessons to students' current or past experiences, which make the lesson more meaningful for students.
6. Relate the lesson to a future event. Students can see purpose in learning a lesson if it relates to them personally.

Lesson development. Here the teacher selects activities to achieve the lesson's purpose, describes these activities, and chooses an instructional model around which to organize the lesson. For each of the model's parts, the educator should plan the appropriate adaptation or intervention, if needed. Frequently, by the time he or she is developing a lesson, the teacher may be aware of intervention points for specific students. For other students, however, the need for identifying an intervention point may emerge as the lesson progresses. The intervention/transition checklist is a useful tool for intervention point identification. As the lesson develops, the teacher should keep several major points in mind:

1. Select strategies for teaching for acquisition, retention, and generalization.
2. Select the appropriate activities for teaching for each part of the model.
3. Be sure that all activities are based on the appropriate objective level.
4. Sequence all activities.
5. Identify any necessary intervention points during the lesson for students experiencing difficulty.
6. Identify the areas that need modification or adaptation: technique, content, technology, or assessment/evaluation.
7. Develop the appropriate modification for the areas identified in item 6.
8. Plan for an adapted learning environment.

Lesson summary. Here the major points of the lesson are summarized and the lesson's events are tied together. The teacher may choose to have students

Research Notes for Classroom Application

Developing lesson plans that allow all students the opportunity to meet the learning objective can be an overwhelming task for teachers, especially those of inclusive, diverse classrooms. A concept called Universal Design for Learning (UDL) can help teachers plan their lessons in such a way that "curriculum can be accessed without the need for specialized modifications and adaptations for particular students" (Thousand, Nevin, McNeil, & Liston, 2006, para. 2).

Most educators want to teach every student the way he or she learns best, and the goal of UDL is "for each student to have access to the curriculum in a way that promotes the most learning for that individual" (Howard, 2004, 27). Teachers can do this in the lesson planning stage by differentiating content and materials, differentiating instructional processes, and providing students with multiple ways for expressing what they learn. One educator has done this by beginning her planning sessions with the following questions (Howard, 2004, 27):

- What is the basic idea that the students need to learn?
- What are different ways to learn this idea?
- If there is reading involved, do they have to read it by themselves, or can they use other tools and strategies to get the information?
- Is a test the best way to find out whether students learned the information?
- In what different ways can students show their understanding? Which will be meaningful for them?

As teachers implement each lesson, they can gather new information about each student as they monitor their performances and products. This can then help them more effectively differentiate instruction in future lesson planning, thus increasing the number of students successful in meeting the learning objective.

Sources: Howard, K. L. (2004, February). Universal Design for Learning: Meeting the needs of all students. *Learning and Leading with Technology*, 31(5), 26–29.

Thousand, J., Nevin, A., McNeil, M., & Liston, A. (2006, November). *Differentiating instruction in inclusive classrooms: Myth or reality?* Paper presented at TED/TAM, San Diego, CA.

Note: From *Reaching the Hard to Teach* by J. W. Wood, 2008, Richmond, VA: Judy Wood, Inc. Reprinted with permission.

describe what they have learned by performing one of several activities, such as answering questions, taking part in a discussion, demonstrating something, or presenting a project.

Resources. In the resources section of the lesson plan, the teacher identifies any materials, media, or technology to be used to achieve the lesson's purpose. Such resources may include pages or chapters in a pamphlet, text, or workbook; video or DVD; guest experts; field experience; special settings; art or cooking supplies; or audiovisual equipment. Assessing the instructional level of materials, matching perceptual learning styles with media, and using a variety of materials or media are all part of developing resources.

Evaluation. Evaluation, the final component of the lesson plan, is designed to measure student outcomes, identify a teacher's need to reorganize lesson plans, and target areas for reteaching. Evaluation may appear to be the last component in the lesson plan format, but actually it is an ongoing process.

During evaluation, the teacher assesses student learning and the success of the lesson. Teachers can assess students by checking behavioral objectives, using informal questions, administering formal pre- and posttests, or having students develop projects or products. A teacher may choose to have students check their own work by providing them with feedback, a model of a completed activity, or an illustration of the lesson's concept or process. Another method is to have students assess one another's work or self-assess. To determine the lesson's degree of success, a teacher may analyze students' reactions during the lesson, the value of the lesson as a learning experience, or the teacher's own teaching performance.

Student assignments are also a major component of evaluation. Assignments are part of the evaluation process as well as an extension of content mastery. They give the teacher an opportunity to see whether the student has mastered the skill and whether reteaching will be necessary.

LESSON PLANNING AND THE GUIDING PRINCIPLES

If teaching is the interaction between teacher and learner, then effective teaching is planning that interaction to incorporate the principles of learning. Teaching occurs in three steps: acquisition, retention, and transfer or generalization. When a teacher teaches a skill, the first stage is **acquisition**—learning a new skill, idea, or concept. When students "acquire" the skill, the teacher continues to teach for **retention,** or remembering the skill. Lastly, educators teach for **generalization (or transfer),** which means using a learned skill in another situation. This three-stage teaching process can be facilitated with the use of specific teaching strategies (see Table 5.1).

Some students acquire a new skill, immediately retain the skill, and can transfer it to other situations. Other students must be purposefully taught to acquire, retain, and transfer. Employing appropriate teaching strategies is a form of intervening. Interventions occur in different forms; one form is to constantly be aware of a student's learning within the cycle. Is the student in acquisition, retention, or generalization?

Table 5.1 General principles of learning and strategies for teaching each principle.

PRINCIPLE	DEFINITION	STRATEGY
Acquisition	The learning of a new skill, concept, or idea.	• Attention and purpose • Demonstration of end results • Whole and parts methods • Amount of material • Sequenced steps • Knowledge of results • Multisensory presentation • Structure • Understanding psychological needs
Retention	Remembering over an extended period of time what was taught.	• Overlearning • Distribution of practice • Recitation • Amount of practice • Type of retention measure • Instructions to recall • Reminiscence/review
Generalization	Taking what is learned in one situation and using it in a second situation.	• Intertask similarity • Overlearning • Multiple career applications • Instructions to transfer

Note: From *Reaching the Hard to Teach* by J. W. Wood, 2008, Richmond, VA: Judy Wood, Inc. Reprinted with permission.

When employing a strategy for teaching a principle, the teacher must develop the strategy into an activity or practical application. Tables 5.2, 5.3, and 5.4 provide practical activities for each teaching strategy found in Table 5.1. For example, Mrs. Divi was beginning a lesson on the parts of a flower. For acquisition she used the teaching technique *attention and purpose*. Mrs. Divi displayed the flower parts on picture cards and placed the "puzzle pieces" together. As the lesson developed, Mrs. Divi continued teaching the acquisition of flower parts employing sequenced steps by using a graphic organizer. When the class acquired the skill, Mrs. Divi continued to teach for retention using the teaching strategy *overlearning*. The students developed games for learning flower parts. For transfer, Mrs. Divi showed the students similarities between the parts of the flower and the parts of other plants.

Table 5.2 Strategies for facilitating student acquisition.

Attention and purpose: Establishing attention and purpose for the task to be learned	• Explain or show pictures or a video of problem situations where concept or skill is needed. • State *what* student will be learning. • Tie what students will be learning to previous learning. Show a connection. • List and state the standard the learning activity will be addressing. • State the learning outcome. • Establish situations in life where problems/situations will be needed. • Focus students' attention on the task by using colors, bold print, etc. • Provide step-by-step directions, placing each direction on one 3 × 5 inch index card. • For younger children use picture cards. • Use tape recorders to give directions with a written checklist to watch as directions are presented orally. • Use wall charts with pictures and word clues. • Review class outlines prior to test. • Be clear with class objective and structures.
Demonstration of end results: Establishing for students what the learning objectives will be and what they will look like	• Repeat objective/outcome/indicators. • Visually display objective/outcome indicators. • Have students explain what they think they are going to learn. • Have students discuss what products/examples they can create that will demonstrate the learning outcomes. • Show examples of prior products that demonstrate learning results.
Whole and parts methods: Whole method presents tasks as a whole; parts method presents tasks in parts	**Whole Method** • Present a word as a whole, then break it down into specific sounds or parts. • Review the outline for the lesson as a whole.

Continued

Table 5.2 (Continued)

	• Address a chapter with a brief summary. • Show the completed product before the student begins to work on the exercise. • Show the video of a novel before the student reads the novel. **Parts Method** • Break skills down into small steps, teaching from lowest to highest skills. • Place each step of an exercise in a checklist so the student can clearly see the parts in progressing order. • Number directions in order. • Tape short segments of a literary work so that the student may listen in parts. • Give tests in small sections. • Focus on parts of the outline or organizer that make up the whole. • Focus on specific steps or segments in a video.
Amount of material: The size of the task and the number of items in the task	• The amount of material may vary depending on the student's ability to handle specific amounts of material. • Work sheets may contain the same information but quantity should be monitored. • Spelling tests may be split in half. • If the student needs more material to learn the task, then the distribution of material should be monitored.
Sequenced steps: Placing steps of activity in sequential order	• Provide visual in handout format of the steps necessary for completing the task. • Place tasks on individual 3 × 5 cards. Give some students only a step or two at a time. • Place the sequence of activities on a bulletin board. • Number all sequences. • Use outlines and graphic organizers.

Knowledge of results: Providing immediate feedback on answers	• Instant feedback is necessary for students to know whether their responses are correct or incorrect. • It has been said that if a student learns the answer incorrectly, it will take 250 times hearing the correct answer to correct the error. • Use computers and/or self-correcting materials. • Provide math problems in puzzle format so that only the correct answer completes the puzzle. • Place the correct response on the reverse side of activity cards. • Develop overlays for tests, such as fill-in-the-blank, multiple-choice, or true-false. • Develop overlays for activities so that correct answers appear either beside or on top of the student's answer.
Multisensory presentation: Using all of the senses for teaching input	• Use outlines and organizers. • Present material visually as well as auditorily. • Let students manipulate objects for concrete learning. • Check the learning styles section in Chapter 6 for an explanation of ideas for multi-sensory presentation. • Use brightly decorated bulletin boards. • Use large print on all transparencies. • Use flashbacks, TV, video, filmstrips, games, and pictures. • Use tape recorders, radios, and recorders with earphones. • Provide recorded books. • Hang mobiles from the ceiling with new information to be learned. • Place information around drinking fountains.
Structure: Organizing the material to be learned so that the student understands the task at hand	• Use acquisition outlines. • Provide organizers. • Review the daily class procedure. • Provide "logical connections" for students between old and new information and explain where the new information fits into the old.

Continued

Table 5.2 (Continued)

	• Remember that just because you understand the material's structure does not mean that the student understands; ask students to explain or demonstrate understanding.
Understanding psychological needs: Understanding what needs the learner has psychologically	• Learning is enhanced when the student's psychological needs are met through instructional/learning activities. • Provide appropriate attention to the student. • Help the student achieve in something. • Help the student to feel secure and safe.

Note: From *Reaching the Hard to Teach* by J. W. Wood, 2008, Richmond, VA: Judy Wood, Inc. Reprinted with permission.

Table 5.3 Strategies for facilitating student retention.

STRATEGY	EXAMPLES
Overlearning: Practicing beyond the point of acquisition the new skill learned	• Provide learning stations or centers with numerous activities designed to teach the newly acquired skill. • Overlearning does not mean boredom. • Let students create ways to practice new skills. • Develop games that reinforce the new skills.
Distribution of practice: The amount of practice required	• The amount of distribution of practice depends on the attention span of the student. • Practice may be mass practice: long periods of practice on a task, or distributed practice, or practice small segments. • Practice vocabulary or spelling words in sets of five. • Practice, rest, and return to practice. • Practice with a friend. • Changing the way information is presented, but not changing the information, will facilitate quicker learning.
Recitation: Practicing a new task after the teacher has removed the original material	• Have students review a new list of vocabulary words with definitions. Have the students use the words without viewing the list. • Present a new word orally and have the students repeat the word within a sentence into a recorder.

	• Let the students play games that use material previously presented by the teacher.
Amount of practice: The total number of practice sessions (the time) students spend to learn a task	• Use games to teach a concept. • Change to another activity teaching the same concept. • Point out practical uses of the concept being taught.
Type of retention measure: Refers to the retention measure a teacher uses to teach material	• The types of retention measures are: **recognition** (the selection of previously learned items from unlearned or false items, for example, a multiple-choice test); **structured recall** (supplying items within a specific context, for example, essay tests or fill-in-the-blank test items); and **relearning** (the time or effort required to relearn previously learned material). • Make a match between how you teach and how you test. • Provide study guides which clearly specify the type of items that will be on the test.
Reminiscence: After a long practice session and rest, the student should have an increase in performance	• Design short check-up tests for students to complete after rest and extended practice. • The practice-rest cycle may have to be repeated several times for some students. • Reward students for information learned even if it is only a small amount. • Students may keep a personal chart of progress.
Instructions to recall: Refers to directing the student to learn with the specific idea of recalling the material at a later time	• Use color-coded notes. • Use note-taking techniques emphasizing specific details. • Provide study guides. • Use outlines and highlight specific details.

Note: From *Reaching the Hard to Teach* by J. W. Wood, 2008, Richmond, VA: Judy Wood, Inc. Reprinted with permission.

Table 5.4 Strategies for facilitating student generalization/transfer.

STRATEGY	EXAMPLES
Intertask similarity: Showing the student the similarity between two different tasks	• Emphasize the similarity between manuscript writing and cursive writing. • Point out how addition and multiplication relate. • Show students how pasting leaves into a book is similar to keeping a notebook in the upper grades.

Continued

Table 5.4 (Continued)

	• Explain how rules in the first or second grade may differ from those in the upper grades. However, rules are rules.
Overlearning: Practice beyond the point of mastery	• Remember that overlearning is not the same as boredom. • Return to skills taught to reinforce the skill. • Use new and creative ways to teach the same skill. • Allow mental/physical rest periods.
Multiple career applications: Generalizing the skills learned to career choice	• Discuss life careers. • Discuss why one selects a career. • Discuss what careers the students are interested in. • List career interest or parent careers on board. • Show connection of skill to career of interest.
Instructions to transfer: Showing the student how learning in one situation will be useful in another	• Show how basic math facts will help the student keep a checkbook. • Point out how reading will help them fill out job forms. • Emphasize how learning to read relates to passing the driver's education class, leading to a driver's license. • Students plan and discuss where they will use what they learned. • Students choose and create a product that uses what they learned. • Relate products to outcomes initially established.

Note: From *Reaching the Hard to Teach* by J. W. Wood, 2008, Richmond, VA: Judy Wood, Inc. Reprinted with permission.

INTEGRATION OF BEST PRACTICE INTO LESSONS

> A teacher level factor that affects student achievement is "instructional strategies." It is perhaps self-evident that more effective teachers use more effective instructional strategies. It is probably also true that effective teachers have more instructional strategies at their disposal. (Marzano, 2003, p. 78)

This text has presented, and will continue to present, strategies that affect student achievement. Because the lesson plan is the starting point for planning and organizing strategies, this would be an appropriate place for discussing categories of research-based instructional strategies and how to incorporate these into lesson planning.

Marzano (2003) reported nine categories of instructional strategies that affect student achievement which he and colleagues researched (Marzano, 1998a; Marzano, Gaddy, & Dean, 2000; Marzano, Pickering, & Pollock, 2001).

These include identifying similarities and differences; summarizing and note-taking; reinforcing effort and providing recognition; homework and practice; nonlinguistic representations; cooperative learning; setting objectives and providing feedback; generating and testing hypotheses; and questions, cues, and advanced organizers (p. 80). Marzano (2003) suggested that educators incorporate these strategies into an instructional framework for units so as not to constrain educators to a day-to-day lesson design. He suggested that general strategies be considered in three categories: "(1) those used at regular intervals in a unit; (2) those focusing on input experiences; and (3) those dealing with reviewing, practicing, and applying content" (p. 85). Marzano went on to list numerous suggestions for implementation. These suggestions have been developed into a checklist for educators found in Figure 5.2. As they develop each lesson within a lesson, teachers can refer to this checklist to ensure that they have incorporated best practice into their unit or lesson.

Figure 5.2 Checklist for integrating best practice into lessons.

Prior to Lesson

- ☐ Prepare a list of questions to help students identify prior knowledge.
- ☐ Prepare logical connections between new content and old content.
- ☐ Provide procedure for organizing new content or thinking about new content.

Goals

- ☐ Establish and identify clear teaming goals. Post standard, benchmark, and indicator.
- ☐ Have students establish self-learning goals.

Class Design

- ☐ Establish individual work based on student ability.
- ☐ Establish cooperative groups.
- ☐ Establish grouping design for lesson:
  - Ability groups
  - Interest groups
  - Creative groups
- ☐ Ask students to revise their mental images.
- ☐ Assign homework:
  - Develop homework and in-class activities requiring students to practice and process new skills.
  - Assign homework and in-class activities that assist students in comparing content with previous knowledge.

During and After Lesson

- ☐ Develop note-taking procedure. Several types may be presented.
- ☐ Have students verbally summarize content.
- ☐ Have students summarize content through written expression. (Some students may not be able to do a complete summary but only write a word summary or sentence summary.)
- ☐ Have students "represent the content as pictures, pictographs, symbols, graphic representations, physical models, or dramatic enactments."
- ☐ Have students use their visual memory to create mental images for content learned.

Lesson Review, Practice, and Content Application

- ☐ Have students revise notes, correct errors, expand information, add details, etc.
- ☐ Ask students to revise graphic representations to correct errors, expand visuals, add details, etc.

Continued

Figure 5.2 (Continued)

Evaluation Measures

- ☐ Establish student self-tracking measures.
- ☐ Establish teacher method of providing student feedback:
  - Item test/reporting back
  - Conferencing
  - Rubric
  - Informal feedback
- ☐ Establish procedures for student comparison of self-evaluation to teacher evaluation.

Develop Projects

- ☐ Assign projects that require students "to generate and test hypotheses through problem-solving tasks."
- ☐ Engage "students in projects that require them to generate and test hypotheses through decision-making tasks."
- ☐ Engage "students in projects that require them to generate and test hypotheses through investigation tasks."
- ☐ Engage "students in projects that require them to generate and test hypotheses through experimental inquiry tasks."
- ☐ Engage "students in projects that require them to generate and test hypotheses through systems analysis tasks."
- ☐ Engage "students in projects that require them to generate and test hypotheses through invention."

Homework

- ☐ Assign homework and in-class activities that assist student in classifying new content.
- ☐ Assign homework and in-class activities requiring students to create metaphors with content learned.
- ☐ Assign homework and in-class activities assisting students in creating analogies with content.

Note: From *What Works in Schools: Translating Research into Action* (pp.85-87) by R.J. Marzano. Alexandria, VA: Association for Supervision and Curriculum Development. Copyright © 2003 by the Association for Supervision and Curriculum Development. Used with permission. The Association for Supervision and Curriculum Development is a worldwide community of educators advocating sound policies and sharing best practices to achieve the success of each learner. To learn more, visit ASCD at www.ascd.org.

DEVELOPING A STANDARDS-BASED LESSON PLAN

Where does an educator physically place interventions within the lesson plan? Table 5.5 presents a sample standard, benchmark, and indicator. Table 5.6 uses benchmark 4 from Table 5.5 and expands it into a sample standards-based lesson plan with preplanned interventions. As Table 5.6 shows, a standards-based lesson plan begins with the broad concept under investigation. Benchmarks are assessed by indicators.

In the "Learning activities/experiences" column in Table 5.6, the lesson purpose is listed, an introduction activity is planned, lesson activity is developed, and the lesson ends with a closing. As seen in the third column, preplanned interventions are inserted into the lesson plan. These interventions are organized according to the SAALE Model: learning environment, teaching/process, content, technology, and products/results. The interventions help the teacher implement the lesson described in the second column. The lesson is assessed according to the indicator listed with the benchmark.

Table 5.5 Standards-based lesson plan.

Broad Concept: Research	**Collaboration Tips: Grade Level Two**
Standard: Students define and investigate self-selected or assigned issues, topics, and problems. They locate, select, and make use of relevant information from a variety of media, reference, and technological sources. Students use an appropriate form to communicate their findings.	
BENCHMARKS	**INDICATORS**
1. Create questions for investigation, assigned topics, or personal areas of interest.	1. Create
2. Utilize appropriate searching techniques to gather information from a variety of locations (e.g., classroom, school library, public library, or community resources).	2. Locate, select, utilize
3. Acquire information, with teacher assistance, from multiple resources about the topic.	3. Acquire
4. Identify important information and write brief notes about the information.	4. Identify and write
5. Sort relevant information about the topic into categories with teacher assistance.	5. Sort
6. Report important findings to others.	6. Report, communicate

Note: From Ohio Department of Education. (2002). *Academic content standards: English language arts k-12.* (pp. 132–133). Center for Curriculum and Assessment. Office of Curriculum and Instruction.

Table 5.6 Standards-based lesson plan.

Broad Concepts: Research		**Grade Level:** Two	
Standard: See Table 5.5		**Benchmark:** No. 4 – Identify	
LESSON PREREQUISITES	**LEARNING ACTIVITIES / EXPERIENCES**	**PREPLANNED INTERVENTIONS**	**ASSESSMENT CONTINUUM**
Key vocabulary:	**Lesson Purpose:** What are we doing today? Benchmark/standard.	**Learning Environment:** • Place in interest groups.	**Identify** • Self-assessment, student reflection.

Continued

Table 5.6 (Continued)

Resources needed: **Hyperlinks:** **Literacy coach/room requests:**	**Introductory Activity:** Put a topic in PowerPoint with a list of short statements. Read and ask what statements are important to the topic. **Lesson Activity:** 1. List topic on an envelope. 2. Using information researched, place important information on small Post-it notes. 3. Drop ideas into envelope. 4. Peers may help. 5. Remove Post-it notes and place on white boards. 6. With group/peer help, identify which is important to topic. **Closing Activity:** • Restate lesson purpose. • Using activity list created by teacher, students check what they have completed. • Star what student needs to rework or continue. • Students self-review.	• Add new words to word wall. **Technique / Process:** • Post intro activity in room as a model. • Print and place model in interest groups. **Content:** • Chop book. • For lesson activity, list activity steps. • Some students may use pictures with code words. **Media/Technology:** • PowerPoint **Products/Results:** • Some students may work alone or write information in phrases or sentences.	• Identified list of important information/teacher observation. • Student highlight important information. • Using the activity list provided to students, make notes for each student for teacher purposes of reteach or back teach. • Completed white boards.

Note: From *Reaching the Hard to Teach* by J. W. Wood, 2008, Richmond, VA: Judy Wood, Inc. Reprinted with permission.

SUMMARY

As teachers prepare lesson plans, they should take time to make adaptations for students with special needs and those at risk. By working collaboratively in the development and implementation of lesson plans, general and special education teachers can provide appropriate instruction for all students. This chapter looked at lesson planning and standards, collaboration during lesson planning, components of a lesson plan, lesson plans and the principles of learning, research-based strategies in lesson planning, interventions in a standards-based lesson plan, the SAALE Model in a standards-based educational system, and simple techniques for lesson delivery. Teachers will discover that when they adapt their lesson plans to the specific needs of learners, students *can* learn the lessons.

RESOURCES

Reading Tree Publications
51 Avesta Street
Springfield, MA 01118-1239
413-782-5839
Fax: 413-782-0862
www.trelease-on-reading.com

SUGGESTED READINGS

Brooks, J. G. (2004). To see beyond the lesson. *Educational Leadership*, *62*(1), 8–12.

Hitchcock, C., Meyer, A., Rose, D., & Jackson, R. (2002). Providing new access to the general curriculum: Universal design for learning. *Council for Exceptional Children*, *35*(2), 8–12.

Rose, D. (2000). Universal design for learning. *Journal of Special Education Technology*, *15*(4), 47–51.

Saphier, J., & Gower, R. (1987). *The skillful teacher: Building your teaching skills.* Carlisle, MA: Research for Better Teaching.

Wong, H. K., & Wong, R. T. (1998). *The first days of school: How to be an effective teacher.* Mountain View, CA: Harry K. Wong.

WEBSITES

The Information Institute of Syracuse. Educators' reference web page offers links to resources and services to the education community. *www.eduref.org.*

Columbia Educational Center Lesson Plans. Lesson plans that have been used successfully by teachers in the classroom. *www.col-ed.org/lessons_page.html.*

Mid-Continent Research for Education and Learning. Provides resources including lesson plans to educators. *www.mcrel.org/resources/plus.*

Teachers.net. Web page offering a Mentor Support Center. *www.teachers.net/mentors.*

REFERENCES

Cooper, J., Hansen, J., Martorella, P., Morine-Dershimer, G., Sadker, M., Sokolove, S., et al. (Eds.). (1977). *Classroom teaching skills: A workbook.* Lexington, MA: Heath.

Marzano, R. J. (2003). *What works in schools: Translating research into action.* Alexandria, VA: Association for Supervision and Curriculum Development.

Marzano, R. J. (1998a). *A theory-based meta-analysis of research on instruction.* Aurora, CO: Mid-Continent Research for Education and Learning. (ERIC Document Reproduction Service No. ED 427 087)

Marzano, R. J., Gaddy, B. B., & Dean, C. (2000). *What works in classroom instruction?* Aurora, CO: Mid-Continent Research for Education and Learning. (ERIC Document Reproduction Service)

Marzano, R. J., Pickering, D. J., & Pollock, J. E. (2001). *Classroom instruction that works: Research-based strategies for increasing student achievement*. Alexandria, VA: Association for Supervision and Curriculum Development.

Tenbrink, T. (1997). Writing instructional objectives. In J. Cooper, J. Hansen, P. Martorella, G. Morine-Dershimer, D. Sadker, M. Sadker, et al. (Eds.), *Classroom teaching skills: A handbook.* Lexington, MA: Heath.

Chapter 6

ADAPTING TEACHING TECHNIQUES

Key Terms

Cognitive Style *(page 90)*
Instruction *(page 87)*
Learning Styles *(page 90)*
Teaching Techniques *(page 97)*

CHAPTER-AT-A-GLANCE

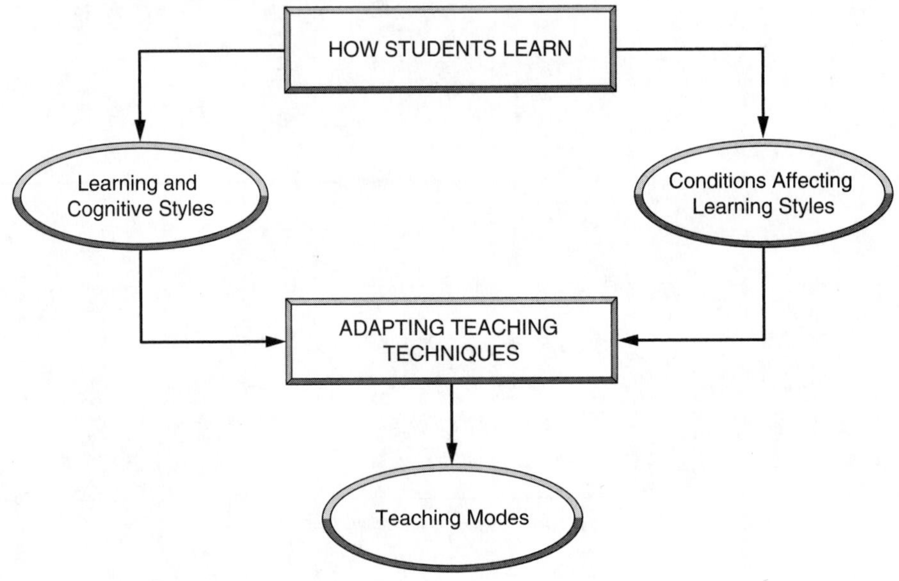

LEARNER OBJECTIVES

After you read this chapter, you will be able to

- *List six learning modalities and techniques for teaching each.*
- *List and discuss the four modes of teaching.*
- *List three teaching techniques for each mode and accommodations for each.*
- *Discuss assessment of teaching techniques.*

VIGNETTE

The faculty of a high school collectively decided to select one intervention that each faculty member would use across the curriculum. After long discussions and reviewing numerous interventions, it was decided that the faculty would each implement a simple outline prior to the beginning of each unit of study. After a few weeks, students began making appointments with the principal. Each student's concern was the same: "What has happened to our teachers? All of a sudden I understand math, science, social studies, and so on. Are they OK?" With great joy the principal reported these comments back to the staff. Their idea was working. It only takes one intervention to make a difference!

Note: From Reaching the Hard to Teach *by J. W. Wood, 2008, Richmond, VA: Judy Wood, Inc. Reprinted with permission.*

Instruction is a teacher's major responsibility to children, school, and community. Good instructional planning paves the way for an organized school day and for the smooth delivery of information vital to children's academic development. But instead of defining instruction as simply imparting specific content, teachers should think of instruction as an ongoing process: The teacher delivers information to children who receive and assimilate it. Teachers who adapt instruction to meet the needs of all students, especially those with mild disabilities, discover that they deliver information more effectively and students learn it more easily. Instruction becomes a continuous process of presenting information, adapting information, representing information, and testing for concept mastery. Making interventions a natural component of this continuum helps students succeed.

The teaching technique is the delivery system that transmits content from teacher to students. If the technique is not appropriate for a student, then most likely the content will never be delivered. This chapter examines learning styles, teaching techniques, adaptations for specific modes of teaching, and how to assess students to match the classroom and the student.

HOW STUDENTS LEARN

Students want to learn to acquire knowledge or skills. Designing and implementing effective instruction so that students learn to their fullest capacity challenges us all. If learning means the acquisition of knowledge or skills, and the teacher wants to help students with that acquisition, then the teacher needs to understand the process of learning in general.

This brings us back to the concept that learning, or the capacity to learn, is based on intellectual ability. The theories of intellect are numerous. Costa & Kallick (2000) presented the following influential theories of intelligence:

1. *Intelligence can be taught.* Arthur Whimbley (Whimbley, Whimbley, & Shaw, 1975, as cited in Costa & Kallick, 2000) introduced the concept that intelligence can be taught and therefore is not exclusively genetically inherited (p. 4).
2. *Structure of the intellect.* Guildford and Hoeptner (1971) reported 120 individual factors of intellect that could also be combined. Twenty-six factors related to school success. These authors asserted that interventions could amplify intelligence (pp. 4–5). During one of my postgraduate

classes, I had the wonderful opportunity to study under psychologist Dr. Raymond Muskgrove. Dr. Muskgrove taught a complete course on theories of intelligence, with the Guilford model being his favorite. It is a fascinating theory that I encourage readers to investigate further. I was impressed that Guilford identified early on the importance of interventions to learning. (Another note regarding my professor, Dr. Muskgrove. He was a colleague of B. F. Skinner and worked beside Skinner in the lab watching the rats scurry about. I was always fascinated with the old pictures of Dr. Skinner and Dr. Muskgrove standing in the lab. Both were so young, and history was written all over those pictures. I salute both great men and will forever be grateful for having the great opportunity to study with the late Dr. Raymond Muskgrove.)

3. *Theory of cognitive modifiability.* Feuerstein believed that intelligence is not fixed, but instead is a function of experience. This theory is the underlying thread of the modern theory that intelligence can be taught and that everyone is gifted to a degree and retarded to a degree (p. 5).
4. *Multiple forms of intelligence.* Howard Gardner (1983, 1999) reported many ways for learning to be expressed. The popular model lists the following intelligences: verbal, logical/mathematical, kinesthetic, musical, spatial, naturalistic, interpersonal, and intrapersonal. These intelligences may be developed throughout one's lifetime.
5. *Intelligence as success in life.* Sternberg, Torff, and Grigorenko (1998) reported three intelligences, which grow throughout life: analytical, creative, and practical (p. 6).
6. *Learned intelligence.* David Perkins (1995) "further supports the theory that intelligence can be taught and learned" (p. 6). He believes that three important mechanisms underlie intelligence:
   - *Neural intelligence* is "genetically determined, hard-wired original equipment" that one has inherited and that determines the speed and efficiency of one's brain. Neural intelligence cannot be altered much.
   - *Experiential intelligence* is context-specific knowledge that is accumulated through experience. It means knowing one's way around the various settings and contexts in which one functions. A person's reservoir of experiential intelligence can be expanded.
   - *Reflective intelligence* is the "good use of the mind; the artful deployment of our facilities of thinking" (p. 264). It includes self-managing, self-monitoring, and self-modifying. Perkins referred to this capacity as "mind-ware," which can and should be cultivated (p. 6).
7. *Emotional intelligence.* Daniel Coleman (1995) simply stated that intelligence and emotions are intertwined. One develops with the other.
8. *Moral intelligence.* Robert Coles (1997) believes that inner character development through interactions with environment and persons within one's environment produce a "moral archeology," a moral code of ethics (pp. 6–7).

Research Notes for Classroom Application

Research surrounding the learning or perceptual styles concept has been conducted for over 30 years. This broad empirical base has provided insight on the subject and given teachers, parents, and students greater understanding of how learning takes place for each individual. Dunn and Dunn have conducted much of this research, and in addition to the auditory and visual learning styles, they identify tactual and kinesthetic learners. Tactual learners "must use their hands to manipulate learning materials," while kinesthetic learners "must engage in whole-body activities and/or real-life experiences to assimilate content" (2005, p. 273).

At least 15% of elementary school students benefit from tactual resources, and more than twice that percentage of poorly achieving students benefit (Dunn & Dunn, 2005). Special education students are predominantly tactual or kinesthetic learners, with many succeeding fairly well when learning through whole-body activities like floor games, simulations, or real-life experiences. Some auditory and visual learners are low- or nontactual. They are in the minority of school populations and are more likely to be female than male.

"Three decades of research suggest that teaching strategies and resources should complement individuals' perceptual strengths when introducing new and difficult academic content" (Dunn & Dunn, 2005, p. 276). Not only are student test scores likely to increase when teachers are able to utilize the proper method for each learner, but student behavior is also likely to improve. Educators must be wary, though, of how they determine each student's learning style. Many of the available learning style instruments have never been validated and tend to measure the respondents' preferences or self-beliefs rather than how they actually learn best (Kratzig & Arbuthnott, 2006). Motivational and situational factors can also influence learning, creating the need to help students acquire effective learning strategies across all perceptual modalities.

Sources: Dunn, R., & Dunn, K. (2005, July/August). Thirty-five years of research on perceptual strengths: *Essential strategies to promote learning. The Clearing House, 78*(6), 273–276.

Kratzig, G. P., & Arbuthnott, K. D. (2006). Perceptual learning style and learning proficiency: A test of the hypothesis. *Journal of Educational Psychology, 98*(1), 238–246.

Note: From *Reaching the Hard to Teach* by J. W. Wood, 2008, Richmond, VA: Judy Wood, Inc. Reprinted with permission.

Learning and Cognitive Styles

Learning styles are students' individual approaches to learning. Knowledge of the different ways students may approach a learning situation and awareness of the influences on these approaches pave the way for successful teaching. Some students with mild disabilities may use one learning style or another, but many reflect a composite of different styles, showing that children learn in many different ways.

In addition to having a distinctive learning style, each student has a **cognitive style.** According to Fuhrmann (1980), "The cognitive components create learning. . . . Each of us develops a typical approach in our use of our cognitive characteristics to perceive, to think, and to remember. This approach constitutes our cognitive learning style" (p. 2). Keefe (1979) placed the many cognitive styles into two major categories: reception styles, which involve perceiving and analyzing functions; and concept formation and retention styles, which pertain to generating hypotheses, solving problems, and remembering.

Conditions Affecting Learning Styles

In addition to an awareness of learning and cognitive styles, teachers should understand the many other conditions affecting the way children learn. The relationships among teaching and learning styles, students' perceptual styles, time, sound, seating arrangements and place, class procedures, group size, and students' attention spans all influence the learning process.

Perceptual Styles. A student's perceptual style refers to the sense through which the student best receives information: visual (seeing), auditory (hearing), or kinesthetic (touching). Most children tend to use one perceptual style more than the others. Visual learners learn best when they can see the information presented (for example, on the chalkboard, through overhead projectors, or with DVDs).

Auditory learners learn best when they can hear the information presented (for example, in a lecture). A classroom teacher who uses the lecture method can help visual learners by recording the lecture for students to play back later.

Some students need kinesthetic feedback to learn. An example would be a teacher providing sandboxes so that students can draw or trace the letters of the alphabet in the sand and get kinesthetic feedback. Teachers need to plan instruction so that it addresses the students' dominant perceptual modes.

Finally, students express the information they have processed and retained, using any of three output components: fine-motor expression, written/motor expression, or verbal expression. Information output can be measured using numerous models. Modifications during the output stage help teachers get the most from the student.

Figures 6.1 through 6.6 provide information on characteristics that may prevail when a student has visual perception, auditory perception, kinesthetic perception, fine-motor, written/motor, and verbal expression problems. Within

Figure 6.1 Visual perception problems and accommodations.

Characteristics of a Student with Visual Perception Problems

- Frequently loses place when reading or copying
- Has trouble discriminating among similar shapes, letters, and words
- Does not enjoy pictures, slides, or books
- Has difficulty reading and copying accurately from chalkboard
- Shows signs of eye strain such as squinting, blinking, and holding head close to page
- Has trouble following written directions from board or printed page
- Works slowly on printed assignments or tests
- Displays poor sight vocabulary
- May use fingers to keep place while reading
- Skips words or reverses words when reading aloud
- Cannot visualize things in mind
- Demonstrates erratic spelling or incorrect letter sequences
- Does not notice details on pictures, maps, and photographs
- Is confused by work sheets containing a great deal of visual stimuli
- Has difficulty remembering what is seen
- May whisper to self while working with visual material

Teaching Tips

- Make sure students are seated close to the teacher, board, or work area.
- Make an effort to write clearly and neatly on the board and on worksheets.
- Try always to give verbal information or explanation along with a visual presentation.
- Use color highlighting on worksheets to cue the student to important words and concepts.
- Introduce new vocabulary in context before a reading assignment.
- Allow students to use index cards to keep their place while reading.
- Pair students for reading assignments.
- Pause periodically during an oral presentation to ask for questions.
- Summarize at the end of the lesson and encourage students to ask questions about what they may have missed.

Note: From *Reaching the Hard to Teach* by J. W. Wood, 2008, Richmond, VA: Judy Wood, Inc. Reprinted with permission.

Figure 6.2 Auditory perception problems and accommodations.

Characteristics of a Student with Auditory Perception Problems

- Has trouble distinguishing fine differences between sounds and words (such as d–t and *pin–pen*)
- Loses interest or concentration during lectures
- Has difficulty following a series of oral directions
- Cannot accurately record notes from oral presentations
- Displays poor receptive vocabulary
- Repeats what is told before acting or responding
- Often repeats the same question

Continued

Figure 6.2 (Continued)

- Asks questions about oral directions and facts previously given
- May watch the speaker's face intently or lean forward toward the speaker
- Does not enjoy listening to music
- Becomes irritated by extraneous noise
- Has difficulty learning and applying phonetic rules
- May have difficulty remembering what is heard

Teaching Tips

- Seat students in a location where sound is clear; avoid seating near distracting sounds or noises.
- Keep oral directions short and simple. Give one-step directions at first. Gradually increase to two-step directions, and so on.
- Accompany oral directions with written directions. List them sequentially using vocabulary appropriate for the students.
- Ask students to paraphrase your oral directions. Call on different group members to do this.
- Alert the students when you are giving directions by setting the stage (e.g., "This is important. I'll give you the directions now."). Additional help can be provided by alerting an individual student through eye contact, positioning toward student, or a gentle touch.
- Be conscious of your rate of speech. Talk slower if students indicate they are having difficulty staying with you.
- Assist student to "stay with you" during instruction by using gestures and changes in tone and pitch of your voice.
- Allow the students to move to a quiet place in the classroom to do their independent work.
- Summarize the key points of your lesson with a visual prop.
- Try to use visual support (pictures, photographs, charts, maps, films, DVDs, overheads) with auditory presentations.

Note: From *Reaching the Hard to Teach* by J. W. Wood, 2008, Richmond, VA: Judy Wood, Inc. Reprinted with permission.

Figure 6.3 Kinesthetic perception problems and accommodations.

Characteristics of a Student with Kinesthetic/Tactual Problems

- Tries things out; touches, feels, manipulates
- Expresses things physically; jumps for joy, pushes, tugs, stomps, pounds
- Gestures when speaking; is a poor listener; stands very close when speaking or listening; quickly loses interest in long verbal discourse
- Starts the day looking neat and tidy but soon becomes disheveled through physical activity
- Seems impulsive
- Prefers to attack problems physically; seeks solutions that involve the greatest activity

- Handwriting that appears good initially but deteriorates as space runs out on the paper and the student exerts more and more pressure on the writing instrument
- Prefers stories with lots of action, especially in the beginning; rarely an avid reader
- Fidgets a lot while handling books
- Often a poor speller; needs to write words to see if they look correct

Teaching Tips

- Provide opportunities for direct, concrete physical involvement in activities.
- Allow opportunities for materials manipulation.
- Allow opportunities for writing on paper and the chalkboard, drawing, hands-on activities with real objects that can be touched.
- Use hand signals, small group discussions, activities that involve emotions and feelings or enable students to move around.
- Play music as a good method of involving movement; sculpture and clay molding are preferable to paintings.
- Plan field trips that enable them to dance or play percussion instruments, or to touch them.
- Try activities that allow for gross motor movement reinforced through visual stimulation.
- Avoid verbal lectures and sedentary classroom activities as much as possible.
- Use sign language to teach sight words.

Note: From *Reaching the Hard to Teach* by J. W. Wood, 2008, Richmond, VA: Judy Wood, Inc. Reprinted with permission.

Figure 6.4 Fine motor problems and accommodations.

Characteristics of a Student with Fine Motor Problems

- Displays poor handwriting and has difficulty forming letters and numbers
- Has difficulty in activities requiring cutting or pasting
- Finds it hard to trace or color within given borders
- Has trouble with speed and neatness in taking notes
- Shows fatigue and restlessness during writing or drawing tasks
- Turns in handwritten work that often appears sloppy and disorganized
- Has difficulty manipulating or using small objects and tools
- Usually works slowly in completing written work
- Has trouble making straight lines for connecting points, matching answers, or labeling maps
- Displays poor copying skills

Teaching Tips

- Strive to set a good handwriting example. A teacher's own handwriting serves as a model for students' writing.
- Place the paper to be copied directly at the top of the students' papers rather than to one side or the other when copying is necessary.

Continued

Figure 6.4 (Continued)

- Teach students how to erase and make corrections without beginning over each time. This is a minor matter that can make a big difference in the appearance of students' papers. Students may be able to eliminate unclear, distracting erasures by using erasable pens.
- Minimize copying activities by providing the information or activities on worksheets or handouts.
- Assign follow-up activities that reduce the students' writing requirement. Paired talking activities, cooperative small group assignments, short answer activity sheets, and instructional games all provide students with opportunities to review skills and knowledge without requiring lengthy written answers.

Note: From *Reaching the Hard to Teach* by J. W. Wood, 2008, Richmond, VA: Judy Wood, Inc. Reprinted with permission.

Figure 6.5 Written/motor problems and accommodations.

Characteristics of a Student with Written/Motor Expression Problems

- Has difficulty writing answers on paper but may be able to give correct answers orally
- Written vocabulary much weaker than spoken vocabulary
- Handwritten work sloppy and disorganized
- Written ideas and concepts usually stronger than writing mechanics (for example, spelling, syntax, vocabulary level)
- Has trouble writing a sentence with a complete thought
- Demonstrates poor spelling skills
- Tests better on objective tests than on tests that require writing (essays and definitions)
- Frequently does not complete written assignments

Teaching Tips

- Allow the students more time to complete written assignments.
- Allow the students to give all short answers to questions (single word or phrase).
- Allow students to check and correct their own worksheets against a model (individually or in a group).
- Permit students to use pictures, drawings, and diagrams as part of their written products.
- Allow students to do taped or "live" oral reports instead of written reports.
- Permit students to work independently in an area free of distractions (away from windows, doors, or traffic areas).
- Try using all-student response cards in small group settings. All students would have the same set of index cards, each card with a specific answer. In response to a question posed by the teacher, each student finds that card with the answer he/she believes is correct and holds up the card to the teacher. The teacher gives the correct answer and explanation to the group if anyone has responded incorrectly.
- Allow students to tape answers or work with peers, tutors, or volunteers who perform the writing tasks.

Note: From *Reaching the Hard to Teach* by J. W. Wood, 2008, Richmond, VA: Judy Wood, Inc. Reprinted with permission.

Figure 6.6 Verbal problems and accommodations.

Characteristics of a Student with Verbal Expression Problems

- Does not enjoy discussions, oral presentations, or reading aloud
- Has difficulty explaining himself or herself clearly and coherently
- Displays poor speech—articulation, fluency, expressiveness
- Unable to vocalize thoughts rapidly
- Uses slang or colloquial terms instead of more precise words
- Has spoken vocabulary that is much weaker than written vocabulary
- Is reluctant to volunteer ideas or respond verbally to questions
- Makes remarks that are often irrelevant, confusing, or inaccurate
- Is uncomfortable speaking in a group
- Has difficulty recalling a word he or she wants to use
- Uses grammatically incorrect sentences

Teaching Tips

- Give students a little extra time to respond. Many students have to struggle inwardly before being able to complete their thoughts verbally.
- Give students a hint to help them along if they are having difficulty.
- Urge students to use outlines or notes when presenting oral reports.
- Encourage students to use visual aids or handouts in conjunction with oral reports.
- Give students the opportunity to read silently before asking them to read orally.
- Structure opportunities for student verbal expression on a one-on-one basis and in small groups. Avoid calling on students to answer aloud in a group as punishment for inattentiveness during discussions.
- Limit the length of oral presentations by students.
- Permit students to sometimes use all-student response cards in small groups instead of giving verbal responses.
- Ask specific, structured questions. This will permit the students to use the elements of the question to organize their answers. For example, "Can you tell me one way that comets and meteors are alike?" instead of "Compare comets and meteors."

Note: From *Reaching the Hard to Teach* by J. W. Wood, 2008, Richmond, VA: Judy Wood, Inc. Reprinted with permission.

each figure accommodations for assisting students within general education classrooms are included. These figures provide valuable information that may be helpful to all educators.

Seating Arrangements. When students first come into a classroom, where do they sit? Do they return to the same places the next day? Teachers attending a class or a meeting prefer certain places—by the window, next to the door, in the front row, or in the back of the room—and children also have such seating preferences. Teachers should try to provide students with a seating arrangement flexible enough for variety, but structured enough for consistency.

Some students lose interest in assigned tasks when they sit in the same seats day after day. Possible variations include having students sit on small mats on the floor, taking students to the library for class, or going outside for the lecture. One secondary school, for example, provides learning stations under the trees and uses logs for seating. Teachers then register for outside stations at the times they want.

When adapting classroom seating arrangements for students with mild disabilities, the teacher must consider any special needs the children may have. Also, many students with disabilities are easily distracted and need to be placed close to the teacher.

Class Procedures. Class procedures are more effective when based on the teacher's awareness of students' various learning styles. It is important to match assignments with learning styles when assigning students to projects, library work, reports, seatwork, or learning centers, especially because the average class assignment is usually too difficult for the student with mild disabilities. The teacher can divide the same assignment into several short segments and use a variety of techniques for presenting the information. Class evaluation procedures also should vary according to learning styles. For example, a teacher can evaluate the work of a student with mild disabilities by simply observing, collecting work samples, or using formative evaluation procedures. Matching the evaluation procedure to the student's learning style helps the teacher evaluate instructional objectives as well as appropriately evaluate the student.

Class procedures must also take into account the emotional aspects of learning styles. Fuhrmann (1980) eloquently summarized the work of Dunn, Dunn, and Price (1979) on these emotional elements: motivation, persistence, responsibility, and structure.

Highly motivated students may need only requirements and resources, but poorly motivated students require special attention to bring out their interest and desire to learn. For example, a student who is poorly motivated by a traditional lecture class may be highly motivated by a programmed text or a small discussion group. The same length and type of assignment is probably not appropriate for all students because both attention span and persistence vary greatly. Furthermore, persistence is related to motivation; the more motivated a student is to achieve in a particular learning experience, the more persistent a student is likely to be in completing the task. Sequenced learning tasks, with clearly defined steps and a final goal, offer the teacher some flexibility in meeting the needs of students with differing degrees of persistence.

Like motivated students, responsible students require only clear assignments and resources to succeed. Irresponsible students, however, often experience failure and discouragement in such an environment. Usually, students lacking responsibility have historically failed to achieve in school and therefore lack the confidence to assume responsibility. Teachers must attend first to their lack of confidence by offering opportunities for them to experience small successes. Individualizing assignments, breaking objectives into smaller components, trying experimental assignments, and using all types of learning aids and resources may encourage such students.

Students also differ in their response to structure—to the specific rules and directions they must follow to achieve certain objectives. More creative students often like a wide variety of options from which to choose, whereas those who are less creative may respond better to a single, well-defined method. Again, the emotional elements are related to one another because the more motivated, persistent, and responsible students require less structure than do the less motivated, less persistent, and less responsible ones (Fuhrmann, 1980).

Teachers, therefore, should make assignments, instruct, evaluate students, and carry out other class procedures on the basis of what they can determine about their students' learning styles and the emotional factors contributing to those styles.

Group Size. The group size most effective for instruction varies according to the learning styles of students and the content and purpose of the instruction. Some students learn better in small groups, some in large groups, and others one to one. Careful analysis of student performance helps the teacher select the most appropriate method. Most students with disabilities do not function well in large groups; instead, very small groups and one-to-one instruction are usually more effective.

Attention Span. Although each student has a different attention span, many students with mild disabilities have short ones. Thus, teachers in inclusive settings should vary teaching techniques and activities accordingly. In fact, teachers who match task to attention span find that students master tasks at a faster rate.

For example, a teacher can divide a math lesson for a student with a short attention span into (a) working problems at the desk, (b) completing additional problems at the board, and (c) going to the learning center to continue with the same math skill but in a different setting. Teachers should first evaluate tasks according to the type of attention span required to complete them. Then they should adapt both their method of delivery and the tasks themselves to the variations of attention spans within the classroom.

ADAPTING TEACHING TECHNIQUES

A **teaching technique** or strategy is a method of imparting knowledge, skills, or concepts to a learner. Historically, colleges and universities have recommended various teaching techniques to educators, who in turn have used those techniques in public and private schools. How teachers teach and what types of strategies they employ depend greatly on previous training, models observed, areas of interest, value judgments, and common sense. According to Jarolimek and Foster (1981), "There is a great deal of disagreement, even among well-informed persons, about what constitutes good teaching and how teaching should take place" (p. 109).

This section, then, does not try to teach teachers how to teach but simply presents a variety of techniques that teachers can use in different situations or modify for particular students. Specifically, the section concerns ways of adapting instruction within teaching modes and techniques.

Teaching Modes

Jarolimek and Foster (1981) identified four major teaching modes: expository, inquiry, demonstration, and activity (Figure 6.7). Each mode has specific teaching techniques common to it, and teachers can adapt or modify all these techniques for students in inclusive settings.

Expository Mode. Teaching in the expository mode centers around the "concept exposition, which means most simply to provide an explanation" (Jarolimek & Foster, 1981, p. 110). This mode, probably the most popular among educators, requires extensive directive teaching. The class focuses on the teacher, who explains or disseminates the information; students are involved only minimally. General education teachers report using this mode 53% of the time during instruction, whereas special education teachers use the expository mode only 24% of the time. Table 6.1 presents the specific teaching techniques used in the expository mode, with suggested adaptations for each. In four of these techniques—lecture, telling, explanation, and discussion—the teacher orally delivers information. These four techniques account for 93% of the time that general education teachers teach in the expository mode and 87% for special education teachers (Wood, 1993).

Presenting new skills or concepts orally (lecturing, explaining, discussing, telling) can make learning extremely difficult for the student who cannot impose structure on learning. Educators can use the following suggestions for adapting these types of techniques.

1. *Multisensory input.* Visual aid materials that address a variety of learning styles should be an important instructional consideration. Because students learn through many sensory systems, educators need to use numerous modes to enhance oral presentations and provide multisensory input for students. Students need to be taught in the different perceptual styles—visually, auditorily, and tactually. Using PowerPoint or the overhead projector to present main points or underline or circle main ideas is an excellent technique for orientation to material.

Figure 6.7 Specific techniques used in various teaching modes.

Expository	Inquiry	Demonstration	Activity
Lecture	Asking questions	Experiments	Role playing
Telling	Stating hypotheses	Exhibits	Constructing
Sound filmstrip	Coming to conclusions	Simulations	Preparing exhibits
Explanation	Interpreting	Games	Dramatizing
Panels	Classifying	Modeling	Processing
Recitation	Self-directed study	Field trips	Group work
Audio recording	Testing hypotheses		
Motion pictures	Observing		
Discussion	Synthesizing		

Note: From *Reaching the Hard to Teach* by J. W. Wood, 2008, Richmond, VA: Judy Wood, Inc. Reprinted with permission.

Table 6.1 Expository mode: Alternative teaching techniques.

TEACHING TECHNIQUES	ADAPTATIONS FOR INCLUSIVE STUDENTS
Lecture	• Provide lecture outlines. • Provide copy of lecture notes. • Use transparencies to provide visual presentation simultaneously with lecture.
Telling	• Keep lecture short. • Be specific about information given. • Be sure you have students' attention. • For students with short attention spans, give information in small segments.
Sound filmstrip	• Provide visuals when possible. • Give earphones to students easily distracted by sounds.
Explanation	• Keep explanations simple and direct. • Give them in simple declarative sentences. • Provide outline of explanation.
Audio recording	• Present recordings with visuals. • Give earphones to students easily distracted by sounds.
Motion pictures	• Orient students to movie before showing. • Be sure length is appropriate. • Place students with auditory problems close to sound. • Review main points of film. • Provide brief outline of main points.
Discussion	• Ask questions you know students can answer. • Keep discussion short. • As points are made, list them on board or transparency. • Divide class into groups for brief discussions. • Keep students on topic. • Involve everyone on appropriate levels. • Use organizer to group ideas and show conclusion drawn.

Note: From *Reaching the Hard to Teach* by J. W. Wood, 2008, Richmond, VA: Judy Wood, Inc. Reprinted with permission.

Videotapes provide instant playback of information for reinforcement. Students who miss a portion of the class will also benefit from a videotape. Audiotape recorders are excellent audiovisual aids for reinforcement of oral materials. Graphic materials such as globes and maps reinforce both visually and tactually the material to be learned. Bulletin boards and websites assist the teacher in presenting new information or providing reinforcement. Presenting information for multisensory input not only enhances classroom instruction but also provides for and addresses the perceptual learning styles of students.

2. *Acquisition outlines.* Acquisition outlines present students with a graphic whole-part-whole method of learning. This method of adapting assists students in seeing the whole of the presentation and then hearing a discussion of the parts. The acquisition outline serves as a formative study guide. The teacher should provide an acquisition outline when presenting new information, concepts, or skills to be learned. Before the unit of study begins, a summative study guide is provided, which sets the stage for studying. The teacher can place the acquisition outline on the overhead projector or give each student a copy to be completed. When introducing the outline, the teacher should follow these steps:

a. Introduce the topic.
b. Explain how the topic for today continues yesterday's lesson and will extend into tomorrow's lesson.
c. Introduce each of the major topics (points 1, 2, 3, and so on).
d. Point out that related topics are listed beneath each major point.
e. Return to point 1.
f. Review the topics listed under point 1.
g. Begin the discussion of point 1.
h. When the lesson is over, return to the whole outline and review the topics.
i. Have the student file the outline in the appropriate notebook section.
j. Save a copy for the teacher's note-taking file.

Acquisition outlines keep students from guessing what will be coming next, help them perceive the organization of the presentation, and serve as a formative study guide for test review. Here are some general tips for using acquisition outlines:

a. The acquisition outline can be developed into one of three formats: blank, partial, or completed. The more difficulty a student has in organizing and absorbing orally presented information, the more information should be provided on the outline.
b. When covering a point that is further explained in a text or a handout, tell the students to write the page number from the text or the name of the handout in the left margin.
c. If some points on the outline require extensive note-taking, the teacher may provide a handout to promote accurate reception of information and save instructional time.

Examples of acquisition outlines appear in Figures 6.8. and 6.9.

Mr. Able was teaching angles to his fifth-grade class. Prior to class he developed an acquisition outline to assist all learners, especially the learners at risk. Figure 6.9 presents the outline Mr. Able used. Mr. Able could complete the lesson quickly with little lesson repeat or reteach. The learners at risk quickly understood the concept of an angle, the definition, and the types.

Figure 6.8 Acquisition outline.

Topic: Vertebrates

I. Mammals—Textbook page 120
   A. Have hair or fur
   B. Feed babies with mother's milk

II. Fish—Textbook page 122
   A. Have gills
   B. Live in water

III. Amphibians—Textbook page 130
   A. Have scaleless skin
   B. Usually live part of life in water and part of life out of water

IV. Reptiles—Textbook page 133
   A. Have dry, scaly skin
   B. Some live on land and some live in water

V. Birds—Textbook page 140
   A. Have feathers, wings, and beaks
   B. Bones filled with air

Note: From *Reaching the Hard to Teach* by J. W. Wood, 2008, Richmond, VA: Judy Wood, Inc. Reprinted with permission.

Figure 6.9 Acquisition outline.

I. Angles
A. Definition: Two rays with a common end point

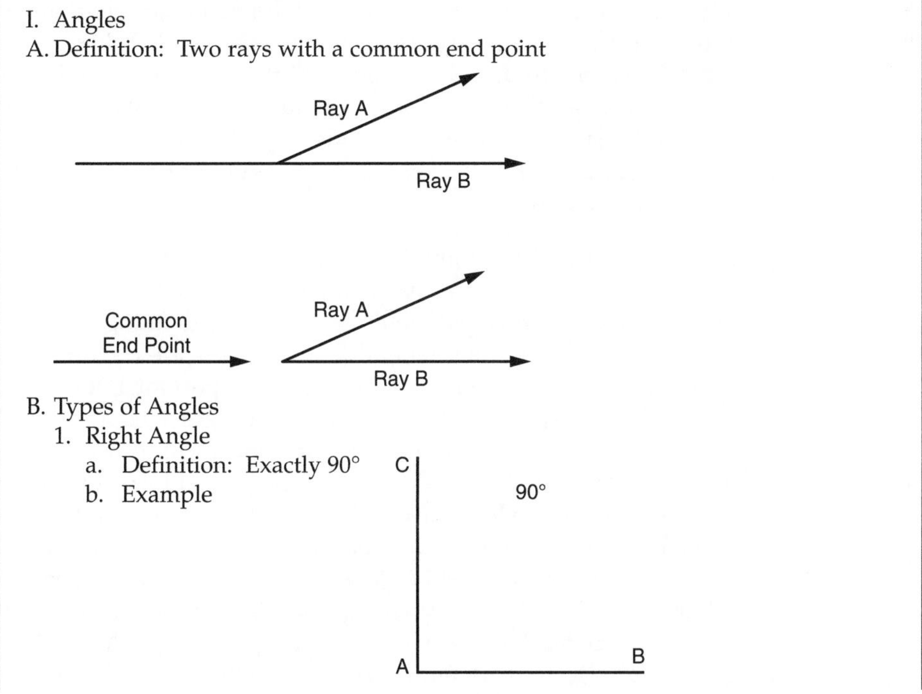

B. Types of Angles
   1. Right Angle
      a. Definition: Exactly 90°
      b. Example

Continued

Figure 6.9 (Continued)

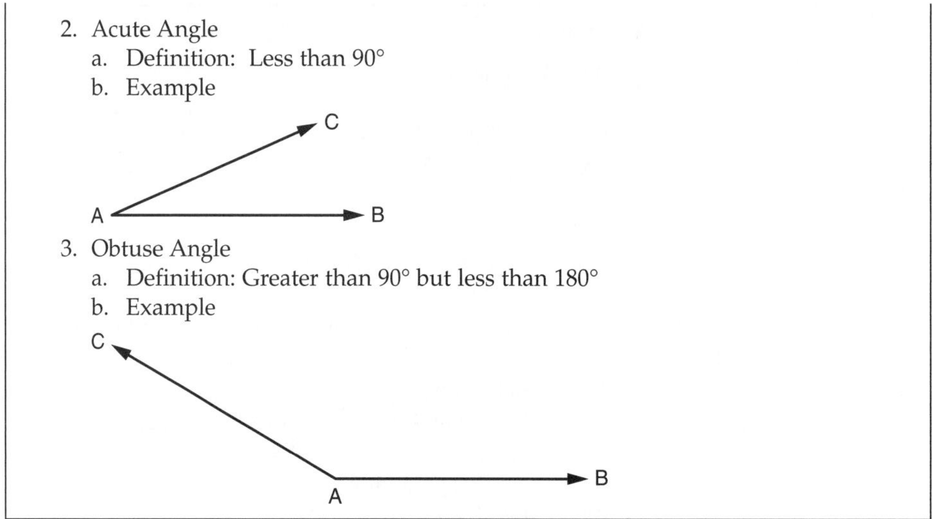

2. Acute Angle
a. Definition: Less than 90°
b. Example
C
A
B
3. Obtuse Angle
a. Definition: Greater than 90° but less than 180°
b. Example
C
B
A

Note: From *Reaching the Hard to Teach* by J. W. Wood, 2008, Richmond, VA: Judy Wood, Inc. Reprinted with permission.

3. *Graphic Organizers.* In classrooms information is most often presented in a linguistic manner. We talk to students or have them read printed text. When nonlinguistic representation is coupled with linguistic, students are better able to think about and recall knowledge (Marzano, Pickering, & Pollock, 2001). Common concepts educators use may be developed into organizers (see Figure 6.10).

4. *Audiotaped presentations.* Frequently students are unable to write down all the important information provided. The student who is a strong visual learner may miss important facts. Letting students tape-record the presentations provides for additional reinforcement at a later time.

Inquiry Mode. The inquiry mode involves "asking questions, seeking information, and carrying on an investigation" (Jarolimek & Foster, 1981, p. 116). This mode of teaching follows five basic steps: "(a) defining a problem, (b) proposing hypotheses, (c) collecting data, (d) evaluating evidence, and (e) making a conclusion" (p. 116). The teacher's guidance is still important, but the inquiry mode allows for more teacher-pupil interaction and encourages a team approach to teaching. For many students, however, the teacher often needs to provide some additional structure. Table 6.2 on page 105 suggests teaching techniques for the inquiry mode.

The inquiry mode is used 23% of the time by general educators and 35% by special educators. Of the techniques listed (see Table 6.2), general education teachers report asking questions 66% of the time, whereas special education teachers ask them 59% of the time. Asking questions of students with disabilities and those at risk can accomplish many things during the lesson. According to Davies (1981), questions help motivate students by getting their attention or gaining their interest, encourage students to think, involve more than one student in the instructional process, and provide feedback for the teacher on students' progress.

The following general suggestions will help teachers determine how to ask questions of students with disabilities and those at risk:

1. Ask questions at the taxonomy level at which the student is functioning.
2. Provide wait time for responses. Extra time is necessary for responses to divergent questions (Kindsvatter, Wilen, & Ishler, 1988). Research shows

Figure 6.10 Acquisition outlines.

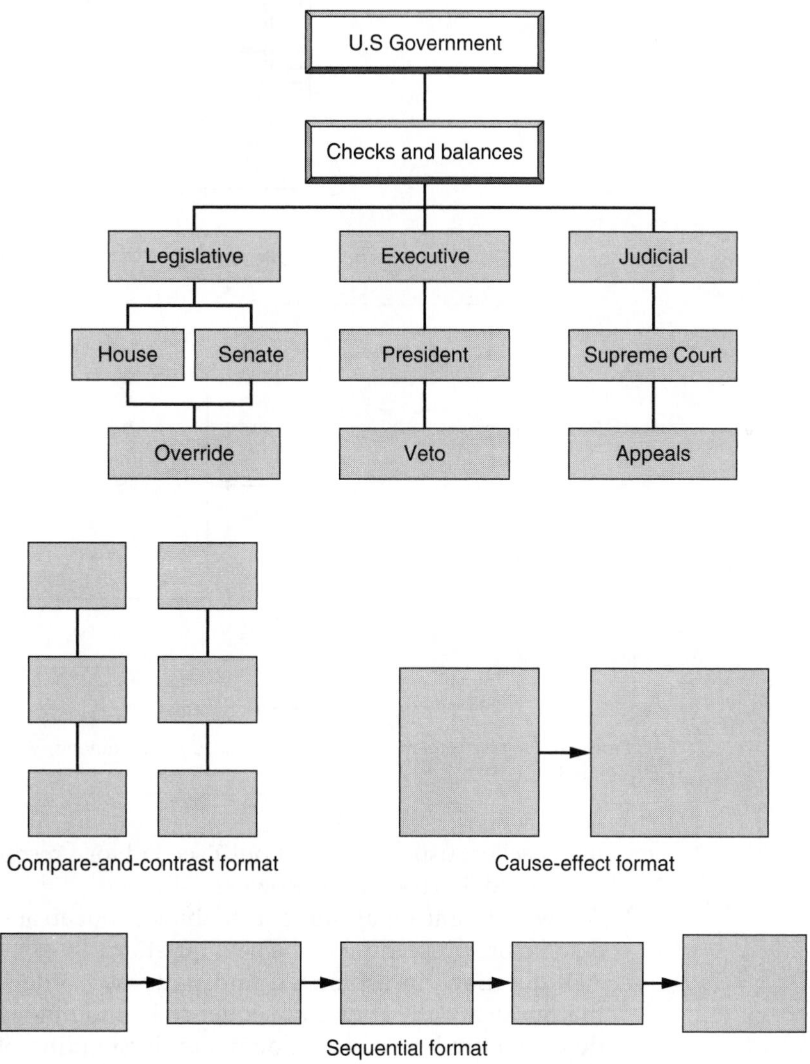

Continued

Figure 6.10 (Continued)

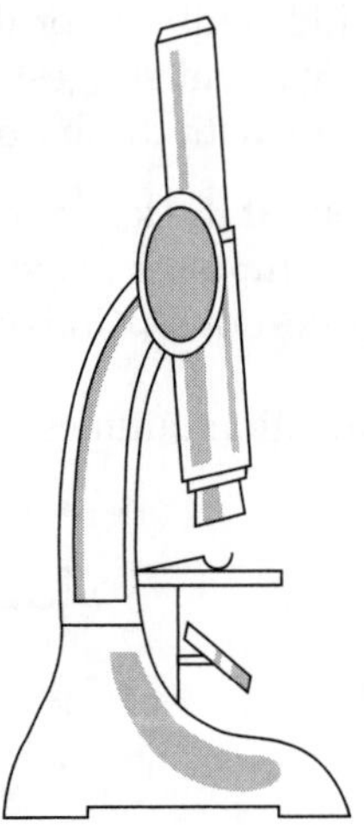

Design format

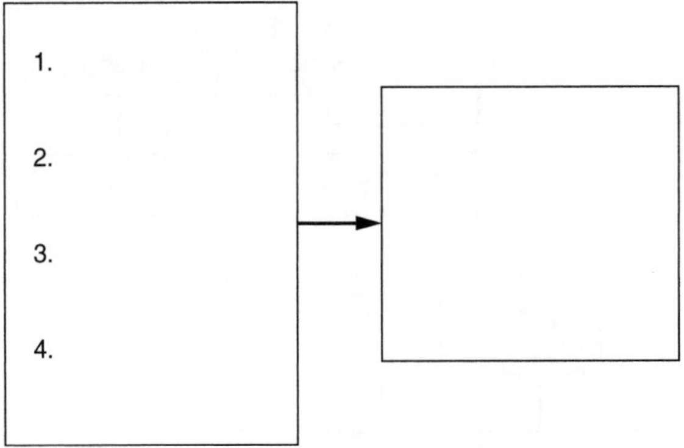

Conclusion format

Note: From *Reaching the Hard to Teach* by J. W. Wood, 2008, Richmond, VA: Judy Wood, Inc. Reprinted with permission.

that teachers usually allow about 1 second for a response, but students typically need 3 to 5 seconds (Rowe, 1974).

3. Allow wait time for all students to think about an answer given by one student before proceeding to the next question.
4. Ask questions in a planned and patterned order or sequence. Factors that influence the choice of sequence include the lesson's objective, student's ability level, and student's understanding of the content covered (Kindsvatter et al., 1988).

Table 6.2 Inquiry mode: Alternative teaching techniques.

TEACHING TECHNIQUES	ADAPTATIONS FOR INCLUSIVE STUDENTS
Asking questions	• Use appropriate wait time. • Ask questions on appropriate level of taxonomy scale; vary questions to meet different taxonomy levels of students. • Call student's name before directing a question to him or her. • Do not embarrass students by asking questions they cannot answer.
Stating hypotheses	• Have students choose from two or three hypotheses instead of having to formulate their own. • Provide model for writing hypotheses.
Coming to conclusions	• Present alternative conclusions. • List information needed for conclusions.
Interpreting	• Assign peer tutor to help. • Present alternative interpretations.
Classifying	• Use concrete instead of abstract concepts. • Provide a visual display with models.
Self-directed study	• Give specific directions about what to do. • Make directions short, simple, and few. • Collect and place resources for study in one area.
Testing hypotheses	• Assign peer tutor.
Observing	• Give explicit directions about how and what to observe. • Provide sequential checklist of what will happen so that student sees steps. • Have student check off each step observed.
Synthesizing	• Assign peer tutor to help. • Provide model of whole.

Note: From *Reaching the Hard to Teach* by J. W. Wood, 2008, Richmond, VA: Judy Wood, Inc. Reprinted with permission.

5. Remember that some sequencing begins with lower-level questions and progresses to higher-level thinking. Some students will start with higher level questions and remain there (Kindsvatter et al., 1988).
6. Because responses to lower-level questions determine student understanding of content, use those responses as an indication of starting points for reteaching.
7. Allow student to formulate questions to ensure active participation in the questioning process (Kindsvatter et al., 1988).
8. State questions clearly and specifically.

9. When asking a question, state the question, call the student's name, and repeat the question.
10. Encourage all students to participate in the questioning process by responding in a positive way to all student responses.
11. Avoid sarcasm, reprimand, personal attack, accusation, or no response at all as teacher responses to student answers (West, 1975).
12. If students hesitate to raise their hands to ask questions in class, tape pockets to their desks containing cards (any color will do). Have students take out the cards and put them on the corner of their desks if they have questions or do not understand. Check for these cards as you walk around the room.
13. Have a question box on the teacher's desk for students who are hesitant to answer questions.
14. Use color responses. All students will have three cards for responding. When a question is asked, each student will put a card at chest level. For example:

    Green: Ask me; I know.
    Yellow: Maybe I know; I'll try.
    Red: Don't call on me; I don't know.

15. Have students respond to questions as follows:

    Four fingers: I know the answer.
    Three fingers: I know the answer, but I don't want to answer.
    Two fingers: I don't know the answer.
    One finger: Please rephrase the question.

16. Have a "ponder period" during which students sit in groups to ponder questions and answers before the question activity.
17. Give each student two chips. This gives a child the opportunity to answer a question or contribute information. When chips are used, the student has made a contribution. This helps the teacher give many children the opportunity to contribute.
18. Tell a student who may not know answers to raise one hand and place the other hand on the desk. Skip that student. When one hand is up and the other hand is not on the desk, the student is signaling that he or she knows the answer to the question. (Wood, 2006)

Demonstration Mode. Essential components of the demonstration mode are "showing, doing, and telling" (Jarolimek & Foster, 1981, p. 120). Like the expository mode, the demonstration mode depends on directive teaching. Because it presents information in a concrete way, this method is essential for teachers to use when instructing students with disabilities.

Table 6.3 presents techniques used in the demonstration mode, with suggested alterations for included students. The demonstration mode is used only 3% of the time by general educators and 6% by special educators. Of the techniques

Table 6.3 Demonstration mode: Alternative teaching techniques.

Teaching Techniques	Adaptations for Inclusive Students
Experiments	• Provide sequential directions. • Have student check off each completed step. If teacher demonstrates, let student assist. • Be sure student fully understands purpose, procedures, and expected outcome of experiment. • Set up incidental learning experiences. • Display materials. • Model the activity. • Provide an outline and a handout/checklist. • Make a list of lab procedures and assign a lab procedure. • Tape instructions and videotape demonstrations.
Exhibits	• Assign projects according to student's instructional level. • Have student select project topic from a short list. • Provide directions and list of materials needed. • Be sure project does not require skills student lacks. • Have student display his or her exhibits.
Simulations	• Do not embarrass the student by requiring him or her to do something that the student cannot do. • Make sure the student understands directions, terms used, and expected outcome.
Games	• Design games making skills, not winning, the priority. • Make directions simple. • Highlight important directions with color codes. • With peer tutor, let student prepare own game. • Design games; emphasize skills needed by student.
Modeling	• Model only one step at a time. • Use task analysis on steps. • Use visual models when possible. • Exaggerate the presentation to make the concept being modeled clear. • Use several short time spans rather than one long demonstration. • Model in hierarchical sequence. • Use video modeling for student to replay. Perform in same manner as the first presentation. • Provide a lecture outline on which the student may take notes.
Field Trips	• Prepare students by explaining destination, purpose, expected behavior, and schedule. • Provide a checklist of expectations.

Note: From *Reaching the Hard to Teach* by J. W. Wood, 2008, Richmond, VA: Judy Wood, Inc. Reprinted with permission.

listed in Table 6.3, general educators use experiments 34% of the time, and special educators use modeling 36% of the time.

Modeling is an excellent technique to use for students who are having difficulty understanding the information presented. Models may be visual (such as a map, chart, or globe) or verbal (such as a language mode). Models may also be participatory: The teacher demonstrates a skill and the students become actively involved. Here are some suggestions for modeling:

1. Exaggerate the modeling presentation.
2. If the steps in the model are lengthy or difficult, use several short time spans rather than one long demonstration.
3. Videotape the modeling demonstration for students to replay and replicate.
4. When repeating the steps in a model, use the same sequence you used in the original presentation.
5. Provide a checklist of the steps in the model for students to follow as you demonstrate.
6. Provide auditory clues along with visual cues.
7. When a student is implementing a model, reward the student's behavior.
8. Use modeling for social, technical, or academic skills.
9. As a student models a desired skill, use the situation to point out the behavior to other students. (Wood, 2006)

Activity Mode. The activity mode of teaching is "a set of strategies that involve pupils in learning by doing things that are, for the pupils, meaningfully related to the topic under study" (Jarolimek & Foster, 1981, p. 127). This method of teaching is best described by an old Native American proverb: "I hear and I forget, I see and I remember, I do and I understand." By using the activity mode, teachers provide students with actual experience and thus a clearer understanding of concepts. The activity mode is used 21% of the time by general educators and 35% of the time by special educators. Table 6.4 suggests activities to accompany the techniques in the activity mode.

The technique of group work is used 66% of the time by general educators and 72% of the time by special educators. Group work is a method of structuring a class so that students work together to achieve a shared academic goal.

Group work has several advantages:

1. Students are responsible for other group members, which encourages liking and learning among students.
2. Assignments can be individualized without working one to one.
3. Teachers can structure students' assignments so that each group member can succeed.
4. Mainstreamed students can be given a short, simple part of the assignment.
5. Group work reduces the time a teacher must spend in preparation.
6. It improves behavior control by minimizing the time focused on one student.
7. It motivates reluctant students through social interaction.

Table 6.4 Activity mode: Alternative teaching techniques.

Teaching Techniques	Adaptations for Inclusive Students
Role playing	• Be sure student understands role. • Short lines or no lines at all may be best. • Respect privacy of student who does not want role. • Let such a student assist another role player.
Constructing	• Select project for students or have them select from a short list. • Try to use projects that include special education objectives. • Provide sequential checklist.
Preparing exhibits	• Assign peer tutor to help. • Use alterations suggested for "constructing."
Dramatizing	• Respect privacy of those who do not want parts. • Let such students help others prepare sets, and so on.
Processing	• Clearly state steps. • Make steps sequential and short. • List steps on board.
Group work	• Assign peer tutor. • Select activity in which students can succeed. • Use variety of grouping procedures (see Chapter 4).
Game/contest	• Be sure game matches lesson objective. • Check game to see if required decision-making skills match students' ability level. • List rules for engaging clearly on board. • Keep pace appropriate. • Assign a buddy. • Provide feedback for game skills as well as for social skills used.

Note: From *Reaching the Hard to Teach* by J. W. Wood, 2008, Richmond, VA: Judy Wood, Inc. Reprinted with permission.

8. It prevents boredom through a variety of group assignments.
9. Students can contribute something from their area of expertise. For example, if they are good in art, they can volunteer (or be assigned) to do the art for the group.
10. Because all students are equally involved in the group's decision, mainstreamed students feel highly motivated. (Wood, 2006)

Role playing is another useful technique in the activity mode. Here are several suggestions for incorporating it into your teaching:

1. Select the role-playing situation.
2. Warm up with some simple charades or another similar exercise.

3. Explain the general situation to participants and observers.
4. State the problem to be worked on, including the setting.
5. Explain the roles that participants will be playing.
6. Explain the roles that the audience will be expected to perform.
7. Start the role playing with a discussion.
8. Follow the role playing with a discussion.
9. Evaluate the exercise. (Wood, 2006)

Role playing has several advantages:

1. Students can express their true feelings without risk.
2. Students can discuss private issues without embarrassment.
3. Students learn to empathize with others by taking on another identity.
4. Students practice alternative behaviors and attitudes.
5. Role playing brings academic subjects to life and thus makes them more meaningful.
6. Motivation and interest increase because they are based on an activity. (Wood, 2006)

Assessing Teaching Techniques

Now that you know that there are four major modes of teaching (expository, inquiry, demonstration, and activity) and that each mode has numerous techniques that belong to the mode, how do you know which technique or mode would be best for a student? Tables 6.5 through 6.8 present each mode, skills a student needs to work in a specific mode, a review of the techniques in the selected modes, responding teachers, and notes.

Expository Mode.

Skills needed. There are numerous skills a student needs for the expository mode. For example, the student must be able to understand material presented auditorily, select pertinent information, process a lot of information at one time, take notes on information presented auditorily, distinguish major and minor parts of information, verbally express self, and attend for long periods of time.

Techniques. Included in the expository mode are the techniques of lecture, telling, sound filmstrips, audio recording, video/DVD, and discussion. Interventions for each of these techniques are found in Table 6.1.

Using the table. If a student has specific difficulty in responding to a selected technique, the teacher (special or general education) may check the appropriate space for the responding teacher. If the teacher has found an intervention that works for the student, the teacher makes a note of the intervention in the note section. Place the table in the student's folder for future reference by another teacher. Using the table for the inquiry, demonstration, and activity modes is the same as using it for the expository mode.

Table 6.5 Expository mode.

Skills Needed for Expository Mode	Techniques	Responding Teacher		Notes
• Can auditorily process and understand material presented • Can select from orally presented information that which is pertinent • Can process a lot of information at one time • Can take notes from information presented orally • Has necessary vocabulary level • Can distinguish major and minor parts of the information • Can express self verbally • Can pay attention for time necessary		SP ED	GEN ED	
	Lecture			
	Telling			
	Sound Filmstrip			
	Explanation			
	Audio Recording			
	Video/DVD			
	Discussion			

- Check teaching techniques in which student has difficulty in responding. If you have found a strategy which the student may use with this technique and be successful, please indicate in notes.

Note: From *Reaching the Hard to Teach* by J. W. Wood. 2008. Richmond, VA. Reprinted with permission.

Table 6.6 Inquiry mode.

Skills Needed in Inquiry Mode	Techniques	Responding Teacher		Notes
		SP ED	GEN ED	
• Has skills required for responding to the expository mode • Can respond at required taxonomy level • Can organize information into groups • Can select alternatives • Can follow a sequence of commands • Can work from whole to parts • Can remain on task for required time	• Asking Questions			
	• Stating hypothesis			
	• Coming to Conclusions			
	• Interpreting			
	• Classifying			
	• Self-Directed Study			
	• Testing Hypothesis			
	• Observing			
	• Synthesizing			
	• Problem Solving			

- Check teaching techniques in which student has difficulty in responding. If you have found a strategy which the student may use with this technique and be successful, please indicate in notes.

Note: From *Reaching the Hard to Teach* by J. W. Wood 2008. Richmond, VA. Reprinted with permission.

Table 6.7 Demonstration mode.

SKILLS NEEDED IN DEMONSTRATION MODE	TECHNIQUES	RESPONDING TEACHER		NOTES
• Understands information presented orally and visually at same time • Selects important information from information presented • Has necessary vocabulary level • Follows instructions given sequentially • Has specific skills needed for selected tasks (such as using microscope) • Works cooperatively in groups		SP ED	GEN ED	
	• Experiments			
	• Exhibits			
	• Simulations			
	• Games			
	• Modeling			
	• Field Trips			

- Check teaching techniques in which student has difficulty in responding. If you have found a strategy which the student may use with this technique and be successful, please indicate in notes.

Note: From *Reaching the Hard to Teach* by J. W. Wood. 2008. Richmond, VA. Reprinted with permission.

Table 6.8 Activity mode.

<table>
<tr><th rowspan="2">Skills Needed in Activity Mode</th><th rowspan="2">Techniques</th><th colspan="2">Responding Teacher</th><th rowspan="2">Notes</th></tr>
<tr><th>SP ED</th><th>GEN ED</th></tr>
<tr><td rowspan="9">• Can follow a sequence of commands
• Has strong self-esteem
• Works cooperatively
• Can organize information
• Thinks creatively
• Can process oral information
• Closes cognitively as well as physically</td><td>• Role Playing</td><td></td><td></td><td></td></tr>
<tr><td>• Stating Hypothesis</td><td></td><td></td><td></td></tr>
<tr><td>• Constructing</td><td></td><td></td><td></td></tr>
<tr><td>• Interpreting</td><td></td><td></td><td></td></tr>
<tr><td>• Preparing Exhibits</td><td></td><td></td><td></td></tr>
<tr><td>• Dramatizing</td><td></td><td></td><td></td></tr>
<tr><td>• Processing</td><td></td><td></td><td></td></tr>
<tr><td>• Group Work</td><td></td><td></td><td></td></tr>
<tr><td>• Games/Contests</td><td></td><td></td><td></td></tr>
</table>

- Check teaching techniques in which student has difficulty in responding. If you have found a strategy which the student may use with this technique and be successful, please indicate in notes.

Note: From *Reaching the Hard to Teach* by J. W. Wood. 2008. Richmond, VA. Reprinted with permission.

Inquiry Mode.

Skills needed. Numerous skills are required by students who can respond to the techniques in the inquiry mode. First, the student must have the skills needed for responding to the expository mode, and the student must be able to respond to the appropriate taxonomy required (knowledge, comprehension, application, analysis, synthesis, and evaluation). Additionally, the student must organize information into groups, select alternatives, follow a sequence of commands, see parts from the whole, and remain on task for a required time.

Techniques. Asking questions, stating hypotheses, coming to conclusions, interpreting, classifying, self-directed study, testing hypotheses, observing, synthesizing, and problem solving are key techniques found in the inquiry mode. Table 6.2 provides interventions for each of the techniques. From the inquiry mode the technique of asking questions is used most frequently by classroom teachers.

Visiting a school in one of the major cities, I experienced a technique I had never seen before. As Mr. Lee, a middle school social studies teacher, asked the class questions, one young boy raised his hand. When called on, the young student replied, "Get back!" I was curious as to what I had just seen and questioned Mr. Lee. Mr. Lee responded, "That young man is disfluent. Sometimes when he starts to answer, he will block or stammer. So together we worked out the intervention 'Get back.'" This is an excellent example of how a responding teacher using Table 6.3 could make a note of the "Get back" intervention for the young man's future teachers.

Demonstration Mode.

Skills needed. As seen in Table 6.7, students must understand information presented orally and visually, select important information from presented materials, have the necessary vocabulary levels, follow sequential directions, have specific skills needed for selected tasks (using the microscope), and work cooperatively in groups.

Techniques. Six techniques frequently used in the demonstration mode are experiments, exhibits, simulations, games, modeling, and field trips. Interventions for each are found in Table 6.3.

Activity Mode.

Skills needed. Table 6.8 presents skills needed when teaching in the activity mode. Following a sequence of commands, having strong self-esteem, working cooperatively, organizing information, thinking creatively, processing oral information, and closing cognitively as well as physically are all required skills a student needs when responding to the activity mode.

Techniques. Techniques frequently used in the activity mode are found in Table 6.8, and interventions for each technique are found in Table 6.4.

SUMMARY

Teaching is a complex issue. As we learned in Chapter 4, the learning environment must be in place. In Chapter 5 we saw the complex process of lesson planning. In this chapter we began to look at understanding learning and learning styles as a prerequisite to the delivery of information. Lastly, educators must understand how they deliver information to help students receive it in an organized manner. Imposing structure on the delivery process and on information helps the learner assimilate and retain information. "Telling is not teaching, and told is not taught." How we deliver instruction and select our delivery system becomes a carefully planned exercise.

RESOURCES

Association for Supervision and Curriculum Development (ASCD)
1703 North Beauregard Street
Alexandria, VA 22311–1714
Service center: (703) 578–9600
or (800) 933–2723, then press 2
Online store: http://shop.ascd.org

Council for Exceptional Children (CEC)
1110 North Glebe Road, Suite 300
Arlington, VA 22201–5704
(888) 232–7733

SUGGESTED READINGS

Kimball, J. W., Kinney, E. M., Taylor, B. A., & Stromer, R. C. (2002). Lights, camera, action! Using engaging computer-cued activity schedules. *Teaching Exceptional Children, 36*(1) 40–45.
Maroneyh, S. A., Finson, K. D., Beaver, J. B., & Jensen, M. M. (2003). Preparing for successful inquiry in inclusive science classrooms. *Teaching Exceptional Children, 36*(1) 18–25.

WEBSITES

Discovery Channel Online. A wealth of information and links to a variety of subjects. *www.discovery.com.*

PBS Online. Website of the Public Broadcasting System showing program scheduling and other information. *www.pbs.org.*

Website contains a discussion of the four areas of perception. *www.ncbi.nlm.nih.gov/entrez/query.fcgi?cmdretrieve&db=pubmed&list_vids=7142799&dopt=abstract.*

Howard Gardner's recent paper on multiple intelligences. *www.pz.harvard.edu/PIs/HG_MI_after_20_years.pdf*

Recent work of Daniel Coleman. *www.amazon.com/working-emotional-intelligence-daniel-coleman/dp/0553378589*

REFERENCES

Coles, R. (1997). *The moral intelligence of children: How to raise a moral child.* New York: Random House.

Costa, A. L., & Kallick, B. (2000). *Discovering & exploring: Habits of mind.* Alexandria, VA: Association for Supervision and Curriculum Development.

Davies, I. K. (1981). *Instructional techniques.* New York: McGraw-Hill.

Dunn, R., Dunn, K., & Price, G. E. (1979). *Learning styles inventory manual.* Lawrence, KS: Price Systems.

Fuhrmann, B. S. (1980, August). *Models and methods of assessing learning styles.* Paper presented at a meeting of the Virginia Educational Research Association.

Gardner, H. (1983). *Frames of mind: The theory of multiple intelligences.* New York: Basic Books.

Gardner, H. (1993). Educating for understanding. *American School Board Journal, 180*(7), 20–24.

Gardner, H. (1999, July). *Multiple intelligences.* Speech delivered at Thinking for a Change Conference, 7th International Thinking Conference, Edmonton, Alberta, Canada.

Guilford, J. P., & Hoeptner, R. (1971). *The analysis of intelligence.* New York: McGraw-Hill.

Hammeken, P. (1995). *Inclusion: 450 strategies for success.* Minnetonka, MN: Peytral.

Keefe, J. W. (1979). *Student learning styles: Diagnosing and prescribing programs.* Reston, VA: National Association of Secondary School Principals.

Kindsvatter, R., Wilen, W., & Ishler, M. (1988). *Dynamics of effective teaching.* New York: Longman.

Jarolimek, J., & Foster, C. (1981). *Teaching and learning in the elementary school* (2nd ed.). New York: Macmillan.

Johnson, G. R. (1976). *Analyzing college teaching.* Manchach, TX: Sterling Swift.

Marzano, R. J., Pickering, D. J., & Pollock, J. E. (2001). *Classroom instruction that works: Researched-based strategies for increasing student achievement.* Alexandria, VA: Association for Supervision and Curriculum Development.

Perkins, D. N. (1995). *Outsmarting IQ: The emerging science of learnable intelligence.* New York: The Free Press.

Rowe, M. B. (1974). Wait time and reward as instructional variables, their influence on language, logic, and fate control. Part 1: Wait time. *Journal of Research on Science Teaching, 11,* 81–94.

Sternberg, R. J., Torff, B., & Grigorento, E. (1998, May). Teaching for successful intelligence raises school achievement. *Phi Delta Kappan, 79,* 667–669.

West, E. (1975). *Leading discussions.* Unpublished paper, University of Minnesota, St. Paul.

Wood, J. W. (1993). *Mainstreaming: A practical approach for teachers.* Upper Saddle River, NJ: Merrill/Prentice Hall.

Chapter 7

ADAPTING THE FORMAT OF CONTENT

Key Terms

Figure-Ground *(page 125)*

Formative Study Guide *(page 135)*

Summative Study Guide *(page 135)*

CHAPTER-AT-A-GLANCE

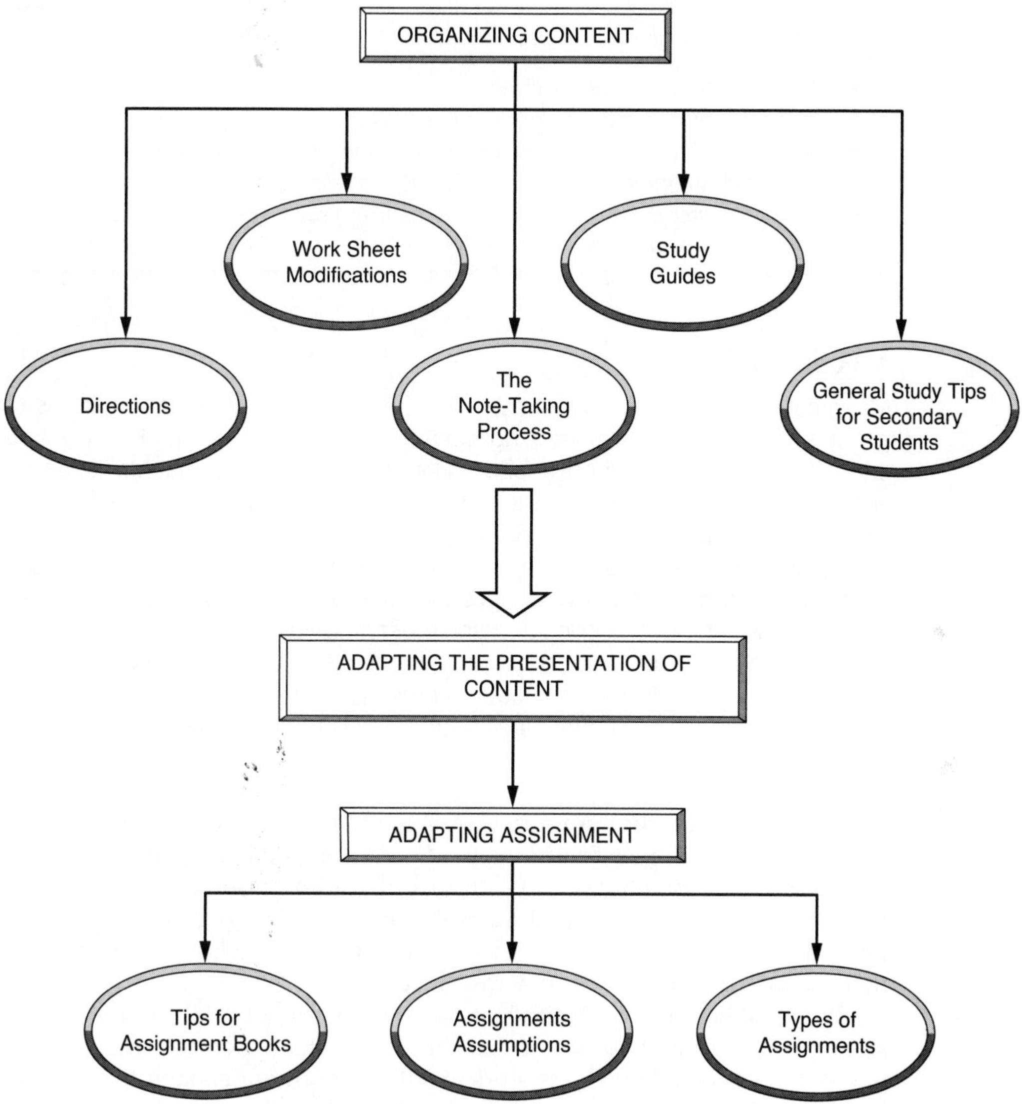

LEARNER OBJECTIVES

After you read this chapter, you will be able to

- *Discuss ways of giving directions.*
- *Provide more appropriate work sheets for students.*
- *Understand the note-taking process and tips for helping students.*
- *Develop study guides.*
- *Develop numerous interventions for presenting the format of content.*
- *Adapt assignments.*

VIGNETTE

Mr. Jimenez was greatly concerned because many of his students in his sixth-grade social studies class were not completing their homework. He spoke to the school counselor and school social worker. Both suggested that Mr. Jimenez visit with each of the students and ask about their home and afterschool activities. Quickly, he realized that many of the students worked afterschool jobs and had numerous responsibilities at home, including watching younger siblings. Mr. Jimenez realized that homework not only must be appropriate and on grade level for each student, but that consideration must be given to students' home life. How can you expect students to do homework when the home does not work?

Note: From Reaching the Hard to Teach *by J. W. Wood, 2008, Richmond, VA: Judy Wood, Inc. Reprinted by permission.*

After teachers select the appropriate teaching technique to deliver the lesson, they may have to consider alternative ways of presenting the academic content. For example, teachers usually teach the subject of reading from a basal textbook and teach math using exercises and examples in a textbook. Assignments to prepare for tomorrow's class may be given at the end of today's class. Work sheets traditionally are used in classrooms across the country.

But what happens to the student who simply cannot achieve success with the strategies and formats used for teaching the content? Sometimes, even if techniques have been adapted, the student still may not understand the material. In such cases, the regular class teacher should ask the following questions:

1. Does the student have the skills to complete the required task?
2. If not, does the student have the prerequisite skills for beginning the required task?
3. Does instruction begin at the student's functioning level?
4. Was the teaching technique appropriate for delivering the instruction to the student?

After answering these questions, the teacher may see a need to modify the strategies and formats used for reorganizing instruction.

This chapter discusses and presents ideas for providing a clear understanding of the content for students. The content is the subjects being taught: reading, math, social studies, science, art, physical education, and so on. There are three major areas of focus when we are analyzing our content or subject: What organizational skills are needed to help the student understand the subject and to be in a constant state of learning for test and review? What strategies can educators use to bring life (understanding) to the content of a subject? When the class is over and assignments are presented, our job is only beginning. How can educators adapt assignments to meet individual students' needs?

ORGANIZING CONTENT

Structure is an important component of content, or subject matter, as it is for other blocks of the SAALE Model. Remember, when educators provide structure, students will eventually, and naturally, learn to impose their own. Organizing content has four important parts: directions, work sheets, note-taking, and study guides.

Directions

Giving directions is one of the first things teachers do in class and also one of the tasks they do most frequently. If students have not heard, listened to, or understood the directions, they are lost from the start. There are three aspects of directions: before giving directions, giving oral directions, and providing written directions (Wood, 2006). Each part is crucial to the process.

Before Giving Directions. Teachers should think about the following suggestions before giving directions:

1. Be sure you have all students' attention. You can get their attention in many ways—wearing a funny hat, holding up a small directions flag, and so on.
2. Allow the class to select the direction clue to be used each month. This gives them ownership in the process.
3. Check to see that everyone has the necessary materials for recording directions (such as paper, pencils, and highlighters).
4. Try not to scold anyone before giving directions. Embarrassment may prevent students from paying attention.
5. Offer small prizes to sections of the class that focus on the direction clue first.
6. Number each direction if more than one is to be used.

Research Notes for Classroom Application

Students may have trouble following directions for a number of reasons (Saunders, 2001). Some may have difficulty understanding certain words. Others may have difficulty attending to, remembering, or processing a long series of instructions. Students with attention problems may not listen when spoken to or may be distracted by background noise. A delay in processing spoken words can also lead to problems in following directions. Students may even receive "extra" directions that were intended for another student. For students with auditory processing difficulties, "challenging listening situations, such as noisy backgrounds or poor acoustic environments, great distances from the speaker, speakers with fast speaking rates, or speakers with foreign accents" pose an even greater obstacle to successfully following instructions (Ciocci, 2002, p. 2).

All teachers, and especially those of inclusive classrooms, must ascertain if a student is not following directions due to a physical or mental barrier or is simply noncompliant. To determine this, they can start with knowledge of the student's receptive and expressive language skills. Students with language deficits are more likely to struggle with verbal messages. Formal assessments provide better information about a student's language abilities and adaptations that can be made to help the student succeed. Teacher observations of student behavior can also provide relevant information. If a student exhibits disruptive behavior immediately following verbal directions, he or she is likely exhibiting frustration at not understanding or remembering the information well enough to follow the instructions.

When teachers are aware of the potential challenges students may have in following directions, they can make adjustments to help individual students and the class as a whole be more successful and reduce frustration felt by struggling students. Simply repeating the instructions using the same words will not be effective if a student did not understand the vocabulary, so simplifying directions and using visual cues are important. Eliminating or reducing as much classroom noise as possible and seating struggling students close to the speaker will help. Some students may require 5–10 seconds or longer before a spoken message is processed by the brain, so pausing before repeating or giving additional instructions is useful. Helping students develop memory techniques and expanding their vocabulary, syntax, and pragmatic skills to facilitate comprehension are among some long-term strategies for addressing students' trouble with following directions.

Sources: Ciocci, S. R. (2002, December). Auditory processing disorders: An overview. *Eric Digest*. Retrieved January 19, 2007 from http://www.eric.ed.gov/ERICDocs/data/ericdocs2/content_storage_01/0000000b/80/2a/38/e8.pdf.

Saunders, M. D. (2001, March/April). Who's getting the message? Helping students understand in a verbal world. *Teaching Exceptional Children, 33*(4), 70–74.

Note: From *Reaching the Hard to Teach* by J. W. Wood, 2008, Richmond, VA: Judy Wood, Inc. Reprinted with permission.

Giving Oral Directions. Here are some tips for giving oral directions:

1. Get students' attention.
2. Eliminate unnecessary words.
3. Speak in short, simple sentences.
4. Give only one direction if possible.
5. Use a visual backup and speak slowly, stopping after each direction if more than one is given.
6. Remember, no matter how slowly you speak or how long you pause, some students can only process one direction and not a series of directions.
7. Ask for volunteers to repeat the directions.
8. Keep visual support present during the activity. In other words, do not erase the visual backup before the activity or assignment has been completed.
9. Have a system in place for students who do not understand directions. In other words, they should know what to do to find out. Do not tell them to raise their hands because some students are embarrassed about doing this. Develop a discreet way for them to get clarity.
10. If repeating directions, restate them exactly the same way (for students with auditory processing difficulties).

Providing Written Directions. I have several suggestions for providing written directions:

1. Use few words.
2. Provide an example.
3. Read the directions orally as the students highlight the written directions.
4. Keep directions on the page that a student is working on. If the assignment is more than one page long, the directions should appear on a card, the chalkboard, or another easily accessible place.
5. Be sure that the students understand all parts of, and all words in, the directions.
6. Have a backup system for students who do not understand the directions. Remember that students who do not understand the directions are usually those who do not want to raise their hands in front of their peers. Find a discreet way for them to get information.

Work Sheet Modifications

I have never been a big fan of work sheets. However, the reality is that work sheets are used frequently in schools. A work sheet should have a definite purpose related to the task at hand and should not be used as busy work.

Work sheets must have a purpose. Teachers should think about that purpose when constructing, implementing, and evaluating them (Wood, 2006).

Construction. Here are some tips for constructing work sheets:

1. Limit the amount of material on each page.
2. Focus on only one concept at a time.

3. Provide large, readable print or type.
4. Make sure the work sheet teaches what you intend it to teach.
5. Do not use work sheets for busy work.
6. Keep directions simple.
7. Do not hand out numerous work sheets at one time.
8. When a student finishes one work sheet, do not just hand out another.

Implementation. Teachers should consider these suggestions before implementing work sheets:

1. Provide short, clear directions.
2. Present all directions both orally and visually.
3. Be sure students clearly understand directions.
4. Have students color code or highlight directions.
5. Present only one work sheet at a time.
6. Allow students to work with a buddy when completing the work sheet.
7. Allow students to complete part of the work sheet or odd/even sections.

Evaluation. Here are three tips for evaluating work sheets:

1. Provide self-correcting work sheets. Answer cards may be used for checking answers, or a completed work sheet may be used.
2. Permit students to correct their own work sheets.
3. If work sheets are turned in, be sure they are reviewed, returned, and deficits retaught.

The Note-Taking Process

Note-taking is a skill that requires instruction, structure, and practice, although teachers often assume that it is an easy task for students. Many students in inclusive settings have difficulty taking notes because of their inability to organize ideas or concepts, distinguish main points or ideas, or transfer information from written or oral formats. Some students also have deficits in processing or in motor skills.

Students must have the correct information in a format useful for study if we expect them to learn class information and pass class tests. The note taking process serves as a study process for many students, especially if the class is organized and systematic. Learning how to take notes in difficult situations is a skill that may be carried not only into other classes but into adult life as well. Learning note taking, learning the method of adaptation that is required, and getting a complete set of notes provide instructional security for students. Their anxiety is reduced when they know that they have the proper information from which to organize their study.

Many students fail tests because of incomplete notes, not because they do not know the material. Test success is extremely dependent on having good notes. Thus, the point of intervention could be working on students' note-taking abilities.

Before providing adaptations for the note-taking process, educators need to consider the sources from which the notes will be given. Will the information be orally presented through lectures, movies, videotapes, or DVDs? Or will it be in written format, using the chalkboard, an overhead projector, a textbook, newspapers, magazines, or PowerPoint? Students should also develop an awareness of the source of the notes and specific adaptations they need for each source.

Second, teachers should tell students about the type of test to expect from the notes, such as multiple choice, essay, or short answer. This helps the student focus on how the material will be presented in the testing situation.

We often think of note-taking as a single skill that students use in the classroom. Actually, there are two distinct types of note-taking, and each requires different skills. Figure 7.1 shows the process of note-taking from both oral and printed presentations.

Taking Notes from Oral Material. Material given orally includes lecture, video, DVDs, and so on. Think of this type of note-taking as a four-step process. First, the student must auditorily pick up the information (figure-ground). (In this case, **figure-ground** means hearing a word and selecting it from a background of other words.) Second, the student must remember what was just said (auditory memory). Third, some sort of organizational processing takes place. Because all information is not equal, students must pinpoint the topic and determine the major and minor parts. Fourth, the student must transfer the material heard into written format. Fine motor abilities come into play here. The process is continuous, not as jerky as it seems in this discussion.

What kinds of trouble do students with special needs have with this kind of note-taking? Imagine that you are a student with poor auditory memory. By the time you write down part of what you heard and return your attention to the speaker, pockets of information are missing from your notes.

The lecture is one of the most common situations in which students take notes from oral information. Students have difficulty taking notes from a lecture for a number of reasons. These include an inability to impose structure, visual processing problems, deficient motor skills, and auditory processing problems. Many students are unable to listen to the teacher, extrapolate the major and minor concepts, and put this information on paper. For them, everything that the teacher says appears equally important. Students with visual processing deficits may not be able to move their eyes from one focal point (the teacher) to a new focal point (the paper) smoothly enough to take notes quickly. Deficient fine-motor control may cause handwriting problems so that students cannot read their own notes. Auditory processing problems may cause students to be unable to hear the lecture clearly and accurately, resulting in incomplete or incorrect notes.

One suggestion for adapting the note-taking process is to provide a lecture outline. An outline gives the student the major and minor parts of the coming lecture, either on a single page or on one or more pages, with space allotted for filling in notes.

Before beginning the lecture, the teacher should follow these steps:

1. Present the topic or objective of the material to be covered.
2. Relate the material to the sequence of material taught yesterday and to the total course sequence.

Figure 7.1 The note-taking process: Oral material and printed material.

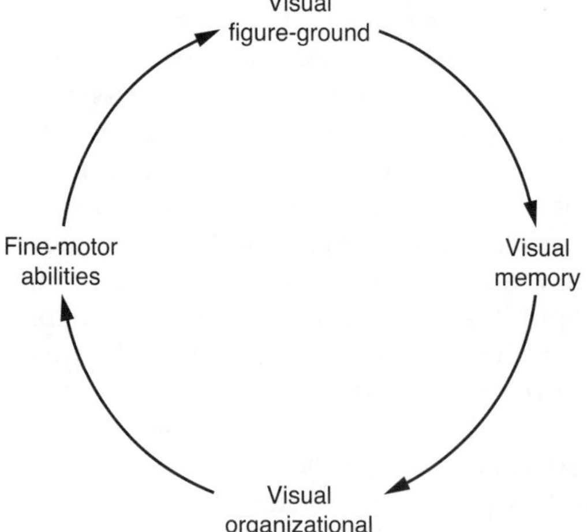

Note: From *Reaching the Hard to Teach* by J. W. Wood, 2008, Richmond, VA: Judy Wood, Inc. Reprinted with permission.

3. Introduce the lecture outline by pointing out the major points (points 1, 2, 3, and so on).
4. Remind students that minor or supporting information will be listed under each major topic.
5. Give the page numbers where students can find the information in the text.
6. Begin the lecture and indicate noteworthy information.

7. Throughout the lecture or discussion, refer to the outline number to keep students on track.
8. At the conclusion of the lecture, briefly summarize the information covered.

Another adaptation for oral lectures is to use tape recorders for recording lectures or discussions. Students may bring their own recorders, or the teacher can record the lecture and allow students to check out tapes at a later date.

During class lectures teachers can also use the chalkboard to help students organize the information. They can start by developing a chart format with headings and then fill in key information during the lecture for students to copy. When the class is completed, students will have a set of notes organized by categories to make studying and review easier.

Good listening is essential for taking notes from lectures, class discussions, reviews, or other oral presentations. Students should be trained to listen. Teachers should remember that, after a while, everything begins to sound the same. Therefore, it is important to take an occasional "listening break." Pause for a stretch, tell a story that is related to the topic, or insert a joke. Breaking the constant flow of the lecture helps the listener attend to noteworthy information.

Teachers can also give signals to let students know what is important to write down. Students who have difficulty with structure may also have difficulty distinguishing major and minor details. When teachers come to parts of the lecture they know students must remember for a test or other reason, they can give a clue, such as, "This is noteworthy." Students should know what the clue words are. They should be instructed to either underline the noteworthy information or put a star in the margin. By giving clues, teachers can (a) keep students on track, (b) help students attend to the important information, and (c) teach the difference between major and minor information.

Taking Notes from Printed Material. Taking notes from printed matter can also be difficult for students. This kind of note-taking falls into two areas: far-point copying and near-point copying. Far-point copying is required when copying from an overhead projector, chalkboard, flip chart, and so on. Near-point copying is required when, for example, copying math problems from a textbook onto paper or copying from one paper to another.

Figure 7.1 displays the four skills required for a student to be able to copy from printed matter. Some students have difficulty finding their place in printed material when they move their eyes from book to paper (visual figure-ground). With such a problem, taking notes can take forever. Because note-taking requires many skills, just one breakdown point can throw the student significantly behind.

Taking notes from the chalkboard requires good skills in visual tracking, handwriting, and organization. If these skills are not fully developed, the student with disabilities may have great difficulty getting the notes. The arrangement of class seating is essential. The teacher should be sure that students are seated so they can see the chalkboard easily as well as to avoid distractions. Teachers who plan to provide a complete set of notes to students who are unable to copy from the board may require them to copy certain sections of the lecture. This will keep them working with the class but take away the stress of trying to get all the notes. Students can then focus on the discussion, knowing that a complete set of notes will follow.

When giving notes from the overhead projector, teachers should keep covered any information they have not yet discussed so that students cannot see it until it is presented. Before discussing the information, teachers should allow time for students to copy it. Talking while students write will result in many of them missing the discussion. Teachers often ask students to take notes from preprinted material such as textbooks, magazines, and newspapers. If the notes are being written for future study and review, students may wish to use the format presented in Figure 7.2. If a student is copying material onto a note card, similar information may be placed on the card. The teacher should make sure to put the page number of the material on the card and number the cards when finished.

General Note-Taking Tips. The information in this section applies to note-taking from any material, whether presented orally or in written form. Figure 7.3 offers a number of note-taking suggestions. (I'd like to thank the following educators for their contributions: Cathy Wobser, Sandra Gilbert, Maureen Thomas, Cathy Perini-Korreck, Marshall Welch, and Ida Crandall.)

Figure 7.2 Format for taking notes from printed matter.

Name:__________ Topic:__________ Source of material:__________ __________ Page numbers:__________	Class:__________ Period:__________ Date:__________
As you develop the outline, put important facts, vocabulary, and dates in this column. The specific page number may also be listed.	Outline material in this section I. A. B. C. II. A. B. C. III. A. B. C.

Note: From *Reaching the Hard to Teach* by J. W. Wood, 2008, Richmond, VA: Judy Wood, Inc. Reprinted with permission.

Figure 7.3 Note-taking suggestions for oral or written materials.

1. Save a set of notes from another class to give to the student.
2. Give the student a copy of the teacher's notes.
3. Let one student copy his or her notes to give to the student who has difficulty taking notes.
4. Use an organizer for taking notes on poems. For example:

Title	Author	Type	Poetic devices used
Summary of poem: **Class discussion:** **What I learned from the discussion:** **Questions I have about the poem:**			

5. Seat the student appropriately to avoid auditory or visual distractions.
6. Provide structured organizers for note taking.
7. Provide a lecture outline for note taking.
8. Develop a who, what, when, where, how, and why outline for note-taking.

Who ———	
What ———	
When———	
Where ———	
How ———	
Why ———	

Who	What	When	Where	How	Why

9. When having students copy from the chalkboard or overhead projector, use various colors of chalk or pens. Each sentence should be written in a different color (blue, pink, green). This method is very useful for all students in finding information in a visual field. But be careful: too many colors overwhelm and distract.
10. After a film, divide the chalkboard into four sections and use words or pictures to review. This is an easy note-taking idea for young children.
11. When handing out study work sheets to be kept in a student folder, have students highlight the important information. Many students can never read all of the material, but will or can read the highlighted information.
12. Be sure all notes to be copied are typed or printed. Cursive writing is extremely hard to read.
13. Use the 1/3–2/3 folding method for note-taking. This may be used for lecture notes or chapter notes. Put main idea or question on left side and answer or detail on right side. For example:

Felony	Crime for which the punishment is one year or longer.

14. Provide a classroom set of clipboards as an incentive for children to get physically involved in note-taking from the chalkboard.
15. Provide a binder available to all students in one place in the room. Have two volunteers/secretaries copy their notes and place them in the binder at the end of each class. The teacher makes 6 to 8 copies of the better set and places them back into the binder. The next day students with note-taking difficulties may get a complete set of notes from the day before.
16. Use a *KIM* sheet for note-taking. It looks like this:

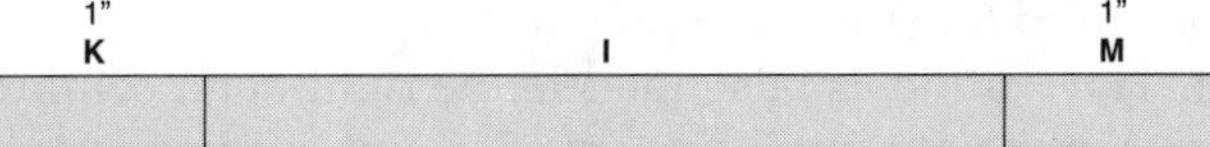

a. Students make their chart using any type of paper.

b. **K** is for key words. **I** is for information about the key word, which can be numbered or lettered. **M** is for a memo to help students remember the information, page, and so on.

c. This method is generic for any class. Students always have the outline when needed. When using the **KIM** sheet to study for a test, you can cover the **K** column and read clues from the **I** column and check answers, or cover the **I** column and use **K** as clues. If writing a report, **K** is your topic, and **I** is the information for each paragraph or sentence.

Continued

Figure 7.3 (Continued)

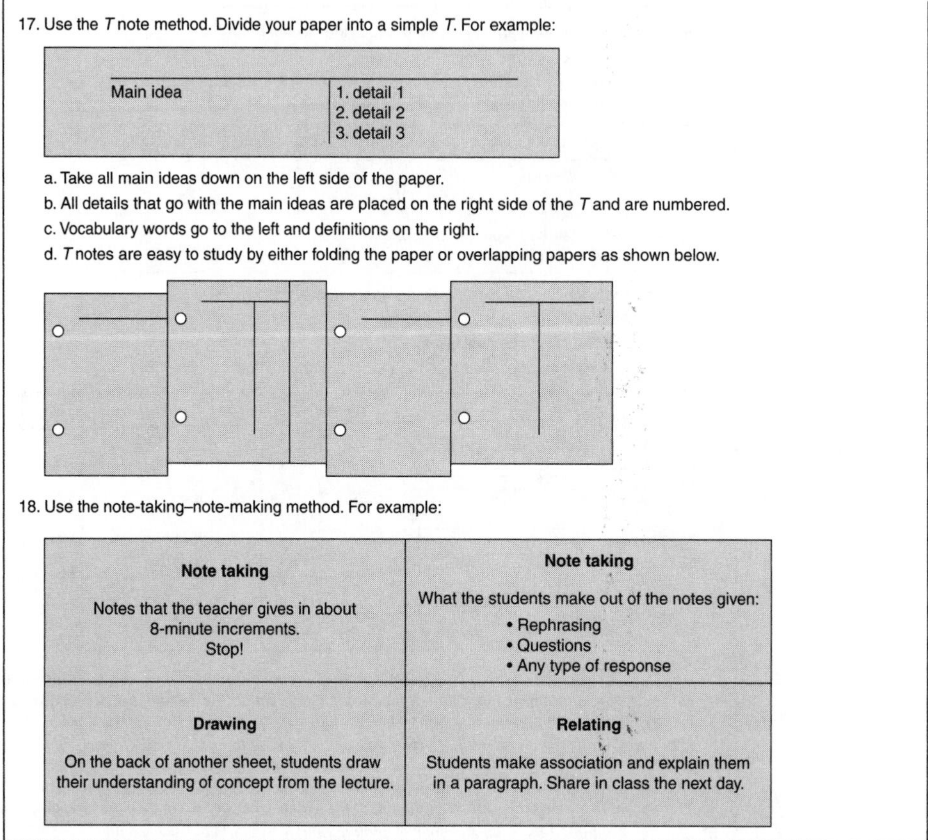

17. Use the *T* note method. Divide your paper into a simple *T*. For example:

Main idea	1. detail 1 2. detail 2 3. detail 3

a. Take all main ideas down on the left side of the paper.
b. All details that go with the main ideas are placed on the right side of the *T* and are numbered.
c. Vocabulary words go to the left and definitions on the right.
d. *T* notes are easy to study by either folding the paper or overlapping papers as shown below.

18. Use the note-taking–note-making method. For example:

Note taking Notes that the teacher gives in about 8-minute increments. Stop!	**Note taking** What the students make out of the notes given: • Rephrasing • Questions • Any type of response
Drawing On the back of another sheet, students draw their understanding of concept from the lecture.	**Relating** Students make association and explain them in a paragraph. Share in class the next day.

Note: From *Reaching the Hard to Teach* by J. W. Wood, 2008, Richmond, VA: Judy Wood, Inc. Reprinted with permission.

To help students improve their approach to note taking, teachers can show them how to format the paper they plan to take notes on. Here are some suggestions about formatting:

1. Teach students to use only two thirds of their paper for note-taking and one third for study and review:
   a. Have students take notes in the right-hand column.
   b. As the notes are being given, point out important dates, facts, vocabulary, and so on; have the student put facts into the left-hand column.
   c. When you have completed a section of notes, stop and ask students to review their notes and list in the left-hand column possible text questions.
   d. Review the questions presented and have the class complete missing information.
2. After note taking, students can work in pairs to study and review notes.

3. Have students develop a format for their notepapers. This will help them to organize, file, and retrieve for later review.
4. Loose-leaf paper means easier filing. However, commercial notebooks can be purchased if you prefer students to keep notes in a spiral-bound book.

Teachers can also help students after the note-taking process. Consider the following suggestions:

1. Teach students how to use the notes for study and review.
2. Assign buddies or study-and-review teams to work together using the notes.
3. Buddies can color code notes. Use three colors: one for vocabulary, one for facts to remember, and one for concepts to study. You can quickly check to see whether important information is highlighted.
4. Buddies can check one set of notes with another and, in the left-hand column, write missing information.
5. Teach students to file their notes in an organized manner. Work on this process for an extended period until students develop the structure themselves.
6. Before the test, refer to notes by dates or topics that should be reviewed. Tell the students the test type for specific notes.
7. It is good practice to keep an extra set of class notes on file in the class. Students who are absent or who have missed sections of notes can refer to this set for assistance. File the notes by class date for easy retrieval.
8. When covering a large amount of material in class, provide students with a basic notes outline and encourage them to add more in-depth information as it is presented. See Figure 7.4 for an example.

Providing adaptations for notes is a crucial support for students. If students are unable to get a complete set of notes, how can we expect them to be successful on tests? The ideas I have presented help bridge the gap between notes and students. Let's look at a few tips that help students help themselves. Figure 7.5 presents note-taking tips that students can incorporate into their own skill base. These are also good ideas for college students.

Before closing this section, I want to leave you with one thought: It is not important that students *take* the notes. It is important that they *get* the notes.

Study Guides

A study guide helps students develop a plan for study and review. As teachers teach, study guides become instruments for improving structure both as the lesson develops and when the lesson is over and test review begins. Study guides benefit students in numerous ways:

1. Provide organization of information for studying purposes.
2. Help students develop a whole-part-whole concept for the material.

Figure 7.4 Student notes given by teacher prior to class.

Basic Water Conservation and Management Principles

1. Intercept the force of the running water.
2. Slow it down.
3. Control it.
4. Reduce the amount of water leaving the land source.

- Sheet erosion moves the soil surface in a large usually unseen thin sheet.
- Erosion takes place anywhere there is bare soil.
- Water beats away at the soil, loosening soil particles and moving them short distances or even far away.
- Erosion causes sediment to fill reservoirs, lakes, and streams that kills aquatic life.
- Erosion can clog water delivery systems that bring water to cities.
- In cities where there is more pavement than soil, water runs off quicker and fills storm drains and sewer systems. This is what causes flooding.

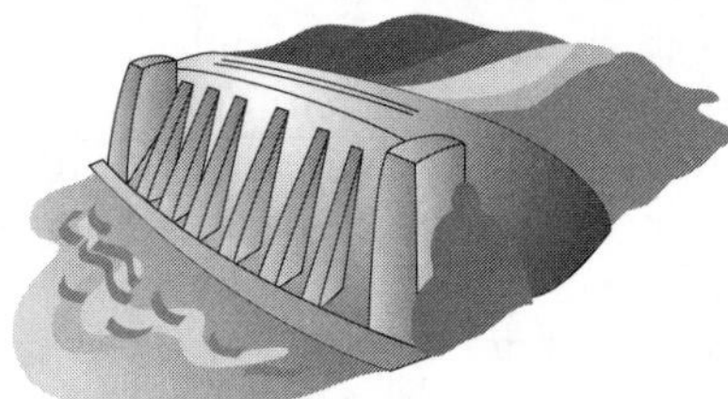

Water and Conservation

Water can generally be managed and conserved as it becomes available through precipitation.

- Water management begins with soil management.
- Soil erosion begins with a drop of water blasting soil particles, like a bomb.

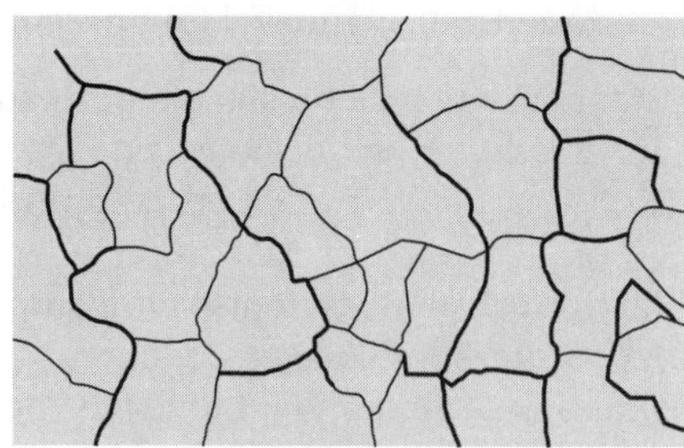

About Water

Water surrounds us. It is in the air as rain, ice, snow, steam, and fog. It is in lakes, streams, rivers, oceans, and glaciers.

Humans are about 65% water
Blood = 80–90%
Muscles = 75%

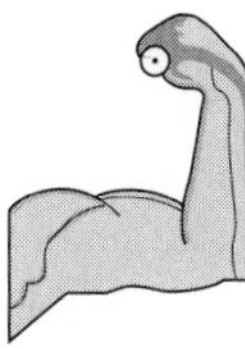

Water isn't ever new, it is recycled time and time again. No new water is being manufactured.
Water is 2 hydrogen molecules and 1 oxygen molecule, H_2O.
The Earth's surface is about 75% water but only 3% is fresh water.
Precipitation falls to Earth from clouds, rain, or snow.

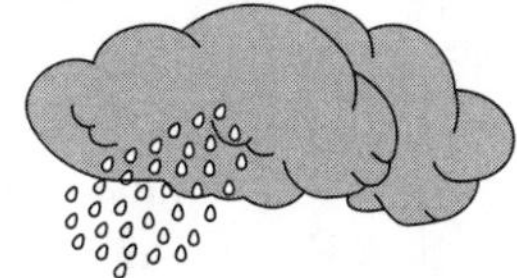

The process then starts over again.

Key Processes of Hydrological Cycle

1. Evaporation: Water goes from liquid to gas stage
2. Transpiration: Water given off through leaves

3. Precipitation: Raining or snowing
4. Infiltration: Fill the pore spaces between individual soil particles
5. Respiration: Breathing
6. Combustion: Burning

The Water Cycle—Nature's Recycling System

Recycling: to pass through a cycle or a part of cycle again

Hydrological cycle: a natural process of water molecules recycling from the land, to the air, and back to the land. Sun's energy warms the water and the vapor goes into the atmosphere.

In the atmosphere the vapor is formed into clouds.

Clouds are carried by weather patterns.

Note: From Science, Spring Oaks Middle School, 2000. A special thanks to Ashly Tardif, Houston, Texas.

Figure 7.5 Note-taking tips for students.

Prepare for the class by completing background reading prior to the class.

Get to class on time so that you don't miss the teacher's opening statements, which are often a statement of the purpose of the lecture.

Don't try to write down every word the teacher says. Focus instead on key phrases, important points, new terms, summary statements, names, dates, etc. Choose one example of a point to record rather than trying to write down each one in detail. Do record all the points in a list.

Keep your mind focused on what the teacher is saying. Try not to look around or think of other things.

Taking notes in outline form will help you focus on main ideas.

Develop your own shorthand system for commonly used words and phrases, for example: b/c for because, w/o for without, $\cong$ for approximately, $\uparrow$ for increased, $\therefore$ for therefore, vs. for versus, $\neq$ for does not equal. Also create a course-specific set of abbreviation, such as: cong. for congressional, adm. for administration, gov't for government, dem/rep for democrats and republicans, etc.

Don't write down small words such as *a the is* that are not needed to understand the informaton.

Remember that your notes are for your own use. Don't be overly concerned about neatness or correct spelling.

If a word is used that you don't know or can't quite understand, write it down phonetically, circle it, and ask a classmate about it or look it up later.

When the teacher uses phrases such as, "This is important." "The main point . . . ," or "An important finding . . . " prior to presenting the information, mark this information by putting a star in the margin of your notes.

When the teacher uses phrases such as "First. . . second. . . third. . . ., ""At this stage. . .," "Finally. . .," recognize these as transitional words that signal a sequence of steps or events.

Notice when the teacher raises the volume of her voice or repeats a word or phrase. This probably signals important information.

Leave plenty of white space in your notes and wide margins for expanding your notes later.

Use a pen rather than a pencil for taking notes. A pen will slide across the paper more quickly and your notes won't smudge and fade like those taken in pencil.

Put the date and day on each set of notes. Draw a line after the last sentence you write and indicate "end."

If you have a question about what the teacher is saying or missed some information, wait until she has completed her thought before interrupting to request repetition or clarification.

If you consistently have difficulty copying lengthy information from overhead transparencies, ask if you can get copies of the transparencies or if you can look at them during a break or after class to fill in information you missed.

If you are going to tape-record a lecture let the teacher know that you plan on doing this. Always try to back up the tape with notes. Review your notes as soon as possible after class, filling in information you missed. Rewriting your notes right after you take them may help you learn the information and also gives you a chance to organize your notes for future study. Arrange for another student to use carbon paper for a second set of notes. This is most helpful if you need to focus on the lecture and not split attention between listening and taking notes.

Note: For practice on note-taking, see Flemming, L. & Leet, J. (1994). *Becoming a Successful Student.* New York: Harper Collins College.

3. Present information in a sequential, logical manner.
4. Tie together the information from yesterday to today and tomorrow.
5. Impose structure on information.
6. Impose a focal point for the teacher.
7. Facilitate collaboration between special and general education teachers.
8. Help parents assist their children in study and review.
9. Aid students in preparing for specific test types.
10. Help students impose structure in other classes without guides.
11. Provide a connection for the students from the lesson or unit to a standard or benchmark.

Types of Study Guides. There are two types of study guides: formative and summative. Each serves a specific function for imposing structure and organizing material.

A **formative study guide** organizes information in short, distributive segments. The guide focuses on specific details of the information covered. An example is the acquisition outline. As a new concept or section of information is presented, students follow the class discussion and record important details in an organized manner. This outline may be on one page or on several pages, and it should have space for notes. The teacher may provide an incomplete outline for students to complete or an outline that has the details already completed. A second option is helpful for students who have difficulty taking notes. Each outline should list the page numbers for the specific information, the title or objective for the lesson, and the lesson date. After the class, students should be instructed to place the outline in the appropriate notebook section. Figure 7.6 presents a sample formative study guide for grade 5.

Summative study guides help students prepare for a quiz or test. They are designed to provide general information about the notes to be quizzed, which lays the foundation for organizing the study effort. The teacher may direct students to put all formative study guides in sequential order by date and place the summative study guide first. The summative study guide provides structure for the student's study effort.

Figure 7.6 Sample formative study guide.

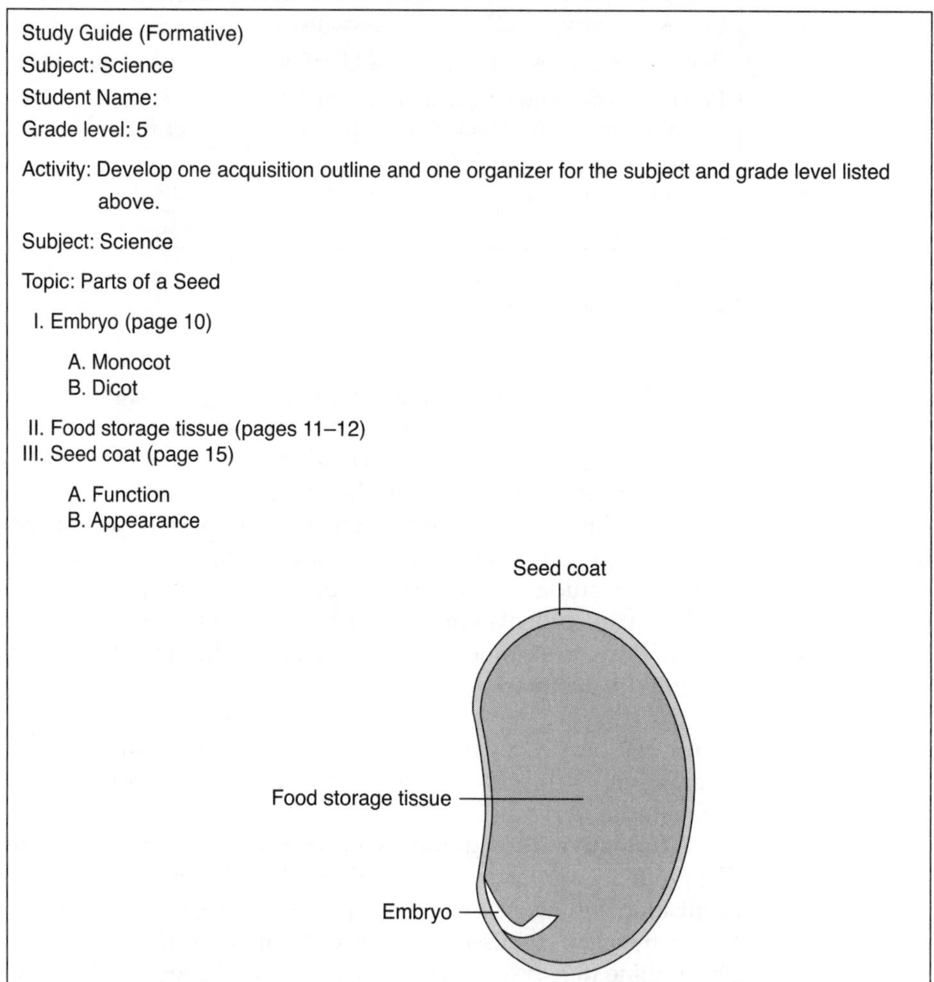

Study Guide (Formative)
Subject: Science
Student Name:
Grade level: 5

Activity: Develop one acquisition outline and one organizer for the subject and grade level listed above.

Subject: Science

Topic: Parts of a Seed

I. Embryo (page 10)
   A. Monocot
   B. Dicot
II. Food storage tissue (pages 11–12)
III. Seed coat (page 15)
   A. Function
   B. Appearance

Note: Thanks to Luanne Berry.

Figures 7.7 and 7.8 present sample summative study guides for secondary and elementary levels. The guides can be completed by the teacher or with the class.

Figures 7.9 through 7.11 present study guides for grades 1 and 5. These examples should give you an idea how formative and summative study guides may be developed for multilevel abilities and subjects.

Students are directed to the study guide to review the lesson or test objective, the textbook, workbook, or handouts to be covered, and key words or vocabulary to be learned. If the test includes short-answer or essay items, review questions are

Figure 7.7 Summative study guide: Secondary level.

Student: ______________________ Date of test: ______________________
Subject: ______________________ Date guide issued: ______________________
Teacher: ______________________

Study Guide

1. Lesson/test objective:
2. Textbook/workbook/manual pages to be covered:
3. Handouts/lectures/films/speakers/demonstrations/labs/maps/charts to be covered:
4. Key words/vocabulary to be learned/location:
5. Review questions for organizing study:
6. Type of test to be given:

	Number of items	Point value
______ Multiple-choice	______________	______________
______ Matching	______________	______________
______ True–false	______________	______________
______ Fill-in-the-blank	______________	______________
______ Word bank included?	______________	______________
______ Short answer	______________	______________
______ Essay	______________	______________
______ Diagrams/charts	______________	______________
______ Maps	______________	______________
______ Word bank for map?	______________	______________
______ List of maps to review	______________	______________
______ Practical tests	______________	______________
Math items:		
______ Computation/equations	______________	______________
______ Word problems	______________	______________
______ Formulas	______________	______________
______ Graphing	______________	______________
______ Proofs	______________	______________
______ Other; please describe	______________	______________

7. Other suggestions for study and review:

Thank you for your help! Student signature: ______________________
Parent signature: ______________________

Note: From *Reaching the Hard to Teach* by J. W. Wood, 2008, Richmond, VA: Judy Wood, Inc. Reprinted with permission.

Figure 7.8 Summative study guide: Elementary level.

Important vocabulary:

Review questions:

Possible short-answer questions:

Important topics:

Parent signature: ______________________

Note: From *Reaching the Hard to Teach* by J. W. Wood, 2008, Richmond, VA: Judy Wood, Inc. Reprinted with permission.

Figure 7.9 Sample formative study guide for science.

Study Guide (Formative)

Subject: Science

Student Name: Betty Barger

Grade level: 1st

Important Vocabulary:

1. Eggs (page 2)
2. Larva (caterpillar) (page 3)
3. Pupa (chrysalis) (page 3)
4. Adult (butterfly) (page 4)

Review Questions:

1. Can you show the sequence of the life cycle of a butterfly? (Use prepared pictures)
2. Can you label the stages in the life cycle of a butterfly? (Prepared cards with words are used)
3. Label the prepared sheet showing the stages in the life cycle of a butterfly with a number 1, 2, 3, 4 showing the sequence in the stages.

Note: From *Reaching the Hard to Teach* by J. W. Wood, 2008, Richmond, VA: Judy Wood, Inc. Reprinted with permission.

Figure 7.10 Test review: Student will label each stage of the butterfly.

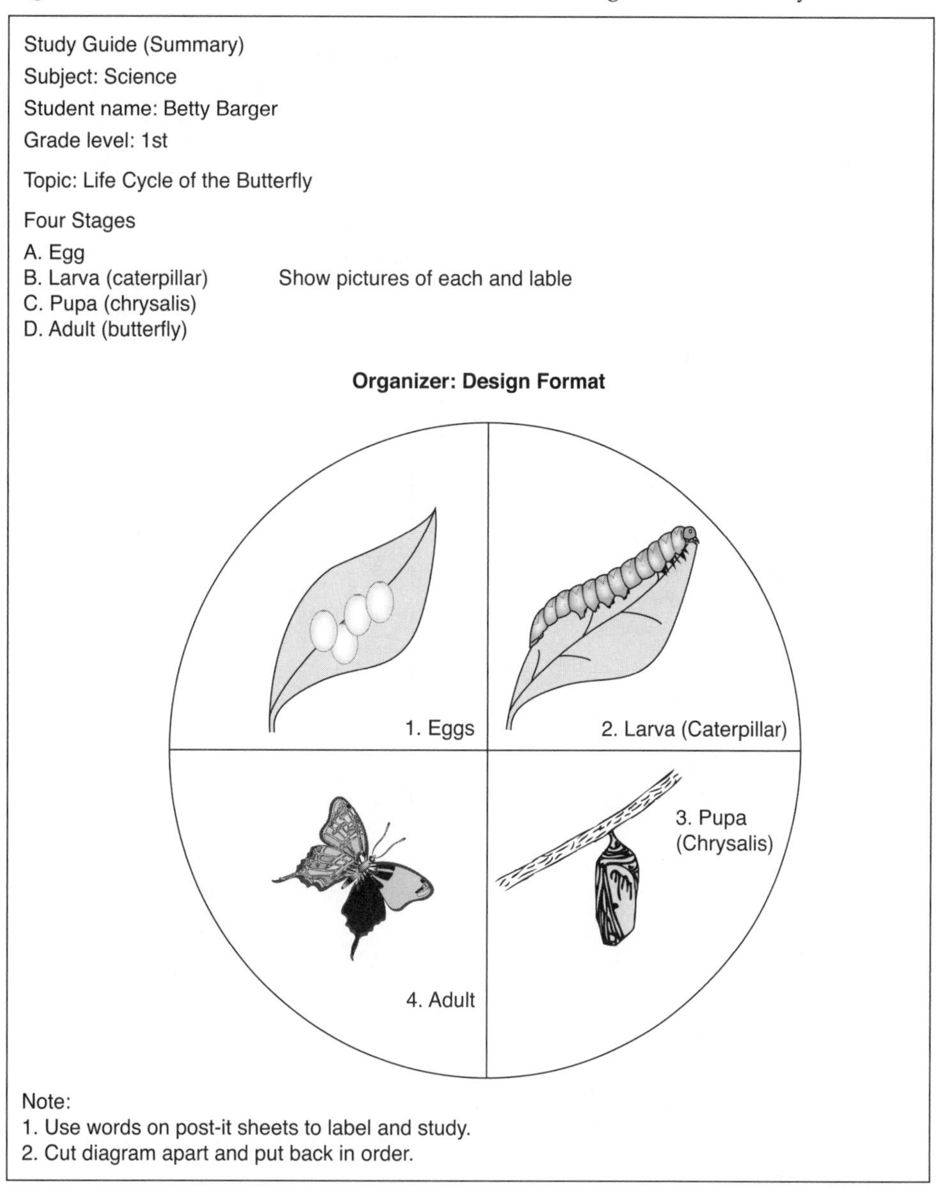

Study Guide (Summary)
Subject: Science
Student name: Betty Barger
Grade level: 1st

Topic: Life Cycle of the Butterfly

Four Stages
A. Egg
B. Larva (caterpillar) Show pictures of each and lable
C. Pupa (chrysalis)
D. Adult (butterfly)

Organizer: Design Format

Note:
1. Use words on post-it sheets to label and study.
2. Cut diagram apart and put back in order.

Note: From *Reaching the Hard to Teach* by J. W. Wood, 2008, Richmond, VA: Judy Wood, Inc. Reprinted with permission.

Figure 7.11 Sample study guide for reading.

Study Guide

Student: ____________________ Date of test: ____________________

Subject: Reading ____________________ Date of study guide: ____________________

Teacher: ____________________

Study Guide
(Summary)

<table>
<tr><td rowspan="2">Needed study materials/pages:</td><td colspan="3">Key points addressed:</td></tr>
<tr><td colspan="3">Test</td></tr>
<tr><td rowspan="2">Key vocabulary words:</td><td>Type</td><td>Number of items</td><td>Point value</td></tr>
<tr><td colspan="3">Suggestions/Comments for study:</td></tr>
</table>

Student signature: ____________________

Parent signature: ____________________

Note: From *Reaching the Hard to Teach* by J. W. Wood, 2008, Richmond, VA: Judy Wood, Inc. Reprinted with permission.

a must. These questions will help the student organize study and review essay questions. The type of test and number of items and point values must also be considered carefully. The type of test reflects the type of retention measure the teacher used while teaching the lesson. In other words, if the lesson focused on specific dates, people, and facts, then the test is a recognition measure. If the lesson focused on general concepts such as "How did the invention of irrigation affect the lives of the people?" then the test is a subjective measure. Just remember this advice: Study guides need to be given out to students before a unit of study or at the beginning of a new chapter.

General Study Tips for Secondary Students

Secondary students can use the following ideas to help them begin their study and make the best use of their time:

- Develop a study schedule for one week to one month in advance.
- Always cross off an assignment when completed. This is an excellent self-motivator.
- Always use an assignment notebook.
- Plan to break up long assignments with a brief rest period, or work on a different subject.
- Schedule rewards for finishing your assignments.
- Sit close to the front of class.
- Make sure you have a complete set of notes.

ADAPTING THE PRESENTATION OF CONTENT

Student success may sometimes depend on the teacher's ability or willingness to adapt the presentation of content. The following activities provide a starting point for developing your own ideas. Many creative educators use inventive adaptations in the class, and the ideas in this chapter represent only a small number of the many possibilities. As much as possible, activities are organized into similar categories. In addition, they are coded *E* (elementary), *S* (secondary), or *E/S* (either elementary or secondary). Here is an example:

Activity (E/S): Alternatives to writing book reports

Adaptations:

1. *Book jacket or bookmark:* Illustrate a cover for the book, or design a bookmark with characters or a setting from the book.
2. *News report:* Summarize the book by writing a news report as if the events in the story actually took place. Pretend to be a TV anchorperson and give the report.
3. *Ending rewrite:* Give the book a new ending. Pursue different ways the story could have ended.

4. *Advertisement:* Dress and act like a character from the book and "sell" the book to the class.
5. *Write to the author:* Write to the book's author in care of the publisher including comments about other books you have read.
6. *Poetry:* Summarize a book by retelling it in poetry form.
7. *Character journal:* Write a journal portraying a character from the book. The journal should be written in the first person and describe the character's thoughts, feelings, and ideas.
8. *Plays:* Rewrite the book in play form. For longer stories, take a chapter or chapters and write an act or scene of the play.
9. *Models:* Make a model of the setting or characters from the book.
10. *Bulletin board:* Use a classroom bulletin board to describe and display the setting, characters, and theme of the book.
11. *Map:* Draw a map of the story setting to show the story action. Use the map as a prop when discussing the book.
12. *Life-size posters:* Make life-size characters to use as props when presenting an oral book report.
13. *Letter:* Write a letter telling a friend about the book. Describe setting, characters, and plot.
14. *Comic book:* Summarize the book in the form of a comic book. This would be a good idea for unmotivated readers who are very interested in drawing and art.
15. *Oral and taped presentation:* This is an easy alternative to written reports. With taped reports, sound effects can be added to interest the audience.
16. *Condensed book:* Write and illustrate a short synopsis of the book. This is similar to what certain magazines do to advertise a book.
17. *Illustrations:* Draw main characters, the setting, or a climactic scene from the book.
18. *Panel discussion:* For students who are reporting on the same book, form a panel and have a question-and-answer period.
19. *Demonstration:* For how-to books, students can demonstrate what they learned. For example, for a book about cake decorating, a student could bring in a cake and show the steps in decorating.
20. *Time line:* Draw a time line of events as they happened in the story. Illustrations may be added to explain events.
21. *Popular music:* Write and perform (or record) rap songs about the book.
22. *Shoe box filmstrips.* Illustrate and summarize the books on cards and then put the cards into a shoe box. When a reader flips the cards, they look like a filmstrip. These filmstrips are kept in the class, and other students look at them and decide whether to read the books.
23. *Tape-recording stories.* Let students tape-record their book reports. You will be surprised how much students know orally that they can't express in a written format.

Frequently, students in inclusive settings can master the academic content presented in general education classes. However, learning will be easier when alternative ways of presenting content become standard procedure in general classrooms. For example, in a class on English grammar, success may depend on the teacher's ability to adapt or modify the presentation of content. A wonderful experience happened in one of my workshops, which clearly explains what I mean by adapting the presentation of content. This story was related to me by teacher A. One day teacher B came into teacher A's room, complaining that a young girl in the class simply could not learn how to do a certain skill. Teacher B said, "I have shown that student how to do the skill *seven* times, and she still cannot get it." Teacher A asked, "Did you show the student the same way each of the seven times?"

"Why, yes," replied teacher B.

Teacher A said, "The problem is that *you* don't get it!"

When a student cannot learn a skill one way, we need to adapt our teaching. This is adapting the format of content.

Activity (E/S): Participating in oral classroom discussion

Adaptation: To help a student listen to questions and give appropriate answers, allow him or her to use a tape recorder. Tape questions with pauses for the student to respond. This gives the student a chance to play back the question and organize the answer. As the student becomes more comfortable with oral discussions, taping can be reduced.

Activity (E/S): Giving oral reports

Adaptations: Allow students who are giving oral reports or speeches to use prompts, such as cards, posters, or visual models. Reports can also be presented using puppets or costumes.

Activity (E): Storytelling

Adaptation: Provide story starters for students who have trouble with original ideas. Allow students to tape-record stories to help them formulate ideas or make presentations.

Activity (E/S): Plays

Adaptation: Allow students with visual tracking difficulties to code or highlight their lines.

Activity (E/S): Comprehension

Adaptation: Highlight *who, what, where* questions in different colors. For example, highlight *where* questions in yellow, *who* questions in blue, and so on.

Activity (S): Understanding idioms

Adaptation: Ask students to demonstrate using concrete illustrations.

Activity (E/S): Understanding compound words

Adaptation: Provide cards with individual words on them and have the student select two. The student puts these two words together or exchanges with a friend. Nonsense words can be created and drawings or magazine pictures used to illustrate the new compound word.

Activity (E/S): Motivating readers

Adaptations: After years of reading failure, students become turned off to reading. Therefore, it is up to the teacher to find reading material that interests them enough so that they find reading acceptable and enjoyable. Figure 7.12 offers a list of motivators for reluctant readers.

Activity (E/S): Organizing and critical thinking

Adaptations: Figure 7.13 offers five tips. (Thanks to Froma Foner and Joan Sanders for their contributions.)

Activity (S): Antonyms and analogies

Adaptation: Figure 7.14 demonstrates a three-step process for prompting students' selection of antonyms and analogies.

Activity (E/S): Making predictions and drawing conclusions

Adaptation: This skill may be modified by (a) reading the passage to the students and (b) presenting several choices of outcomes from which students select the correct answer.

Activity (E/S): Reading graphs and maps

Adaptation: Use high-interest information on the graph or map such as favorite TV shows.

Figure 7.12 Motivation materials for reluctant readers.

Joke and riddle books	Greeting cards
Album jackets	Comic books
Comic strips	Tongue twisters
Travel brochures	Transportation schedules
TV schedules	Catalogues
Advertisements	Classified ads
Telephone book, Yellow Pages	Cookbooks
Society columns, Dear Abby	Biographies
Sports page	How-to books
First-aid books	Driver's education manual
Magazines	The Internet

Note: From *Reaching the Hard to Teach* by J. W. Wood, 2008, Richmond, VA: Judy Wood, Inc. Reprinted with permission.

Figure 7.13 Reading tips.

1. Most needlework stores carry plastic sheets or strips that are easy on your eyes when working on a pattern (such as counted-cross stitch). The usual colors are yellow and blue. These strips or sheets may be placed on the reading material.
2. The gels (colored plastic sheets that are placed over theater lights) may be placed over reading material. Let the student select the color of choice and place over the page to be read. This helps for focus.
3. Place a Yellow Pages information guide in your classroom. Use a wide three-ring binder with tabs. After students have read a book they must complete an activity: sociogram, diorama, opinion/proof, cartoon, report, and so on. When each of the activities is explained, make an example and place it in the Yellow Pages behind the activity-labeled tab. You may place a student example behind your example with detailed requirements and directions. Thus, the teacher only has to explain once, and students have an ongoing prompt.
4. Here is a way to organize story elements:

S + Ch + Co + Pl + Cl + Th

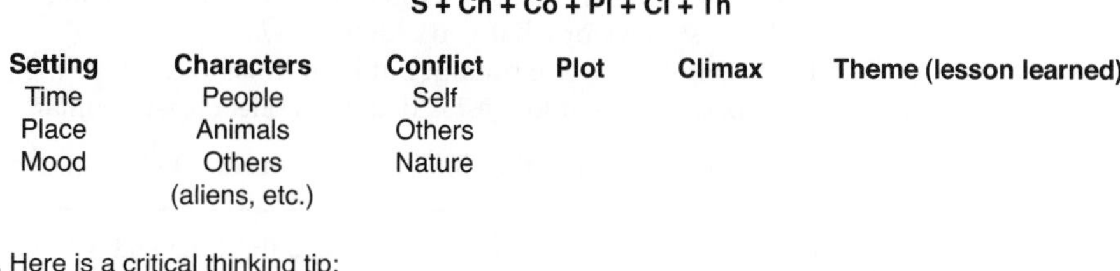

Setting	**Characters**	**Conflict**	**Plot**	**Climax**	**Theme (lesson learned)**
Time	People	Self			
Place	Animals	Others			
Mood	Others (aliens, etc.)	Nature			

5. Here is a critical thinking tip:

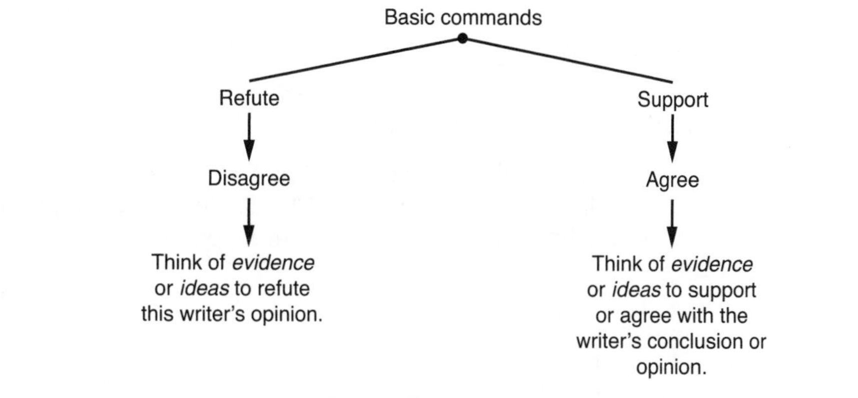

Note: From *Reaching the Hard to Teach* by J. W. Wood, 2008, Richmond, VA: Judy Wood, Inc. Reprinted with permission.

Activity (E/S): Draw a chapter

Adaptation: As children read a novel, have them draw pictures of each chapter to help them remember events in the story. They can keep the drawings in their journals as a ready reference for sequence and events.

Activity (E/S): Understanding the four kinds of sentences

Adaptation: Provide a basic sentence key: four cards with the type of sentence on one side and an example on the back.

Figure 7.14 Antonyms and analogy prompts.

1. What you know
2. What you are reasonably sure of (an educated guess) through
   a. Association
   b. Prefixes
   c. Base words
   d. Personal creation within sentence
3. What you don't know
   Strategy for SWAG (Scientific Wild Donkey Guess)
   a. If you know the prompt:
      - Pick answer you don't know.
        i. If more than one, choose B, C, or D.
        ii. If more than one in B, C, and D, pick longest.
   b. If you don't know the prompt, and don't know some choices
      - Pick as above or what you didn't know.
   c. If you don't know the prompt but know all choices, take the longest answer from B, C, and D. If longest is tied, then select least familiar.

If in doubt, guess the longest of B, C, and D. This has 33 to 40% accuracy.

Note: From *Reaching the Hard to Teach* by J. W. Wood, 2008, Richmond, VA: Judy Wood, Inc. Reprinted with permission.

Activity (E/S): Sentence writing

Adaptation: Prepare substitution tables for teaching sentence structure (Anderson, Greer, & Odle, 1978). Begin with a simple sentence substitution table using the subject-predicate pattern.

1	2
Girls	play.
Boys	run.
Children	sing.

This activity can be extended from teaching simple agreement between subject and predicate to more complicated sentences.

1	2	3
I'm	going	to the White House.
You're	going	home.
He's	going	to school.
She's	going	to Frayser.
It's	going	to Dixiemart.

We're	going	to the grocery.
You're	going	downtown.
They're	going	to the post office.

Activity (E): Punctuation

Adaptation: Using newspaper cartoons, replace the cartoon bubbles with assigned sentences and allow the student to punctuate them. You may want to provide a choice of punctuation marks.

Activity (E/S): Punctuation

Adaptation 1: Tape-record sentences. Provide a work sheet that has the same sentences with punctuation marks omitted. As students listen to each sentence, they follow along on the work sheet and add the correct punctuation. You may want to include two or three choices of punctuation marks at the end of each sentence so students can circle correct responses. For example, "Is your house on fire (. ! ?)"

Adaptation 2: Give students a punctuation key to use when punctuating sentences. The key consists of four cards, each containing a punctuation mark and sample key words or sentences.

Adaptation 3: In preparing work sheets or listing sentences on the board, group sentences by punctuation types. For example, list all sentences requiring question marks or periods together. After students have acquired the skill, begin to mix the sentences, first using only two types of punctuation marks and then adding a third.

Activity (E/S): Compound words

Adaptation: Give students a word list with three columns. Tell students to select the first words from columns 1 and 2 and combine them in column 3. After students have learned the concept, mix the words in columns 1 and 2. Then have students select the appropriate word from column 1 and match with a word from column 2 to make a compound word in column 3.

1.	2.	3.
After	noon	afternoon
Some	one	someone
With	out	without
Any	body	anybody

Activity (E/S): Spelling

Adaptation 1: Divide the spelling list into halves or fourths for the students with mild disabilities. Often they can learn how to spell the words, but not as quickly as other students.

Adaptation 2: Provide "structure spellers" for students who have trouble remembering all the words on the spelling list.

interesting i__ t __ __ e __ __ __ __ g
America __ m e __ i __ __

Activity (S): Pluralizing irregulars

Adaptation: Develop a format for making plurals on transparencies. Students can use the format over again for each new word. Figure 7.15 suggests one possible approach.

Activity (E/S): Creative writing

Adaptation: Don't be overly critical of grammatical errors in creative writing activities. Be concerned about the creativity, praise the efforts, and provide assistance with rewriting.

Activity (E/S): Finding reference materials

Adaptation: Teach students to use a variety of reference materials. Provide a list and a map that shows the location of these items in the library.

Figure 7.15 Pluralizing irregulars.

Make *elf* plural
Take off *f*
Add *v*
Add *es*
Elf becomes *elves*
el
elv
elves

Make *shelf* plural
Take off *f*
Add *v*
Add *es*
Shelf becomes shelves
shel
shelv
shelves

Note: From *Reaching the Hard to Teach* by J. W. Wood, 2008, Richmond, VA: Judy Wood, Inc. Reprinted with permission.

Activity (E/S): Collecting reference information

Adaptation: Give students a reference check work sheet to help keep track of reference information.

Activity (S): Writing a business letter

Adaptation: Give students a visual model with lines to be filled in at appropriate parts of the letter. This prompt can be reduced by using dotted lines in place of solid lines.

Activity (E/S): Writing multiparagraph papers

Adaptation: Figure 7.16 presents an organizational format for helping students develop a framework for writing multiparagraph papers. (Thanks to Tonya Evers for her contributions.)

Activity (E/S): Proofreading checklists

Adaptation: Figures 7.17 and 7.18 suggest two types of checklists for use in the proofreading stage.

Figure 7.16 Group activity for writing a multiparagraph paper.

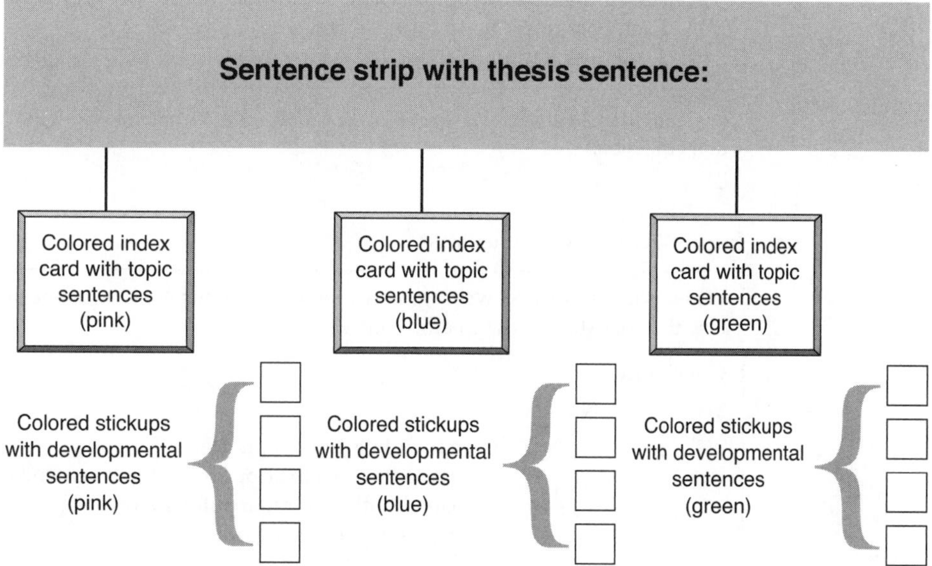

Directions:

1. Put up the organizer on the class wall as it is developing.
2. Before writing or organizing let students ask questions regarding topic or objective.
3. Students can move cards and stickups around to develop or change sequence of material.

Note: From *Reaching the Hard to Teach* by J. W. Wood, 2008, Richmond, VA: Judy Wood, Inc. Reprinted with permission.

Figure 7.17 Proofreading checklist.

Form

1. I have a title page with centered title, subject, class, name, and date.
2. I have a thesis statement telling the main idea of my paper.
3. I have an outline that structures the major topics and minor subheadings.
4. I have footnoted direct quotations and paraphrased material.
5. I have made a footnote page using correct form.
6. I have made a bibliography, using correct form, of all reference materials.

Grammar

1. I have begun all sentences with capital letters.
2. I have put a period at the end of each sentence and a question mark at the end of each question.
3. I have used other punctuation marks correctly.
4. I have checked words for misspelling.
5. I have reread sentences for correct noun-verb agreement and awkward phrasing.
6. I have checked all sentences to be sure each is complete.

Content

1. I have followed my outline.
2. I have covered each topic from my outline thoroughly and in order.
3. Each paragraph has a topic sentence.
4. The paper has an introduction.

Note: From *Reaching the Hard to Teach* by J. W. Wood, 2008, Richmond, VA: Judy Wood, Inc. Reprinted with permission.

Figure 7.18 Essay checklist.

When you've finished writing, you should read your essay to make sure it's complete. Use the checklist below to edit your work.

Check one

Yes	**No**	
___	___	I began with a topic sentence.
___	___	I provided details to support the topic sentence.
___	___	I finished with a summary statement.
___	___	All my sentences are complete.
___	___	My handwriting is legible.
___	___	My spelling is correct.

If you checked yes for all of the statements, you've mastered the steps in writing a good essay response!

Note: From *Reaching the Hard to Teach* by J. W. Wood, 2008, Richmond, VA: Judy Wood, Inc. Reprinted with permission.

Activity (S): Organizing research material

Adaptation: Use a graphic organizer:

1. List the topic to be researched on the first line.
2. After reading or taking notes on the topic, divide information into major headings.
3. On index cards, list all words that represent the major headings.
4. Organize words into major areas.
5. Place words under appropriate subheading.
6. Place the words into the organizer format.

Figure 7.19 illustrates a graphic organizer.

Activity (E/S): Vocabulary

Adaptations: Figure 7.20 presents 17 ways for modifying the teaching of vocabulary. (Thanks to the following educators for their contributions: Alyce Goolsby Kennard, Midway [TX] Independent School District, Saharli Cartwright, Andie Brown, Rodney Conrad, John W. Wilkie, Jr.,

Figure 7.19 Graphic organizer.

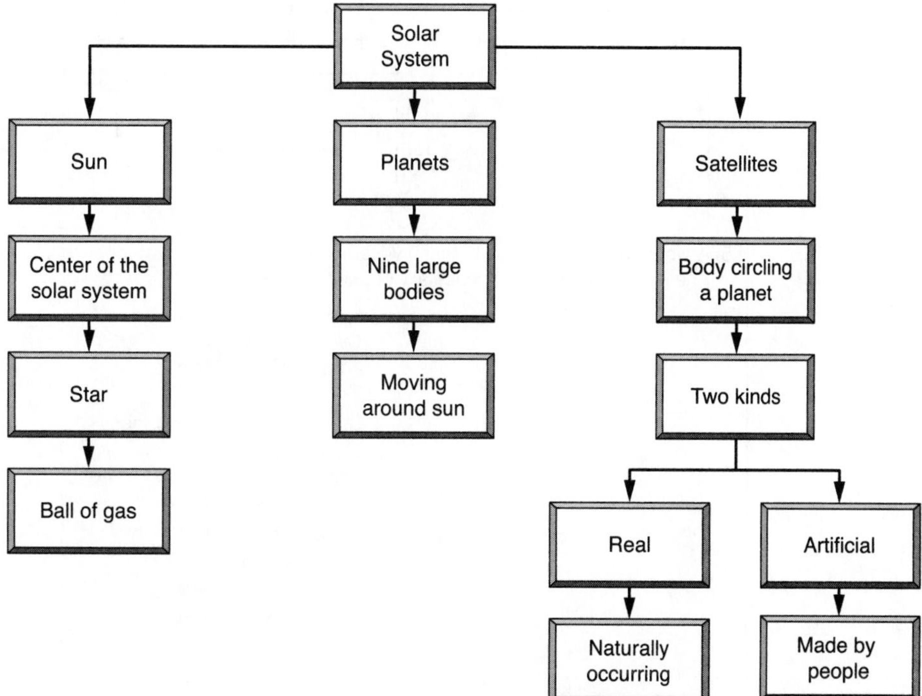

Note: From *Reaching the Hard to Teach* by J. W. Wood, 2008, Richmond, VA: Judy Wood, Inc. Reprinted with permission.

Figure 7.20 Teaching vocabulary.

1. Enlarge the diagram of a plant, or perhaps an animal cell. Place the correct vocabulary word on a sentence strip backed with tacky paper. Let the student place the correct word on the correct diagram part.
2. The same technique may be used in social studies. The correct CONTENT may be stuck on the correct place on the map: OCEAN, STATES, and so on.
3. Have students place a vocabulary word on one side of the page and the definitions on the other. The paper may be copied by the teacher and placed in the student's notebook or in a class notebook. The original paper can be cut into flash cards. For example:

Vocabulary Word	Definition
Vocabulary Word	Definition
Vocabulary Word	Definition
Vocabulary Word	Definition

4. Have students draw a picture to go with the vocabulary word as a clue. For example:

Key	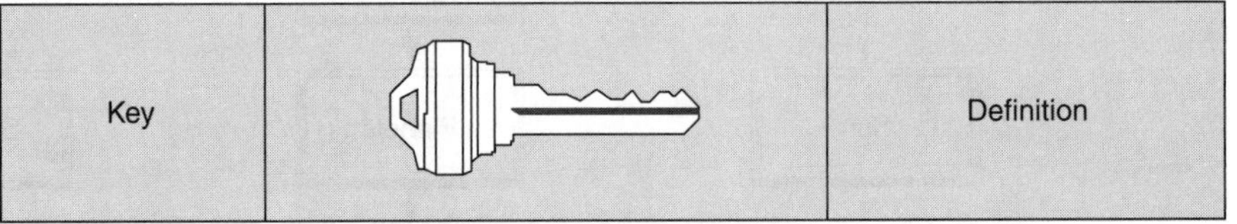	Definition

5. A wonderful and fun way to teach vocabulary and to keep all of those words and definitions in one place is to make a vocabulary booklet. For example:

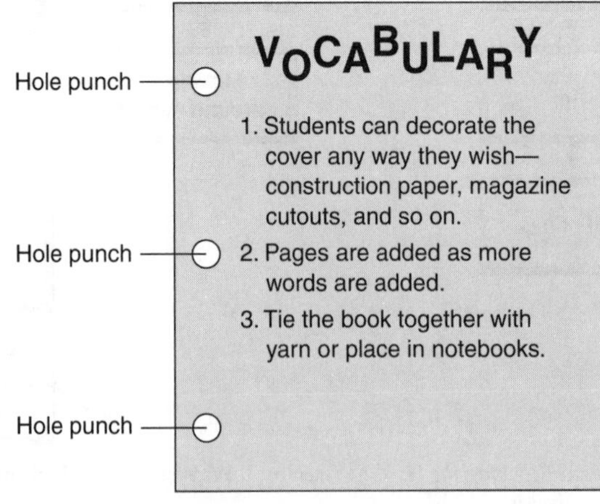

VOCABULARY
Hole punch
Hole punch
Hole punch
1. Students can decorate the cover any way they wish—construction paper, magazine cutouts, and so on.
2. Pages are added as more words are added.
3. Tie the book together with yarn or place in notebooks.

Now let's look inside.

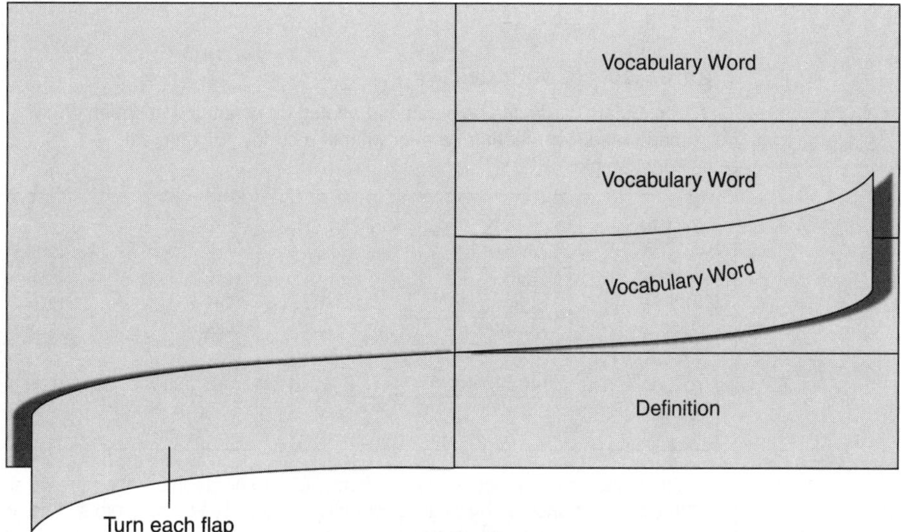

6. Use color coding to keep track of vocabulary cards. The different colors represent different subjects: blue for history, pink for reading, and so on. Because the white cards are less expensive, use highlighter pens to color code or use small stick-on dots. In the corner of the card, write the chapter, number, and/or period.

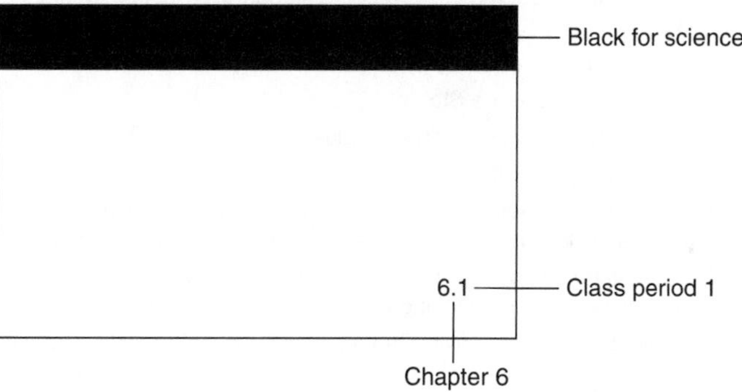

7. For storing vocabulary cards, use sports card holders. Punch holes and put into folders or notebooks. The cost is approximately \$3.99 for 25 sheets. The 3″ × 5″ cards will have to be cut to the size of baseball cards.
8. Vocabulary cards may also be stored in baggies. Place tape on the baggie to label each set of cards.
9. In preparing vocabulary cards, write the word on the blank side and the definition and a sentence using the word in context on the lined side.
10. Tape-record words, definitions, and sentences. Listen while getting ready for school, before going to bed, while waiting for the school bus, or when riding in the car.

Continued

Figure 7.20 (Continued)

11. Vocabulary cards can be typed and printed on construction paper, cut with a paper cutter, and made ready for students, with or without a buddy, to complete.
    For example:

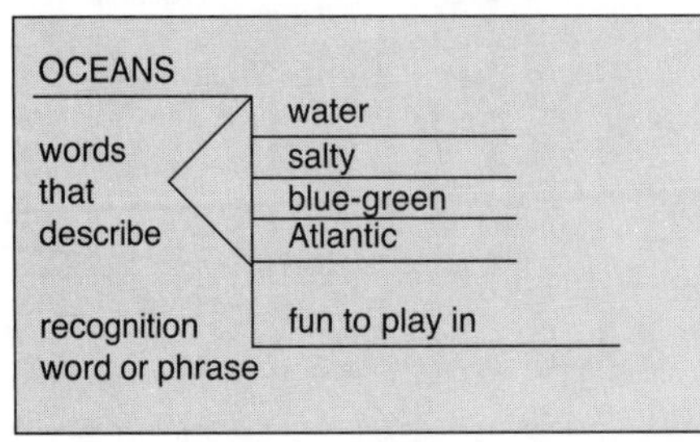

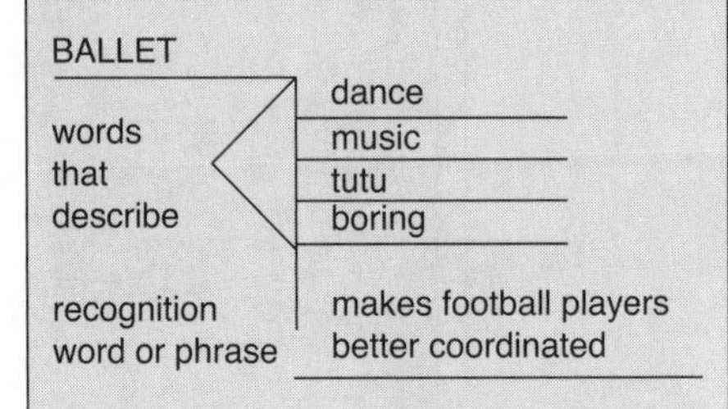

12. When flash cards (vocabulary or information) go home, have the parents sign a note saying that the child has answered all cards correctly and give five bonus points to be added to the test score. Students with no parent in the home, or one who is having difficulty, may ask someone else to sign his note. The student still gets the five points and you have a measure of the student's ability level.
13. For flash cards, put the word on one card and the definition on a separate card (not on the back of the word card). This makes it easy to match the word to the definition. Also, put little numbers on the back of each card so that the student will get immediate feedback of response.
14. Make sure that you teach all vocabulary that is interchangeable and explain why it is interchangeable or use only one set of vocabulary and test it. For example:

    War between the States:

    North = Union = Yankees = Blue

    South = Rebels = Confederate = Gray
15. Watch the vocabulary tests that come with teacher guides. Frequently, the definitions we discuss in class look nothing like the definition in the test guide.
16. Some students do not know how to decode the words in the definition and thus do not understand the words even after looking up the definition. Go over the definition and decode all words.
17. Let students design Trivial Pursuit questions to share with each other and with their parents.

Note: From *Reaching the Hard to Teach* by J. W. Wood, 2008, Richmond, VA: Judy Wood, Inc. Reprinted with permission.

and Lisa Pharr.) Figures 7.21 through 7.23 suggest other ideas for vocabulary practice.

Activity (E/S) Understanding rules and laws

Adaptation: Students can role-play selected rules or law-breaking vignettes and then discuss what consequences are suitable for certain crimes. This is a good opportunity to discuss why certain rules and laws exist and look at their positive aspects.

Activity (E/S): Understanding different cultures

Adaptation: Students with disabilities often have trouble visualizing life in other countries. When studying different cultures, allow students to "live"

Figure 7.21 Vocabulary: Sentence and picture.

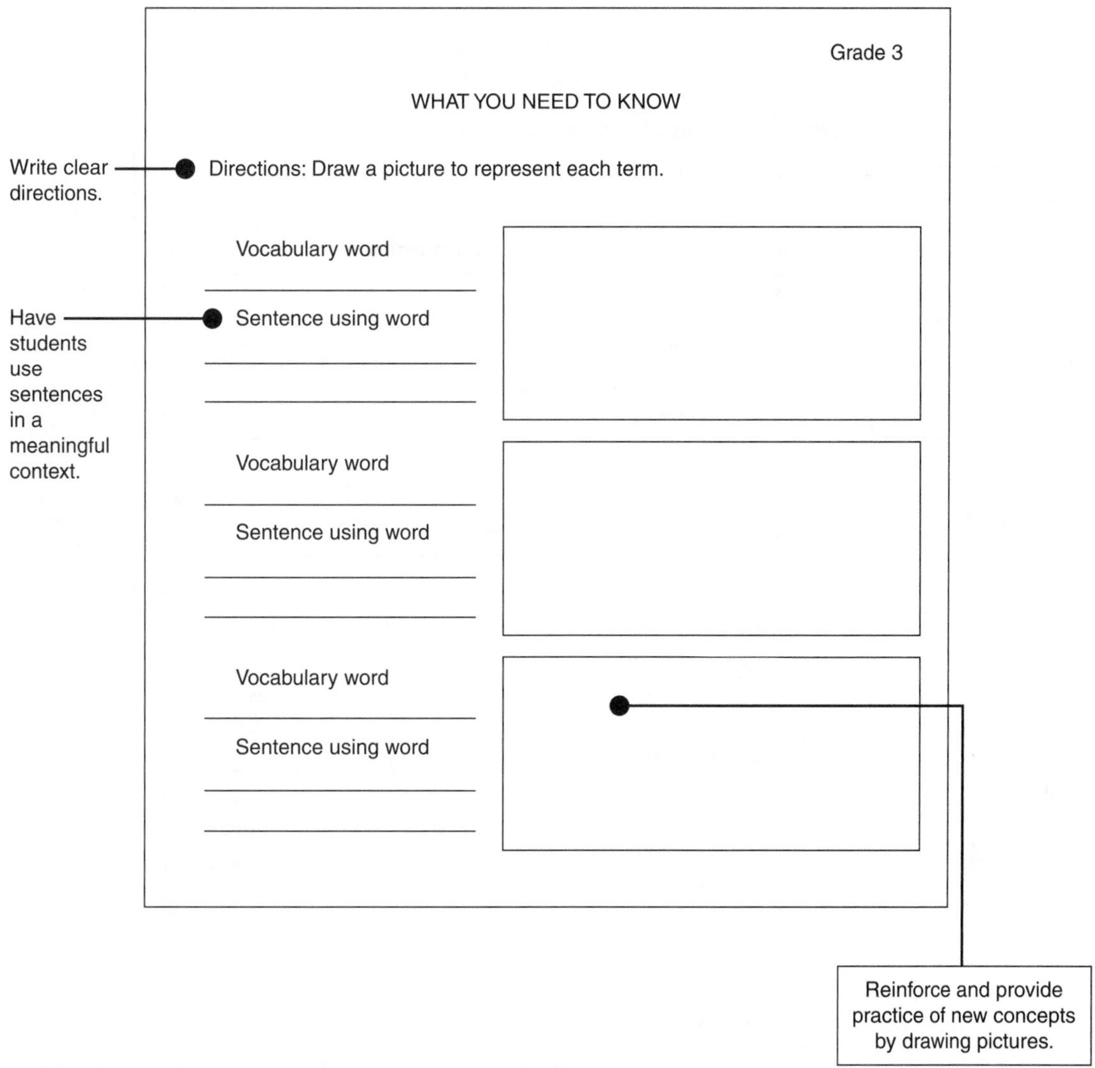

Note: From *Reaching the Hard to Teach* by J. W. Wood, 2008, Richmond, VA: Judy Wood, Inc. Reprinted with permission.

in that culture. Encourage them to dress, act, speak, eat, work, and play in the culture. Class periods could be devoted to experiences such as cooking and eating authentic meals, making costumes, or learning the languages. Discuss what is important to the culture and how it would feel to be a person from that setting.

Figure 7.22 Vocabulary: Word and meaning.

Write clear directions.

Provide category words to help students organize information and remember it.

Provide page clues to help students locate information.

Allow sufficient space for writing meaning.

WHAT YOU NEED TO KNOW
Social Studies

Chapter 11 "Jacksonian Democracy" (pp. 200–204)

Directions: Read the pages in your text and write the meaning of each word in the space provided.

Vocabulary	Page	Write the meaning of each word below
CONCEPTS		
Utopian Movement	200	
Reform	200	
PUBLICATIONS		
Liberator	201	
PEOPLE		
Mary Lyon	202	
Horace Mann	202	
Dorothea Dix	204	
SYSTEMS		
Underground Railroad Spoils Systems	200	

Note: From *Reaching the Hard to Teach* by J. W. Wood, 2008, Richmond, VA: Judy Wood, Inc. Reprinted with permission.

Activity (E/S): Using maps

Adaptation: Begin with something familiar to the students. Make a map of the school and have students label specific points. Then have them map out their neighborhoods. Eventually progress to states, sections of a country, and finally whole countries.

Activity (E/S): Reviewing maps

Adaptation: Make an overhead transparency of a blank map. Project the map onto the chalkboard and have students write in specific information being reviewed, such as states, capitals, and rivers. Students can erase and repeat until they've learned the material.

Figure 7.23 Vocabulary: Word and picture.

WHAT YOU NEED TO KNOW
Math

Geometry Terms

Directions: Draw a picture to represent each term. Number 1 is done for you

Term	Picture
1. Angle	∠
2. Midpoint	
3. Point	
4. Parallel lines	
5. Plane	
6. Ray	
7. Congruent segments	
8. Line segment	
9. Line	
10. Intersecting lines	

Write clear directions.

Have students draw pictures as a way to illustrate the concept in a semi-concrete way.

Give an example that will serve as a model for students.

Allow sufficient space for drawing picture.

Note: From *Reaching the Hard to Teach* by J. W. Wood, 2008, Richmond, VA: Judy Wood, Inc. Reprinted with permission.

Activity (E/S): Understanding graphs and charts

Adaptation: Use high-interest information such as favorite TV shows, foods, and sports. Figure 7.24 gives an example.

Activity (S): Understanding a sequence of events on a time line

Adaptation: First, have students list important events in their lives and the approximate date when each occurred. Provide a time line and have students transfer the information onto it. Figure 7.25 gives an example.

Activity (E): Studying products made in different sections of the United States

Adaptation: On the bulletin board, draw an outline of the United States. Develop a series of transparencies with shading for different areas of the

Figure 7.24 Favorite foods.

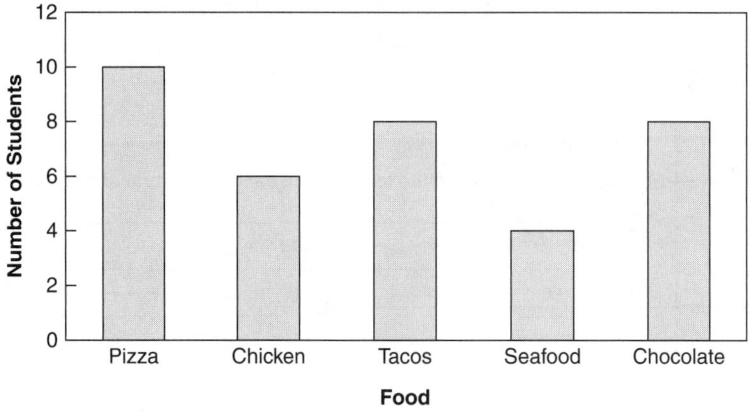

Number of Students

12
10
8
6
4
2
0

Pizza Chicken Tacos Seafood Chocolate

Food

Note: From *Reaching the Hard to Teach* by J. W. Wood, 2008, Richmond, VA: Judy Wood, Inc. Reprinted with permission.

Figure 7.25 Time line.

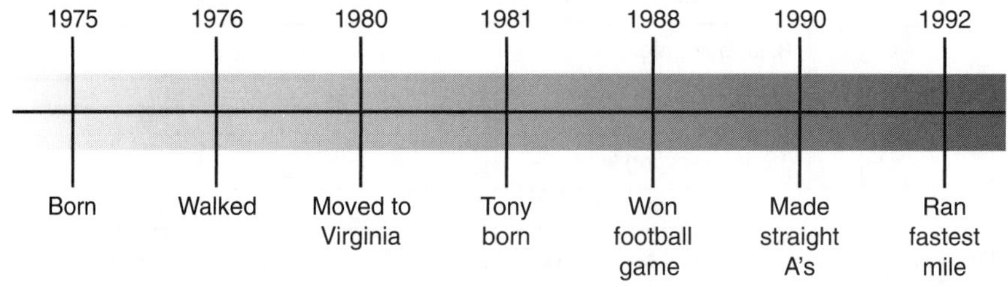

Note: From *Reaching the Hard to Teach* by J. W. Wood, 2008, Richmond, VA: Judy Wood, Inc. Reprinted with permission.

country. Pose a question such as, "What are the major corn-producing states?" A student will select the correctly shaded transparency to project onto the U.S. outline on the bulletin board.

Activity (E/S): Solving word problems using structured organizers

Adaptation: Figure 7.26 offers a suggestion. (Thanks to Diane Damback for her contributions.)

Activity (E/S): Solving word problems

Adaptation: Use Figure 7.27.

Activity (E/S): Steps in problem solving

Adaptation: See Figure 7.28. (Special thanks to Helen Giestie.)

Figure 7.26 Solving word problems using structured organizers.

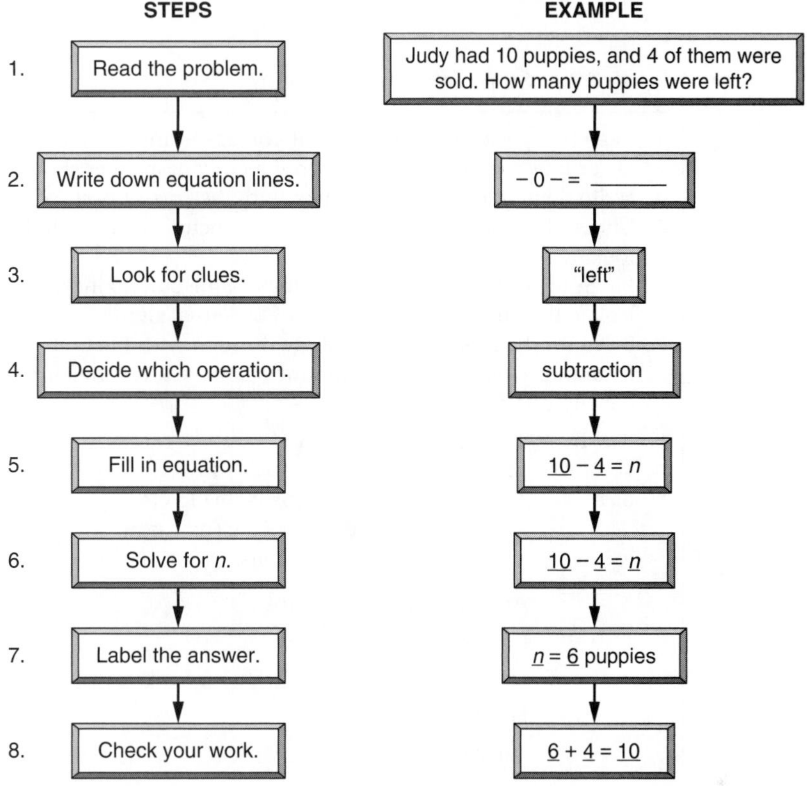
STEPS
EXAMPLE
1. Read the problem.
Judy had 10 puppies, and 4 of them were sold. How many puppies were left?
2. Write down equation lines.
– 0 – = ______
3. Look for clues.
"left"
4. Decide which operation.
subtraction
5. Fill in equation.
10 – 4 = n
6. Solve for n.
10 – 4 = n
7. Label the answer.
n = 6 puppies
8. Check your work.
6 + 4 = 10

Note: From *Reaching the Hard to Teach* by J. W. Wood, 2008, Richmond, VA: Judy Wood, Inc. Reprinted with permission.

Figure 7.27 Solving word problems.

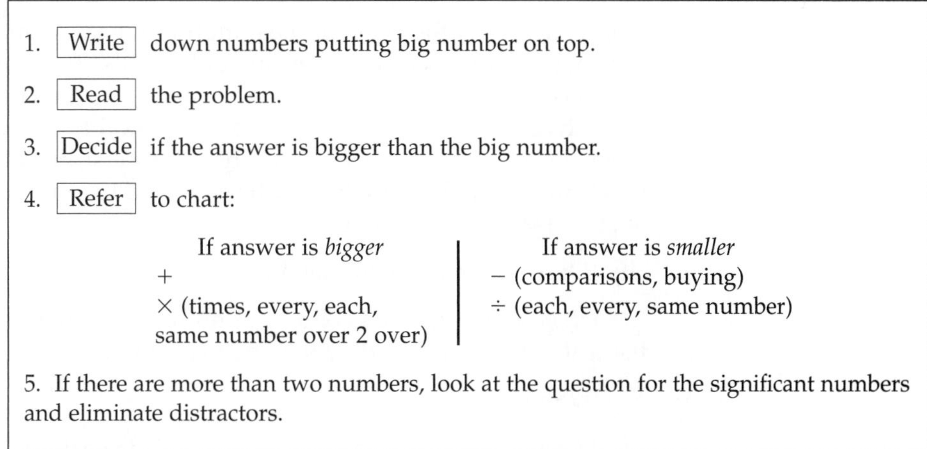

1. Write down numbers putting big number on top.
2. Read the problem.
3. Decide if the answer is bigger than the big number.
4. Refer to chart:

If answer is *bigger*	If answer is *smaller*
+	– (comparisons, buying)
× (times, every, each, same number over 2 over)	÷ (each, every, same number)

5. If there are more than two numbers, look at the question for the significant numbers and eliminate distractors.

Note: From *Reaching the Hard to Teach* by J. W. Wood, 2008, Richmond, VA: Judy Wood, Inc. Reprinted with permission.

Figure 7.28 Steps in problem solving.

1. Read the question and *circle* what you are trying to find.
2. Determine the unit of measure in which your answer should be expressed.
3. Write down the values you know with the correct units of measure.
4. Choose the correct formula, one which includes what you know and what you are looking for with no other gaps.
5. Fill in the formulas with your values, being sure to include the correct units.
6. Isolate the unknown on one side of the equal sign.
7. Solve for the unknown and follow through with the units.
   Example: What mass of aluminum will have a volume of 15 cm^3? Aluminum has a density of 2.7 g/cm^3.

   density = 2.7 g/cm^3 $D = m/v$
   volume = 15 cm^3
   mass = ? $2.7\ g/cm^3 = m/15\ cm^3$
   $(15\ cm^3)(2.7\ g/m^3) = m$
   $40.5g = mass$

Answer Sheet for Prompt

Looking for ______________________

Know ______________________

Formula Calculation ______________________

Answer ______________________

Note: From *Reaching the Hard to Teach* by J. W. Wood, 2008, Richmond, VA: Judy Wood, Inc. Reprinted with permission.

Activity (E): Money

Adaptation: Make the concept meaningful by using paper money. Begin by using several pretend paper one-dollar bills. To show that two half-dollars constitute one dollar, cut one paper dollar in half. Then place the two halves on the whole paper dollar and ask the student to put the cut paper dollar together. This activity functions just like putting parts of a puzzle together. The activity may be extended to other fractions of a dollar such as fourths or tenths.

Activity (E): Addition and subtraction

Adaptation: Block off each column of numbers so that students don't get distracted visually. Figure 7.29 gives an example.

Activity (E/S): Division

Adaptation: Use a model to teach division. Fade parts of the model as students begin to understand where each number belongs. Figure 7.30 gives an example.

Figure 7.29 Blocking columns of numbers.

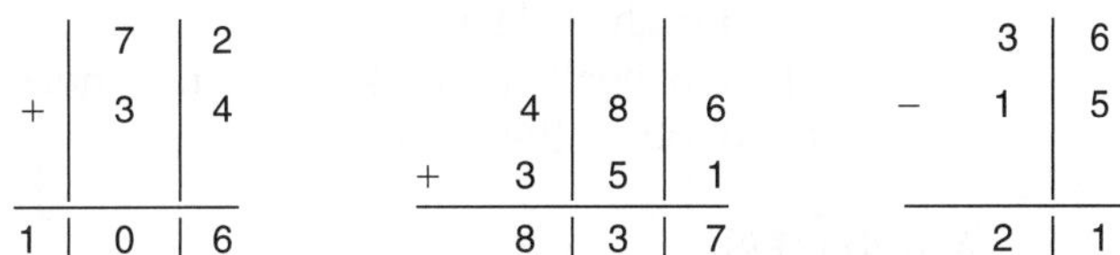

Note: From *Reaching the Hard to Teach* by J. W. Wood, 2008, Richmond, VA: Judy Wood, Inc. Reprinted with permission.

Figure 7.30 Division model.

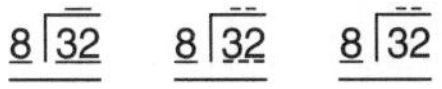

8 | 32   8 | 32   8 | 32

Note: From *Reaching the Hard to Teach* by J. W. Wood, 2008, Richmond, VA: Judy Wood, Inc. Reprinted with permission.

Activity (E/S): How to study for a math exam

Adaptation: Give students the following advice (thanks to Lee Cairel):

1. Start early. Don't be afraid to ask review questions in class. Probably six more students have the same question.
2. Find out when your teacher is available for extra help out of class. Then go see him or her.
3. Scan the last chapter exam to review skills already learned.
4. Know exactly *what* the exam will cover and *when* it will be. (Chapter exam? definitions? solving problems? must show work? part credit given?)
5. Think about the name and objective of the chapter. (What is the chapter talking about?) Draw pictures in your mind and think about them. Draw pictures on paper, too.
6. Review each section and do a few problems in each homework assignment. (Do some odd-numbered problems; they usually have answers in the back of the book.) Also, ask your teacher about problems that you forgot how to do or didn't get the right answers for.
7. Study important properties and vocabulary words and know how to use them.
8. Review any notes you have taken; go over any examples and quizzes from the chapter.
9. Look over the chapter review at the end of the chapter; go back again to sections that are fuzzy. Ask questions.
10. Take the chapter test at the end of the chapter as if it were an exam. For any problems that are difficult, ask your teacher.

11. Finally, look over the chapter test again the night before, and get a good night's sleep.
12. Have a healthy breakfast in the morning and come ready to do a good job on the exam.

Activity (E/S): Division

Adaptation: Develop a "check-off" chart for helping students divide (see Figure 7.31).

Activity (E/S): Sequential graphics

Adaptation: Use color coding (see Figure 7.32).

Activity (E/S): Division

Adaptation: Use steps of assisting with division (see Figure 7.33).

Figure 7.31 Graphics.

```
   25
3 |75      ÷ divide
  -6↓      × multiply
   15      − subtract
  -15      ↓ bring down
   00
```

Note: From *Reaching the Hard to Teach* by J. W. Wood, 2008, Richmond, VA: Judy Wood, Inc. Reprinted with permission.

Figure 7.32 Color coding.

When using sequential graphics, add color.
For example, *green* for the beginning step, *yellow* for the middle, and *red* for the end.

Example: Solving algebra equations

```
| 2 + x = 8 |  ← green

| 2 + x = 8 |
| − 2    −2 |  ← yellow
|  0  x   6 |
      1

|   x = 6   |  ← red
```

Note: From *Reaching the Hard to Teach* by J. W. Wood, 2008, Richmond, VA: Judy Wood, Inc. Reprinted with permission.

Figure 7.33 Steps for division.

Dividing

Steps:

1. Divide the dividend by the divisor in the greatest place value position possible.
2. Multiply.
3. Subtract.
4. Bring down the next digit or digits.

Repeat steps 1 to 4 until the remainder is less than the divisor.
To check, multiply the quotient and the divisor, add the remainder to get the dividend.

Examples

```
               58  ← quotient                 158R3
divisor → 6)348  ← dividend                5)793
            -30↓                              5↓|
             48                               29|
            -48                               25↓
              0  ← remainder                   43
                                               40
                                                3  ← remainder
```

Think About It!

Answer the question and solve the equation.

(a) How many fives in 10? → $10 \div 5 = a$
(b) How many fours in 16? → $16 \div 4 = b$
(c) 30 students in the class
6 students on a team.

How many teams are there?
$30 \div 6 = N$

Complete this table

Since	We know that
$6 \times 5 = 30$	$30 \div 5 = \underline{6}$
$7 \times 6 = 42$	$42 \div 6 = \underline{7}$
$24 \times 17 = 408$	$408 \div 17 = \underline{24}$
$52 \times 36 = 1872$	$1872 \div 36 = \underline{52}$

Mental Math

Try to move across each row without using pencil and paper.
If you do your work correctly, you will end with the starting number.

1.	24	÷4	6	×2	12	÷3	4	×5	20	+8	28	÷7	4	×6	24
2.	40	÷5	8	+7	15	+5	20	÷4	5	×7	35	+7	42	−2	40

Note: From *Reaching the Hard to Teach* by J. W. Wood, 2008, Richmond, VA: Judy Wood, Inc. Reprinted with permission.

Activity (E/S): Math prompts for math vocabulary

Adaptation:

Multiplication	Division
Cue words:	Cue words:
multiply	divide
product	quotient
times	divided by
twice (32)	halved (divide by 2)
doubled (32)	quartered (divided by 4)
tripled (33)	equal parts
quadrupled (34)	

Activity (E/S): Choosing the correct operation

Adaptation: Use the four-step method:

Step 1 Understand the problem.
Step 2 Make a plan.
Step 3 Carry out the plan.
Step 4 Check the answer for reasonableness.

Activity (S): Lab assignments

Adaptation: Many schools ask students to complete part of a lab assignment sheet before the teacher's demonstration and to finish the sheet after the demonstration. Table 7.1 shows how to adapt a lab assignment for the inclusive student.

Teachers also need to prepare the physical environment for a lab. They should (a) plan ahead to accommodate students with disabilities and (b) interview students concerning their needs, keeping communication open. Student needs may involve the following:

1. Adjustment of table height so that students using a wheelchair can pull up to the table
2. Accessible sinks for cleanup
3. Microscope stands at eye level and within arm's reach
4. Display models or chemistry sets at seat level
5. Adequate space around tables and entrances to allow access by wheelchairs, walkers, and so on
6. Flexible arrangement of lab space to allow changes when needed
7. Transition time to and from various activities to accommodate students who may take longer to move from one area to another

Table 7.1 Adapting a lab assignment.

LAB ASSIGNMENT OUTLINE	STANDARD STUDENT RESPONSE	ADAPTATIONS FOR INCLUSIVE STUDENT
Title of lab	Student completes.	Fill in for student.
Materials	Student completes from observing teacher or reading text.	Complete for student or let peer tutor assist.
Purpose of lab	Student completes from text or lecture.	Complete for student.
Lab procedures	As teacher demonstrates, student records the procedure.	List procedures on the board so student can follow each step. Provide a check sheet and have student check off each step.
Observations	Student records the observed experiment.	Let student tape-record the observed demonstration.
Conclusion	Student records.	This step requires the evaluation level of Bloom's taxonomy, so the teacher may choose to omit it for an included student.
Analysis/questions	Student responds.	Provide answers for the mainstreamed student.

Note: From *Reaching the Hard to Teach* by J. W. Wood, 2008, Richmond, VA: Judy Wood, Inc. Reprinted with permission.

When preparing students for a lab, teachers should do the following:

1. Prepare materials being used in advance. (For example, open jars if screw tops are difficult for students with physical impairments.) Waiting for activities to begin can be frustrating for students with ADHD.
2. Encourage students to speak to you about directions that may be unclear to them, or state instructions several times throughout lab activities.
3. Keep lab activities structured and limit directions.

4. Be open to the use of tape recorders or other forms of backup support.
5. Summarize and review information covered at the end of each session.
6. Consider alternative test-taking and grading procedures.
7. Keep overhead transparencies or written materials simple and free of clutter.

Here are some lab tips for students:

1. Speak with your lab instructor concerning your individual needs and concerns.
2. Allow yourself extra time to get prepared and comfortable before the lab begins.
3. If you are using a tape recorder or any other device, discuss it with the instructor in advance.
4. Cue yourself using key terms or phrases if you have difficulty maintaining focus.
5. If information is unclear to you, speak with your instructor or ask questions.
6. Review your lab notes immediately after class to help retain information.
7. Limit distractions to help you focus on tasks and schedules in the lab.
8. If you have difficulty following the sequence of steps in a procedure, ask for a printed copy of the procedure prior to class so that you can familiarize yourself with the steps. As you complete each step, mark it off.
9. Supplement your notes with diagrams to illustrate concepts, procedures, and so on. Develop and use a shorthand method for noting technical terms that appear often in your notes.
10. If you are aware of physical accommodations or technological adaptations that will enable you to use the lab more fully (e.g., a straight chair fastened to a platform on casters or foot-operated rather than hand-operated equipment), discuss these with your instructor.

Activity (S): Teaching students with disabilities to drive

Adaptation: Here are some tips:

1. Our attitude toward persons with disabilities is their biggest handicap.
2. Sincerity is sensed easily by a person with a disability.
3. Find something to praise, no matter how small the accomplishment, especially during the early lessons. This builds rapport and relaxes the student.
4. Be honest. For example, if the student needs to stay off the expressway and out of rush-hour traffic, tell him or her to plan driving times during the least busy times of the day.
5. Students do not want sympathy; they want independence. Be objective and positive and expect their best performance.

6. Follow up on students to ensure that the correct vehicle modifications are made.
7. During the final phases of driving, encourage parents and other members of the family to observe the student's driving. Explain the purpose and importance of each piece of equipment.
8. It is very easy for us to help the student in his or her efforts to drive (for example, learning to use the key quad to turn the ignition), but the real reward is seeing the student successfully and independently achieve this goal. Don't rush to help. Be patient and look at the expression on the student's face when he or she finally succeeds. The time is worth it.
9. When you must tell a student you are unable to help him or her at a particular time, never say *never.* Tell the student, "I am placing your evaluation on file at the present time and will contact you as soon as I am able to help you." Research and modern technology are constantly changing. At the same time, if you truly sense that the person will never drive, don't give false hope. Be honest and explain in detail. At this time, the person's emotions will surface, so be gentle.
10. Ninety percent of driving depends on vision. If you detect a visual problem during the evaluation, require that a medical evaluation be sent to you to ensure that this can be corrected.

ADAPTING ASSIGNMENTS

This section is divided into three parts: tips for assignment books, assignment assumptions, and types of assignments.

Tips for Assignment Books

Before any assignment is given, students need to establish an organization process for keeping assignments. Figure 7.34 suggests tips for assignment books.

Assignment Assumptions

Educators make many assumptions about assignments. While I was visiting a sixth-grade social studies class, the teacher gave the assignment for the next day as the class was coming to a close: "Bring in one article that reflects what we studied in class today."

The bell rang and all the students, except for one young man, hurried out of class to the next one. The young man walked up to the teacher and said, "We don't have a newspaper for an article in my home."

The teacher quickly replied, "Oh, just use a magazine article. Any article will do. Now hurry, or you will be late for your next class."

As I watched the young man walk down the hall, I imagined a zero for class tomorrow. I wanted to say to the teacher, "Don't you have ears?" That student was

Figure 7.34 Tips for assignment books.

Selecting/organizing assignment books

1. Many school supply sections in stores sell assignment books. When selecting a book:
   - Be sure the size is appropriate for the student's notebook or book bag.
   - Check the assignment book to see if the sections are appropriate for the student.
2. Many schools have assignment books preprinted for students. Here are some suggestions and a list of advantages:
   - All students will have the same assignment book.
   - Because everyone will be using an assignment book, no student will feel awkward.
   - Let the students design the cover for the assignment book. Conduct an election to vote on the class choice. This introduces ownership in the assignment book.
   - The book could include a space for the yearly schedule.
   - Include a letter from the principal, student body president, or another "famous" person.
   - Each year the letter could come from a "mystery writer" to be held in strict confidence until the books are handed out.
   - A guessing contest with prizes could be used to see who this year's mystery writer will be.
   - The book could contain general information, school rules, services, activities, and a monthly calendar listing all important events.
   - The last section could provide weekly divided sections for assignments, due dates, class periods, and a special reminder section.
   - One benefit of a school-provided assignment book is that no one does without because of cost.
3. Use a teacher's plan book as an assignment notebook. Set it up for a student's individual schedule.

Note: From *Reaching the Hard to Teach* by J. W. Wood, 2008, Richmond, VA: Judy Wood, Inc. Reprinted with permission.

trying to tell his teacher that he was willing to complete the assignment but had no materials at home. The teacher's assumption? Students have at home what they need to complete assignments.

We simply cannot make assumptions about students. Figure 7.35 lists other assignment assumptions.

Types of Assignments

Assignments, the learning tasks that reinforce concepts taught during class instruction, are crucial to skill acquisition. However, for various reasons, some students may not be able to complete an assignment.

Figure 7.35 Assignment assumptions.

1. We assume that students can copy the assignment from the board correctly.
2. We assume that students can complete the assignment.
3. We assume that the assignment is not too difficult.
4. We assume that the assignment is not too long.
5. We assume that students understand the assignment because they do not raise their hand when we say, "Are there any questions?"
6. We assume that students have materials needed to complete the assignment.
7. We assume that students have the money necessary to buy the materials to complete the assignment.
8. We assume that the students' parents will help them with the assignment.
9. We assume that the students' parents can do the assignment.
10. We assume that the students have parents.
11. We assume that the parents are home.
12. We assume that the parents care.
13. We assume that students have a home.
14. We assume that students have time to complete the assignment.
15. We assume that the students care if they complete the assignment.
16. We assume that the students or parents have the language skills necessary to complete the assignment.
17. We assume that the students have proper places to complete the assignment.
18. We assume that we are the only teachers giving homework.

Note: From *Reaching the Hard to Teach* by J. W. Wood, 2008, Richmond, VA: Judy Wood, Inc. Reprinted with permission.

There are two types of assignments: control and no control. Control assignments include in-class assignments and other assignments over which the teacher has complete control. These include class discussions; problem solving; group experiments; group projects; and independent seatwork assignments such as reading from the text, answering questions, and completing work sheets. When students are working on these assignments, the teacher has the power to make any necessary adjustments for a student. The teacher can answer questions or observe a student's work. If an assignment is too difficult, lengthy, or confusing, the teacher can immediately remedy the situation.

When students take assignments home, the teacher begins to lose control. No-control assignments are those that are no longer under the supervision of the teacher.

Homework falls into this category. The teacher has now lost all control or power to provide direct assistance during students' work on the assignment.

Homework is assigned for a number of reasons (Turner, 1984):

1. Homework facilitates learning through practice and application.
2. Homework individualizes learning for all students.
3. Homework is assigned for work not completed during the school day.

4. Homework teaches independent study skills and helps develop good work habits.
5. Homework communicates to parents which concepts and skills are taught in class.

Figure 7.36 suggests tips for adapting assignments. (Thanks to Julie Duff for her contributions.)

Figure 7.36 Tips for adapting assignments.

1. Be sure that student has the correct information on the assignment (page numbers, date due, and so on).
2. Review the assignment and check for questions.
3. The assignment should be geared to the level of each student.
4. Structure each assignment so that all students can experience success.
5. Provide immediate feedback on all assignments.
6. If the assignment requires students to look up answers to questions, use an asterisk to distinguish implied fact from literal questions requiring a stated fact.
7. If the assignment is lengthy, provide class time to complete it partially or divide assignment time into two or more days.
8. Identify an assignment buddy for each student. The buddy may be another student within the class, a student in another class, or a friend or parent outside of class. This provides a support system for the student who may not know how to complete the assignment.
9. Assignments may be given to two or more students. It is suggested that class time be given for shared assignments and that split grading be used.
10. Teach students the concept of grade averaging with and without zeros. Many students do not realize the difficulty of trying to raise an average after just one zero on an assignment.
11. Allow students the option of dropping one or more low assignment grades per grading period.
12. Establish assignment passes earned for good work, which can be cashed in when an assignment is forgotten or a low grade is received.
13. Be consistent in placing the assignment for class or homework in the same place each day.
14. Provide written and oral directions for assignments.
15. If an assignment requires several steps or stages (such as projects), provide a checklist for the students.
16. If the assignment is to be copied from the board, provide a copy for the student who may have difficulty copying.
17. If the assignment is to be copied from the text, allow the student who has difficulty copying or who copies slowly to copy only the answers.
18. Work sheets should be clear and uncluttered. Watch for the overuse of work sheets. Don't make the reward for completing one work sheet another work sheet. Also, giving a stack of work sheets can be overwhelming.

19. Tell students to put books they need to take home in the locker with the spine to the back of the locker and on the right side of the locker. At the end of the day, the student reaches into the locker and retrieves all spine-back books to take home.
20. Require a method of recording assignments.
21. Make copies of the assignments for a week and give the student and the resource teacher a copy.
22. After the class assignment is completed, tell the student where to put the assignment and what to do next.
23. Do not punish the student by making him or her finish assignments during free time, recess, or after school.
24. For in-class assignments, give a warning when it is almost time to turn in the assignment.
25. Orient students to the major points of the assignment.
26. Begin all assignments with a planned opening and a purpose.
27. Practice for assignments should be distributed instead of given in a mass.
28. Relate all activities within an assignment directly to the objective of the assignment.
29. Assess the assignment for the appropriate instruction level.
30. Use feedback from previously completed assignments to indicate the quality of the next assignment.
31. To assist students with organizing assignments, have every content area on a different color of paper. Each assignment will get placed in the appropritе section.
32. At the end of each class let students have 15 minutes to start on their homework. Circulate around the class to see who needs help. Just before the bell rings, ask each student to circle the last problem they completed. Assign everyone to do five more problems for homework. This allows for differences in the number of problems students can complete in a given period of time. Everyone doesn't have to do 1 through 30, but everyone gets independent practice.
33. Do you have trouble with students not being responsible for homework? Try giving them a clipboard with the assignment sheet and all homework sheets attached. It must be returned the next day and signed by a parent.
34. To make sure that students clearly understand assignment in class or out of class, have each student turn to a buddy and repeat what he or she thinks the assignment is and how to respond.
35. Allow students to do auditory homework.
36. Let students turn in homework early, then grade homework early, and return to student for correction before final grading.
37. Have one night during the school week for "no homework" night (K–12). This gives families a break or provides a catch-up time for students.
38. Have all major tests, projects, spelling tests, book reports, and so on due on Wednesday. This gives the weekend for catch-up.
39. Start spelling units on Wednesday and test on the unit the following Wednesday. This really helps the child and parent. Weekends can be used for studying.

Continued

Figure 7.36 (Continued)

40. Each Monday provide an assignment grid with all assignments/tests indicated. Place on bulletin board. This helps organize study time. For example:

	Monday	Tuesday	Wednesday	Thursday	Friday
Social studies					
Science					
Reading					
Spelling					
Math					

41. Assign projects to be completed at school. Teacher may provide display boards, materials, help, and so on. Children have equal opportunity regarding socioemotional level. This also avoids parent project participation stress.

Table 7.2 Types of homework and suggested adaptations.

Type of Homework	Example	Suggested Adaptations
Preparation: homework assigned to assist students' preparation for the next day's lesson/class	• Reading a chapter • Reviewing a film	1. Provide recorded materials for materials to be read. 2. Review in class before the lesson to assist students who cannot prepare ahead of time. 3. Allow students to prepare with a buddy. 4. Provide a summary of material to be read. 5. Provide a checklist for steps on procedures to be reviewed.
Practice: homework assigned to reinforce the skills taught during the day's lesson	• Working on math problems • Answering questions about class lecture	1. Be sure that the student understands the assignment. 2. Review assignment directions.

		3. Review the assignment. 4. Provide a model. 5. Provide guided practice before independent practice. 6. Check for student functional level and match assignment. 7. Provide alternative amounts of assignments to students who cannot complete the same quantity as others.
Extension: homework assigned to extend or transfer skills taught	• Book reports • Practicing computer skills	1. Provide models for required reports. 2. Provide a checklist of procedures. 3. Allow buddies to work together on a shared assignment. 4. Be sure that students have been taught for acquisition and retention before requiring transfer.
Creativity: homework that requires synthesis of skills and concepts previously taught.	• Term papers • Research assignments	1. Allow partners on projects. 2. Provide a clearly explained checklist with examples for all projects. 3. Do class projects that model each step of an independent project before assigning the latter. 4. Remember that students who have difficulty with structure need guidance with assigned projects, papers, and research projects. 5. Consider alternative assignments for students who may not be at this level.

For a no-control assignment, the teacher must be absolutely sure that the student has the skills necessary to be successful. Lee and Pruitt (1970) divided homework into four categories: preparation, practice, extension, and creativity. Table 7.2 shows each category and suggests adaptations for teachers to use with students experiencing difficulty with homework.

SUMMARY

This chapter has been developed to help you "uncover subject matter." We are assigned subjects, or content, to teach, and in conjunction with our teaching, we are constantly developing strategies for adapting the format. If a student cannot divide, for example, the teacher should find an organizational strategy to help the student understand the skill.

RESOURCES

Audio Book Contractors/Classic Books on Cassettes
P.O. Box 40115
Washington, DC 20016
(202) 363–3429

Books on Tape
Box 25122
Santa Ana, CA 92799–5122
(800) 626–3333

National Braille Association (NBA)
3 Townline Circle
Rochester, NY 14632
(716) 427–8260

National Braille Press
88 St. Stephens Street Boston, MA 02115
(617) 266–6160
(800) 548–7323

SUGGESTED READINGS

McKenna, M. C. (2002). *Help for struggling readers.* New York: Guilford.

Kuder, S. J., & Hasit, C. (2002). *Enhancing literacy for all students.* Upper Saddle River, NJ: Pearson Education.

Tucker, B. F., Singleton, A. H., & Weaver, T. L. (2002). *Teaching mathematics to all children: Designing and adapting instruction to meet the needs of diverse learners.* Upper Saddle River, NJ: Merrill/Prentice Hall.

WEBSITES

Discovery. A site listing information about television's Discovery Channel, The Learning Channel (TLC), The Science Channel, and much more. *www.discovery.com.*

Scholastic. A wide variety of resources and activities for kids, parents, teachers, administrators, and librarians. *www.scholastic.com.*

Wright Group. Resource products for pre-K to adult teachers and administrators. *www.wrightgroup.com.*

The National Council for Social Studies. A site with a lot of resources for social studies content. *www.socialstudies.org.*

National Science Teachers Association. Features teacher resources, professional information, and a science store. *www.nsta.org.*

PBS Kids. *www.pbskids.org.*

Puzzlemaker. Puzzlemaker is a puzzle generation tool that allows you to create and print word searches, math and crossword puzzles. *www.puzzlemaker.school.discovery.com.*

REFERENCES

Anderson, R. M., Greer, J. G., & Odle, S. J. (1978). *Individualizing educational materials for special children in the mainstream.* Baltimore: University Park Press.

Lee, J. F., Jr., & Pruitt, K. W. (1970). Homework assignments: Classroom games or teaching tools? *Clearing House, 1,* 31–35.

Turner, T. (1984). The joy of homework. *Tennessee Education, 14,* 25–33.

Wood, J. W. (2006). *Teaching students in inclusive settings: Adapting and accommodating instruction.* Upper Saddle River, NJ: Merrill/Prentice Hall.

Chapter **8**

ADAPTING ASSESSMENT, EVALUATION, AND GRADING

Key Terms

Alternative Assessment *(page 182)*
Classroom-Embedded Assessment *(page 183)*
High Stakes *(page 178)*
School Improvement *(page 178)*
Standards *(page 178)*
Statewide Assessment *(page 178)*

CHAPTER-AT-A-GLANCE

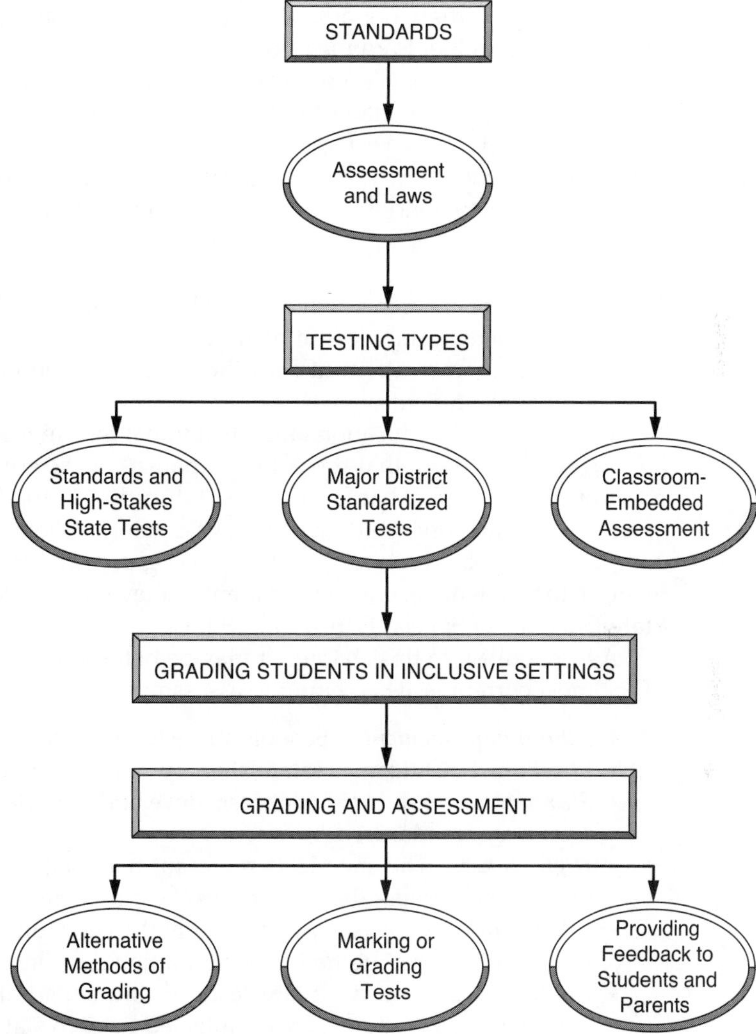

LEARNER OBJECTIVES

After you read this chapter, you will be able to

- *Discuss standard high-stakes testing.*
- *List three major testing types.*
- *List classroom-embedded assessment measures.*
- *Discuss grading issues and alternative grading measures.*

VIGNETTE

Sara has been failing all assessments in her fourth-grade class. Sara's parents are extremely worried because the teacher at the last parent conference expressed concern that Sara may not be promoted to the fifth grade. Even though Sara has not been identified as a student with special needs, her teacher asked that the building intervention team provide suggestions for assessing her. The team suggested that other methods of assessment be used for Sara to evaluate her progress accurately. This chapter provides that information.

Note: From Reaching the Hard to Teach *by J. W. Wood, 2008, Richmond, VA: Judy Wood, Inc. Reprinted with permission.*

For the past 35 years, general and special educators have been working together to modify curricula, adapt lesson plans, and alter classroom environments to meet the needs of students with mild disabilities. Today, attention has been given to the evaluation of all students.

The emphasis in education and educational reform is accountability. "It is not an exaggeration to say that the core component of the educational reform movement of the 1990s [was] accountability. Education in the United States has been criticized for allowing students to leave school without the skills necessary to compete in a global economy, and increasing pressure is being applied to every level of the system to improve student achievement" (National Association of State Directors of Special Education, 1997).

As we move into this chapter, it may be helpful to develop an understanding of the most current issues relating to assessment:

- ***School improvement.*** Schools strive to improve all aspects of their system.
- ***Standards.*** Outcomes established by states. All students must achieve.
- ***Statewide assessment.*** State tests developed to determine whether students meet state standards.
- ***High stakes.*** The state tests represent high stakes for educators, students, and parents because they affect pass/fail rates, graduation rates, and funding.
- *School superintendents.* Must have high scores on state tests for their districts. High scores are tied to accreditation, funding, and community pride.
- *Alternative assessment.* State tests for students with selected disabilities. Alternative assessments are established by each state.
- *School principals.* Are pressured to have their schools meet the standards to compete within their district.
- *Teachers.* High student scores on state tests reflect good teaching and sometimes determine job tenure.
- *Students.* Personal high scores on state tests are needed for grade advancement and high school graduation.
- *Parents.* Their children's high scores on state tests result in personal pride.
- *Community.* School districts with excellent student scores on state tests draw populations, have high real estate values, and have an overall sense of community pride.

STANDARDS

School improvement is tied to accreditation, and accreditation is tied directly to funding and community pride. We continually hear about standards. Regardless of whether you are in Virginia, with their "standards of learning," or in another state, there is a state assessment of children and their achievement. Every state is more focused on outcome-based results. In the past, generally, students with special needs were excluded from participation in these assessments, or if they were allowed modifications, their scores were not included in the total picture for that district. Today, all students are assessed, and students with disabilities must be included in statewide testing.

A common saying in the education field is, "What gets measured gets taught." Much of the focus of the national reform movement has been in the area of general education because there was no systematic collection of data on the achievement results of students with disabilities. Therefore, monies to improve education were intended for general education purposes. With the reauthorization of IDEA and the reforms of the No Child Left Behind (NCLB) Act, students with disabilities are to be included in this state assessment, with accommodations if appropriate. Alternative assessments are provided for students who cannot participate in the state assessment.

Standards are a hot topic today, and they are important. They have helped unify the curriculum used across a state. In the past the curriculum in one part of the state could be very different from that in another part of the state. We are becoming a very transient population. If we want to prepare students to be part of a global society, then curricula shouldn't be extremely different even from state to state. For this reason, we should view standards in a positive light.

A phrase used more consistently now in discussions on standards is that they apply to *all* students. This has been, and will continue to be, a major challenge for education. All students are part of the accountability system, and they all benefit from instructional changes and educational reforms that are implemented in response to information on assessment results.

The idea that all students should be included in the accountability process is based on three assumptions:

1. All students can learn.
2. Schools are responsible for measuring the process of learners.
3. The learning process of all students should be measured. (National Center on Education Outcomes [NCEO], 1997)

Assessment and Laws

Nationally, legal mandates are in place to ensure appropriate education and now assessment for students with disabilities as for all students served in American education systems. The two laws now on the surface of educational concern are the Individuals with Disabilities Education Act and the No Child Left Behind Act.

Individuals with Disabilities Education Act (IDEA, PL 105–117). Since the reauthorization of IDEA in 1997, federal funds continue to support the education of students with disabilities. Changes that address assessment include the fact that "IEPs must now document how the student's disability affects involvement and progress in the general curriculum; individual modifications needed for students to participate in state and district assessments; and, if the student is unable to participate in the general assessment, why and how learning will be assessed. Public reporting requirements are also included in the reauthorization of IDEA" (Thurlow, Elliott, & Ysseldyke, 2003, p. 261).

No Child Left Behind Act (NCLB, PL 107–110). On January 8, 2002, President Bush signed into law the No Child Left Behind Act, the latest reauthorization of the Elementary and Secondary Education Act. Stronger accountability for student results is a major emphasis of this law. Now states must do the following:

- Have strong academic standards for reading, math, and science.
- Administer tests in each grade from grades 3 through 8, and during high school.
- Produce annual state and district reports that show assessment for each designated student group.
- Monitor the extent to which students in each group are making adequate yearly progress toward proficiency.
- Assign real consequences to districts and schools that fail to make progress. (Thurlow et al., 2003, p. 261)

TESTING TYPES

Testing falls into three major types: standard high-stakes state tests, district tests, and classroom-embedded assessment. This section will address each test type, problems students have in each test type, and accommodations teachers may use.

Standards and High-Stakes State Tests

Each state can determine what it considers to be "high-stakes" tests or barrier tests. "High stakes accountability refers to decisions that are made on the basis of the results of the assessment" (Turnbull, Turnbull, Shank, & Smith, 2004, p. 49). These could include "whether the student is eligible to progress through the grades, attend a magnet school, or even graduate and, if graduated, the type of diploma awarded" (Turnbull et al., 2004, p. 49). Standardized high-stakes testing is designed to measure general education achievement and the achievement of standards of learning in content areas. The National Center on Education Outcomes (1997) made the following findings:

- In the states where high-stakes testing was required, more students were retained.
- Of those students retained, indirect evidence might suggest that more of the students drop out of school. (pp. 9–10)

Schools today are busy aligning standards to the curriculum, teaching students the curriculum, and hoping students will reach the standards and succeed on the state test. However, many problems prevent students from doing their best on state tests. Some of these issues are addressed by states during statewide testing; others are not.

Problems Students Encounter During Statewide Testing. Before putting pen to paper, many students encounter problems that can result in test failure. The teacher needs to understand the problems that can arise before students even enter a testing situation. Many states provide accommodations for some of these problems. Some accommodations are allowed for district assessment; however, teachers may provide any necessary accommodation for classroom-embedded assessments.

Thurlow and colleagues (2003) researched statewide accommodations allowed for students with disabilities and organized them into five categories: setting, schedule, timing, presentation, and response. Table 8.1 presents these five categories along with problems encountered by students in each.

Table 8.1 Problems encountered by students during statewide testing.

Accommodation Area	Definition	Student Problem
Setting	Changes in assessment place	Lack of focus Need for special equipment
Timing	Changes in duration or organization of time during testing	Need for extra time to use certain equipment Fatigue Processing difficulties
Scheduling	Changes in when testing occurs	Writing difficulties Need to coordinate assessment with the effects of medication Frustrates easily
Presentation	Changes in how an assessment is given	Need for assistive devices Modality needs Difficulty with directions Need for large print or Braille Clarification of directions Difficulty with reading level
Response	Changes in how a student responds to an assessment	Has physical or sensory disabilities Process difficulties

Note: Adapted from M. L. Thurlow, J. L. Elliott, and J. E. Ysseldyke, 2003, *Testing Students with Disabilities: Practical Strategies for Complying with District and State Requirements* (pp. 51–69).

Alternative Assessment. When students are unable to participate in the traditional district or state assessment, an **alternate assessment** measure is provided. Approximately 1% of the total student population, or 10% of the students with disabilities, may qualify for alternative assessments. Alternative assessments were required to be in place by July 1, 2000. Each state develops its own assessments, which are in continuous transition. "Students who participate in the alternative assessment should be those for whom regular assessment is not appropriate for two major reasons: (1) any and all accommodations that might be provided to students still do not enable them to participate, and (2) students are working on instructional goals that are not assessed by the assessment" (Thurlow et al., 2003, p. 78). Table 8.2 provides possible measurement approaches for an alternative assessment.

Major District Standardized Tests

Standardized state and national tests are a big issue everywhere in the country. By definition, "a standardized test consists of a set of items administered to all students, under the same conditions, scored in the same way, and with results interpreted in the same way" (Wilson, 2002, p. 28). Because every student is tested the same way, the test is said to be "standardized." These standardized conditions

Table 8.2 Possible measurement approaches for an alternate assessment.

OBSERVATION	INTERVIEWS AND CHECKLISTS
Marking occurrence of specific behaviors	Interviews: teachers, peers, parents, employers
Written narrative of what is observed	Rating scales or checklists: mobility and community skills, self-help skills, daily living skills, adaptive behavior, social skills
Notation of the frequency, duration, and intensity of behavior Videotape Audiotape	Peer and/or adult rating scales or checklists
TESTING	**RECORD REVIEW**
Performance events	School records
Portfolios	Student products
Curriculum-based measures	IEP objectives and progress

Note: Adapted from M. L. Thurlow, J. L. Elliott, and J. E. Ysseldyke, 2003, *Testing Students with Disabilities: Practical Strategies for Complying with District and State* Requirements (p. 79).

allow comparisons to be made among students and groups of students. Based on these tests, schools make major decisions regarding student placements in academic groups and yearly promotions or retentions. Teachers are under tremendous pressure for their classes to score high. Principals are pressured to have building scores in line with or better than those of other schools. School superintendents are pressured when local and state papers publish their districts' test scores. Colleges select prospective students from test scores.

Problems Students Have During District Testing. Problems experienced by students taking district standardized tests parallel those problems experienced during statewide tests. Please refer to the discussion in the preceding section on statewide assessment.

Accommodations Allowed for District Testing. According to Thurlow and colleagues (2003), districts and states have written policies on the use and type of accommodations allowed during testing. "These policies are quite general (e.g., allowing whatever the student uses during instruction) and other times quite specific (e.g., extended time may be used during one assessment, but not during another, and if used, the student's score will not be included in summaries of performances)" (p. 40). All teachers should become acquainted with their district's and state's requirements.

Classroom-Embedded Assessment

Because instruction and assessment are developed together, **classroom-embedded assessment** measures can help teachers evaluate their teaching methods while also serving as a grading measure. Although assessment and grading are often considered together, every assessment measure does not require a grade. On-demand assessments and extended-time assessments, discussed later, may serve as a method of assessing skills taught and may or may not be given a grade. As we walk through various methods of assessing, remember that all assessment is curriculum based. Initially, curriculum-based assessment (CBA) was designed to fill the need for an assessment process based on the student's progress through curriculum. A major goal of CBA was to eliminate the mismatch between low-achieving students and the sometimes unreasonable demands of the curriculum. Today, when planning instruction, educators consider the student who may not respond to certain curricular demands and attempt to align the assessment with the instruction.

Classroom-embedded assessment is an important aspect in the big picture of educational assessment. Most assessment is provided by the classroom teacher day by day. These assessments must be aligned with standards, and standards must be aligned with the information taught. Standards-based assessment measures, then, validate the results of classroom assessments.

Reteaching or teaching to mastery relies heavily on classroom-embedded assessment. Thus, the assessment must measure not only what the student learned, but also the student's ability to respond to the assessment. If a student cannot respond in writing, an essay test would not be appropriate. The student would be better assessed through product development, recording answers on a tape recorder, answering the essay with voice-activated computer software, and so on. Most important is that the assessments provide the teacher with information on the student's understanding of the content. If the student has not mastered the content, then reteaching is essential. Therefore, thoughtful consideration should be given to classroom-embedded assessment.

Model for Assessment Considerations. A model for assessment consideration is presented in Figure 8.1. Looking at the big picture of assessment, there are three major places where accommodations can occur: test construction or preparation, test administration, and test site. As stated earlier, allowed accommodations for statewide and district assessments are very specific. However, for classroom-embedded assessments, accommodations are at the teacher's discretion.

Educators generally agree about the appropriateness of instructional accommodation. Issues arise, however, when testing accommodations are mentioned. Teachers should recognize the appropriateness of making accommodations for both instruction and testing.

Figure 8.1 Assessment considerations for testing.

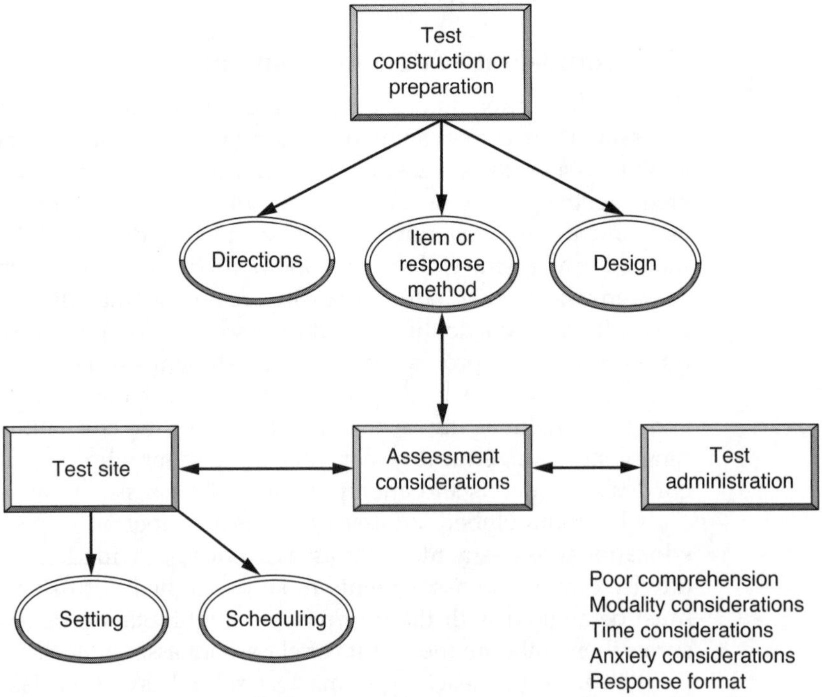

Note: From *Reaching the Hard to Teach* by J. W. Wood, 2008, Richmond, VA: Judy Wood, Inc. Reprinted with permission.

Test Construction or Preparation. Test construction or preparation is the first step in assessment considerations. This step includes writing test directions, choosing the test item or response method, and designing the test.

Test directions. Test directions that are not clear and understandable may cause failure for students before they even try to complete the test. Consider the following suggestions for making test directions clear for all students:

1. Keep directions short.
2. Keep directions simple; avoid unnecessary words.
3. Type directions.
4. If directions are not typed, print neatly.
5. Place all directions at the beginning of each separate test section.
6. When giving more than one direction, list them vertically.
7. List only one direction in each sentence.
8. Underline the word *directions* to focus students' attention.
9. Avoid using words such as *never, not, always,* and *except.* If you must use these words, underline and capitalize them.
10. Define any unfamiliar or abstract words.
11. Color code directions.
12. Avoid making oral directions the only means of communicating the purpose of the test to the students. Read directions orally and write them clearly on the test.
13. Tell students the reason for or purpose of the test.
14. Go over each direction before the test. Be sure that students understand what they should do.
15. Remember that students who do not clearly understand the directions will be the last to raise hands and ask for clarification.
16. While the test is in progress, walk around the room and check to see that students are following directions.
17. Teach students that they should only lose points for not knowing items on the test. They should avoid losing additional points for not following or understanding the test directions.
18. Teach students how to approach tests in a systematic manner. Look over the total test.
19. Read directions to the class at least twice.

Test item or response method. The second aspect of test construction is choosing a test item or response method. These methods can be divided into two categories as shown in Table 8.3: On-Demand Assessments and Extended-Time Assessments. On-demand assessments require students to respond within a certain period of time. Extended-time assessments provide a longer period of time for completion.

Table 8.3 Classroom-embedded assessments.

ON-DEMAND ASSESSMENTS	EXTENDED-TIME ASSESSMENTS: STUDENT DRIVEN
Student Response: Forced Choice • Multiple choice • True–false • Fill in the blank with a word bank • Matching questions	• Performance/products (individual or groups) • Oral reports • Student self-assessment • Portfolios
Student Response: Constructed Response • Brief essay • Expanded essay • Short written responses • Reading comprehension • Definition questions • Extended-response item • Computational problems • Work problems • Lab practicals	• Observations • Interviews • Anecdotal records • Assignments • Homework • Multiple intelligences • Authentic assessment

Note: From *Reaching the Hard to Teach* by J. W. Wood, 2008, Richmond, VA: Judy Wood, Inc. Reprinted with permission.

On-demand assessments include forced choice and constructed items. Forced choice is used to assess student knowledge. Knowledge is the lowest level on Bloom's taxonomy and is a necessary measurement to ensure that students have the necessary knowledge to build a foundation for higher order responses. Items in this area include multiple choice, matching, true–false, and fill in the blank with or without a word bank (a list of words from which students select a response to place in the blank). All of these, with the exception of true–false, are *recognition tests* that require students to examine a group of choices and select a quick answer. Because the correct answer is presented within a list of distracters, recall can be prodded. The student may recall after seeing the correct choice. Class instruction should focus on retention of specific information such as facts and data. Study guides should require students to focus on specific ideas.

Structured recall requires the student to recall the answer to a question without a visual prompt. This type of recall is heavy on memory load. Class instruction should focus on general information such as broad topics or ideas. Study guides should include focus questions designed to help students organize the study process around the general area the test questions will cover. A true–false item requires structured recall.

Multiple-choice items are some of the most useful types of objective test questions. The following suggestions may prove helpful for teachers who are constructing them:

1. Avoid frequent use of fillers. For example:
   a. Either . . . Or
   b. All of the above
   c. None of the above
2. Let the student circle the correct answer rather than place the answer on an answer sheet or blank form. This reduces the possibility of copying errors when transferring letters to the blanks.
3. Arrange the correct answer and the distracters (incorrect answers) vertically on the page. Example: You have a board 48 inches long. If you cut off a 6-inch piece, how much is left?
   a 38 inches
   b. 42 inches
   c. 48 inches
4. Be sure that all choices are grammatically consistent. Example: Because of poor land and a short growing season, the New England colonies were forced into the economic choice of
   a. Exporting food,
   b. Trading and shipbuilding, or
   c. Growing and exporting cotton.
5. Avoid using more than 10 multiple-choice questions per test.
6. State question and answer choices clearly.
7. Avoid using unnecessary words.
8. Give credit to students if they marked out the choices they know are incorrect answers, even if they did not mark the correct answer. This is an alternative for multiple-choice items that involve thought. Perhaps students cannot determine what is correct, but they can process what's not possible. Both require knowledge of the material.
9. Mark out one or two choices (of four choices) with a black marker for some lower level students before handing out the test. Usually the choice eliminated is very close to the correct answer and involves thinking.

The matching exercise is designated to measure factual information based on simple association. It is a compact and efficient method of measuring simple relationships. The following suggestions may be helpful when selecting matching items for tests:

1. Place all matching items and choice selections on the same page.
2. Leave extra space between items in columns to be matched.
3. Use homogeneous material for each matching exercise.
4. Use small groups of matching questions. Avoid long matching lists.

5. Have one extra response in one of the columns. For example, if you have 10 items in column A, place 11 choices in column B. This statistically puts the question in the student's favor.
6. Have only one correct answer for each item.
7. Avoid having students draw lines to correct answers. This may be visually confusing.
8. Keep all matching items brief. The student who has comprehension and reading problems may not be able to process long, wordy items.
9. Place the responses, such as names of explorers, on 3″ × 5″ cards. These become a manipulative exercise. Students can match items to the correct answer by placing the card next to the item. (Thanks to Janice Mael for her suggestion.)
10. Place the list with more lengthy items, usually the descriptive items, in the left-hand column. This makes for less reading and will assist the slow reader.
11. Make a **mini–letter** bank under the blank to reduce the number of choices.
12. Place the blank for the response after each item in column A.
13. For tests with columns that are reversed, teach students to begin the test working from column B to column A.
14. Teach students to answer questions in reverse.
15. Place the blank before the number in column B.
16. Put responses to matching test items in alphabetical order on the left-hand side to facilitate location of the answer.

Here is an example of a matching test:

Column A	**Column B**
1. The island continent	a. Africa
2. Bordered by the Atlantic	b. Asia
3. Located north of the Mediterranean Sea	c. Atlantic Ocean
4. Bordered by Africa and Asia	d. Australia
5. The largest ocean	e. Europe
6. Bordered by the Atlantic and Pacific, north of the equator	f. Indian Ocean
7. The largest continent	g. North America
8. Bordered by the Atlantic and Pacific, south of the equator	h. Pacific Ocean

The most common use of the true–false test is to measure the student's ability to identify the correctness of statements of fact or definition. The following suggestions for modifications may help teachers construct these items:

1. Avoid stating questions negatively.
2. Avoid long, wordy sentences.
3. Avoid statements that are trivial or do not assess student knowledge.
4. Allow students to circle the correct answer.
5. Avoid using too many true–false questions at one time, preferably no more than 10 items per test.
6. Avoid using *never, not, always,* and *except.* If you must use these words, underline and capitalize them.
7. Avoid having students change false statements to true statements unless you have taught this skill.
8. Place the words *true* and *false* at the end of each sentence.
   Example: Imperialism was a cause of World War I. True False

Fill-in-the-blank or completion questions are suitable for measuring knowledge of items, specific facts, methods or procedures, and simple interpretation of data. Because this type of test requires structured recall, it is difficult for many inclusive students and should be used sparingly, if at all. In many cases, multiple-choice items may be more appropriate. If teachers still want to use fill-in-the-blank items, they can attempt to reduce their complexity by following these suggestions:

1. Write simple and clear test items.
2. Avoid using statements directly from the textbook. Taken out of context, they are frequently too general and ambiguous to be used as test questions.
3. Provide large blanks for students with poor handwriting or motor control problems.
4. Be sure that the blank size matches the response. If the blank is too long or too short, students may think that their response is incorrect.
5. Place the blank at the end of the sentence.
6. Provide word banks for the test.
7. Provide a **mini–word** bank immediately under the response blank. This reduces memory load and can be implemented on a test that is already constructed.
8. Allow students to circle the correct choice in the **mini–word** bank.
9. Before the test, tell students whether they will have a word bank on the test.
10. Use a floating word bank that is detached from the test. The student can move the word bank up and down the right side of the page to check for the correct word, placing the words close to the blanks.
11. Have another teacher read your test to check for clear understanding of each item.
12. Place one extra word in the word bank, which statistically puts the test in the student's favor.

13. If a word will be used as a response more than once, list it the appropriate number of times in the word bank.
14. Break the test section into two parts: five questions and a six-word word bank. Repeat for each section. For example:

(1)	(2)	(3)
jump	stomp	throw
run	stop	catch
hop		

(3) 1. Johnny will __________ the ball to Jim.
(1) 2. After Jim hits the ball he will __________ from base to base.

The second category of on-demand assessments is constructed response. These items require that a student create an answer. Forced choice items provide choices for student selection (i.e., multiple choice). In constructed item tests students have a prompt (a question or problem to answer) and must create an answer from recall of information previously learned, or develop a response from created information. Constructed items include brief or expanded essays, short written responses, reading comprehension, definition questions, extended-response items, computational problems, word problems, and lab practicals.

Teachers use brief or expanded essays and short written response questions to measure learning that cannot be evaluated by objective test items. These items may be used to assess higher-order thinking. Most essay or short written response items require the student to recall relevant factual information, mentally organize ideas, and write an extensive or short response. Tests of this type may require skills that students with poor organization abilities, memory problems, or deficient writing skills do not have.

Reading comprehension tests require students to read a passage and respond to it in some way, either by answering questions about it or by giving their impressions or opinions of it. Students won't be able to study for the exact questions that will be asked on the test, but they can practice finding the important information in a passage.

Teachers can use reading comprehension questions to assess students' abilities to locate and retrieve information from the printed page. These questions are also a good way to find out how well students interpret what they read. Students may become frustrated if they haphazardly search for answers rather than use a systematic approach to recognize important information.

Following are suggestions for teaching reading comprehension to elementary students:

1. Read the story twice. Underline words that tell who and what.
2. Read the story twice. Underline words that tell when and where.
3. The main idea tells what the story is mostly about. Ask yourself what big idea the sentences in the story tell about.

If the emphasis in daily classroom activities is on word recall, students will have even greater difficulty with reading comprehension tests that require them to make inferences or draw conclusions. Classroom activities should include both oral and written practice with the same question-and-answer formats that students will find on tests.

To help students perform better on reading comprehension questions, teachers should consider the following when writing tests:

1. Ask a reasonable number of questions per paragraph. Too many items results in questions that are repetitive or irrelevant. Too few items results in overlooking important points.
2. Mix question types for each paragraph.
3. Use a consistent format on all reading tests.
4. Avoid introducing new vocabulary in reading passages. If you do, provide a definition key and type key words in boldface on the test.
5. Space passages so students have enough room to underline important information.

Defining words and using words in context is an expectation of teachers across all content areas. Some teachers use definition tests for weekly spelling vocabulary assessment. Others require students to respond to definition items in social studies, literature, or science.

Although popular with teachers, definition tests can be difficult for many students because they require structured study and memorizing. The format itself is very flexible; however, it can vary from requiring simple recognition responses to structured recall formats. Matching, true–false, multiple choice, sentence completion with or without word banks, and sentence dictation are the most popular formats for definition tests.

Teachers can help their students by explaining about the importance in real life of understanding definitions and why teachers across all content areas expect their students to define words and use words in context. Definition items may appear in various test formats, but they all require extensive study and memorization.

The key to success on definition tests is studying and memorizing. The following 21 study tips will help students prepare for definition tests:

1. Practice a three-step approach to learning definitions. Write the words and definitions you want to learn on a sheet of notebook paper. Divide the paper into three vertical sections. Put the word in section 1 and the definition in section 2. Fold section 3 over section 2 while you're studying.
2. Use flash cards to study. Put the word on one side of an index card and its definition on the other side. Use the cards to study by yourself or with a partner.
3. Use a memory strategy for remembering words and definitions. Use the Look, Say, and Write strategy for learning definitions:
   - Look at the word and study the definition.
   - Say the word and its definition.
   - Write the word.

4. Study words and definitions in groups of five. Study five words and definitions at a time. After you've learned the first five words and definitions, study another group of five. Then, review all ten words. Continue studying groups of five words and definitions at a time. After studying each group of five, go back and review all the words you've studied before adding any new word groups.
5. Find a study partner. After you've used the Look, Say, and Write strategy for studying the words, have someone say the words and you give the definitions.
6. Vary the study technique you use with your partner. You might also want to have someone give you the definitions and you name the words.
7. Think of short definitions for words. Try to think of a one- or two-word definition for a word rather than a long phrase or sentence. For example, instead of memorizing *to accumulate gradually* for the word *gather,* use the word *collect* as your definition.
8. Highlight prefixes, suffixes, and root words. When you learn the meanings of common prefixes, suffixes, and root words, this will help you define words you're unsure of. Look at the following example for the word *preexistence.*
   - *Pre* is the prefix. It means "before."
   - *Exist* is the root word. It means "to come into being."
   - *Ence* is the suffix. It means "a state of being."

   By looking at the prefix, suffix, and root word, you can figure out that *preexistence* means "to come into being before something else."
9. Learn basic root words. Learning root words can help you figure out the meanings of words you're unsure of. For example, the root word *magni* means "great" or "big." If you know this, it can help you figure out the meanings of words like *magni* fy, *magni* ficent, and *magni* tude.
10. Learn prefix meanings. Even if you don't know the meaning of the root word, knowing its prefix can give you a clue to the word's meaning. For example, what do you think the word *dissatisfied* means? If you know the prefix *dis* means "not," you can guess the meaning of this word as "not satisfied."
11. Learn suffix meanings. Even if you don't know the meaning of the root word, knowing its suffix can give you a clue to the word's meaning. For example, what do you think the word *reliable* means? If you know the suffix *able* means "able to," you can guess the meaning of this word as "able to rely on."
12. Use visualization and association to help recall definitions. When you visualize something, you try to picture it in your mind. When you associate something, you try to link it to something it's like. For example, you might use visualization and association to remember the meaning of the word *cowl,* which is a monk's hood. To do this, picture the hood coming down in a point over the monk's forehead, like the markings on an owl's face.

13. Make up jingles to help learn definitions. For example, you can think of a jingle for the word separate, which means "to keep apart." You might think, "The crowd will separate if a rat appears."
14. Look for small words within words. Long words are often made up of two or three smaller words. Looking for the small words can help you learn to spell the long words. For example, the word *separate* has the words *par* and *ate* in it.
15. Match your study techniques to the type of test. Will the test be a sentence completion test? Will it have a word bank? Will you be asked to take dictation? Will you be asked to provide an antonym or a synonym for a word? Always ask your teacher how the test will be given so you'll know how to study.
16. Complete the definitions you know first. Then you'll know how much time you have to answer the ones you don't know.
17. Use the number and length of blanks as a clue to the answer. If the definition is given as an incomplete sentence, check the number and length of the blanks. Sometimes this is a clue to the size and the number of words.
18. Look for *a* or *an* right before the blank. If the definition is given as an incomplete sentence, check the word right before the blank. This can be a clue to the word you are looking for. *A* usually comes before a word that starts with a consonant. *An* usually comes before a word that starts with a vowel.
19. Decide which part of speech is missing from an incomplete sentence. If the definition is given as an incomplete sentence, check the part of speech that's missing. Subjects and verbs must agree. Look at these examples:

    A pilot is the person who flies the plane.

    Pilots are people who fly planes.
20. Use context clues. All of the words in a sentence depend on the others. If you don't know the meaning of a word, look at the words around it for a clue. This kind of clue is called a *context clue.* There are five types of context clues:
    - Synonyms
    - Definition or description
    - Association
    - Tone and setting
    - Cause and effect
21. Ask your teacher if there's a penalty for incorrect answers. If there isn't a penalty, always guess at definitions you're unsure of. (Lazzari & Wood, 1994, pp. 89–92)

Extended-response items are becoming more frequent on state assessment measures. This response item may appear in different domain areas and require higher order thinking skills. An effective solution requires that the student complete all parts of the task and clearly communicate and justify the answer. In some cases, writing skills are evaluated. General tips for helping students respond to constructed-response items are helpful when practicing for extended-response items. Following is an example of an extended-response item for the domain area of math:

Solve the Problem: Rhonda has 23 CDs in her music collection. She gives away 8 of them.

a. Write a number sentence that shows one way to find the number of CDs she has left in her collection.
b. What is the solution to your number sentence?
c. Write a story problem of your own that could be solved by the master sentence shown below. $15 - ? = 8$
d. Show how to find the solution to your number sequence.

Computation problems usually require the student to apply an algorithm or a formula to find a numerical answer. Consider the suggestions in Figure 8.2.

Figure 8.2 Adaptations for computation problems.

1. Provide manipulative objects that make the problems more concrete.
2. Avoid mixing different problem formats in the same section. For example, a student with organizational or visual tracking difficulties may be able to solve problem A but may not be able to align the numbers in problem B.

Problem A	*Problem B*
$\begin{array}{r} 468 \\ 83 \\ +\ 1894 \\ \hline \end{array}$	$670 + 40 + 2861 =$ _____

3. Avoid mixing vertical and horizontal problems in the same section. For example, for the student with visual tracking problems or one who has difficulty changing gears from one process to another, the shift in presentation from problem C to problem D may be confusing. It would be better to test the student's knowledge of the two processes in two separate sections of the test.

Problem A	*Problem B*
$\begin{array}{r} 8 \\ \times 5 \\ \hline \end{array}$	$5 \times 6 =$ ______

4. Give formulas and meanings of symbols.
   < means *less than*
5. Give a set of written steps for applying algorithms.
   Long Division
   1. Divide
   2. Multiply
   3. Subtract
   4. Check
   5. Bring down

Note: Adapted with permission from *"Adapting Test Construction for Mainstreamed Mathematics Students"* (*Mathematics Teacher*), copyright May 1988 by the National Council of Teachers of Mathematics.

Word problems can be very difficult for students with disabilities. The suggestions in Figure 8.3 are helpful during evaluation.

Lab practicals can be used to assess students with mild disabilities. If students have been learning how to operate Bunsen burners, for example, a test could involve giving them a checklist to work on throughout the lab (see Figure 8.4). Students who need individual help can work with a lab partner or in a small group. Teachers can follow up with more specific questions, which students should complete with the burner turned off. Teachers can write similar checklist tests for the use of other lab equipment, such as balances, graduated cylinders, and microscopes.

Many students can answer questions better orally than in writing. To test students' safety knowledge, teachers can make slides of people using improper safety procedures. They can then show these slides and ask students to describe orally which rules are being broken. Another adaptation is to read tests aloud to students with reading disabilities.

For students who learn best through hands-on experiences, teachers can design tests that evaluate students in a hands-on manner. For example, instead of labeling a diagram of an atom on a test, students can construct a three-dimensional model of an atom using plastic foam balls. The students can indicate on the model the location and charge of neutrons, protons, and electrons.

Wilson (2002) presented five constructed-response pitfalls students may encounter.

Figure 8.3 Adaptations for word problems.

1. Use simple sentences. Avoid words that may cause confusion.
2. Use a problem context that is relevant to the student's arsenal of experience.
3. Underline or circle key words—for example, *less, more.*
4. Use no more than five word problems per test because they require greater effort to read and understand.
5. Give formulas as reminders of operations to be used.
6. Be sure that the reasoning skills being tested are appropriate to the student's comprehension level. Avoid the use of word problems (with some students) because this may be testing language and measuring skills above the student's level. For example, a student with a mild disability who has poor reading and comprehension skills may not be able to understand a complex word problem without assistance.

The following example incorporates many of these suggestions:

John lives 3 and $\frac{7}{10}$ miles from Fair Oaks elementary school.
Trish lives 2 and $\frac{3}{4}$ miles from school.
Which one lives farther from school?
How much farther?

Note: From *Reaching the Hard to Teach* by J. W. Wood, 2008, Richmond, VA: Judy Wood, Inc. Reprinted with permission.

Figure 8.4 Lab practical for the Bunsen burner.

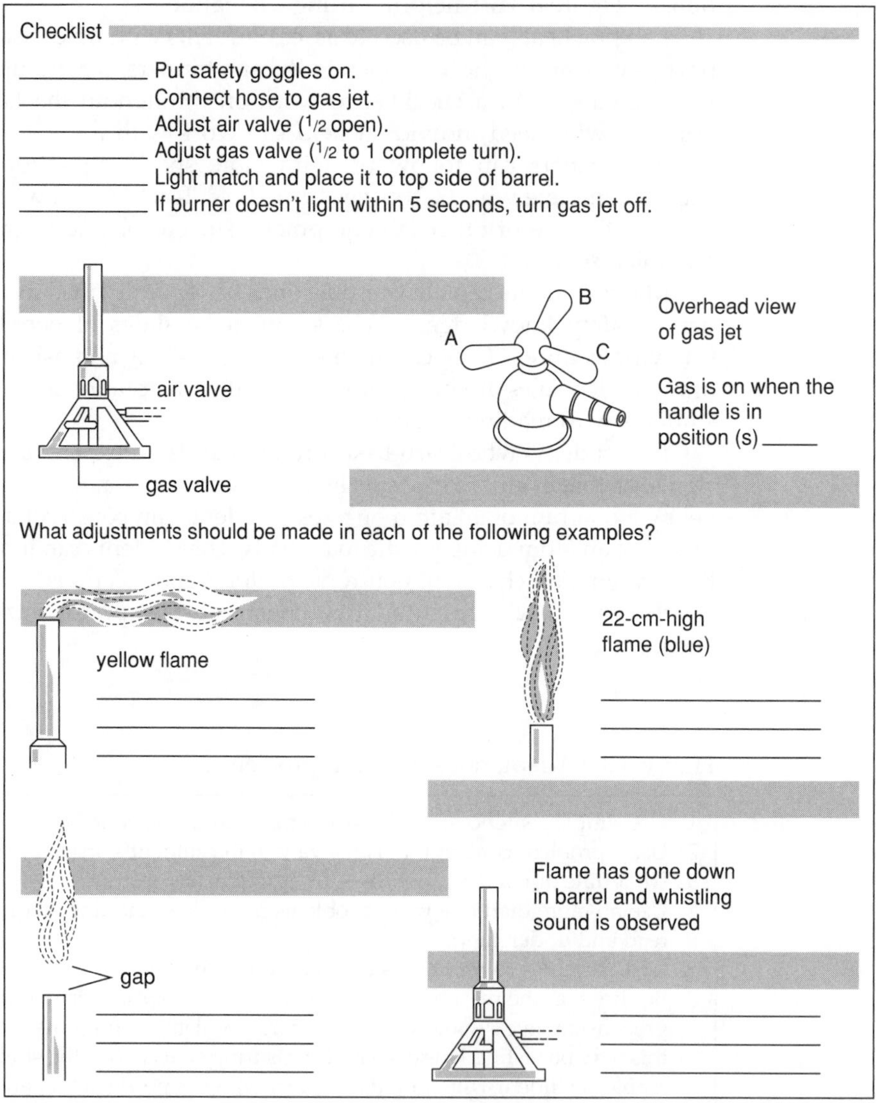

Checklist

_______ Put safety goggles on.
_______ Connect hose to gas jet.
_______ Adjust air valve (1/2 open).
_______ Adjust gas valve (1/2 to 1 complete turn).
_______ Light match and place it to top side of barrel.
_______ If burner doesn't light within 5 seconds, turn gas jet off.

air valve
gas valve

A B C

Overhead view of gas jet

Gas is on when the handle is in position (s) _____

What adjustments should be made in each of the following examples?

yellow flame
____
____
____

22-cm-high flame (blue)
____
____
____

gap
____
____
____

Flame has gone down in barrel and whistling sound is observed
____
____
____

Note: Adapted with permission of NSTA publications from "Stress the Knowledge, Not the Student," by Wood et al., from *The Science Teacher,* November 1988, published by the National Science Teachers Association, Arlington, Virginia.

1. All sections of the question must be answered. Some problems have more than one step. Therefore, the student must reread the question after answering the question. An extended-response item is an example of a multiple-step question.
2. Be sure to show all of your work. Some problems are graded on a point system and a step omitted could result in a loss of points.

3. Provide all evidence to support your answer. Younger children may assume that the grader knows the answer and therefore, there is no need to provide details. Have students reread their answer from another student's point of view.
4. Practice with the class using scoring rubrics so that students begin to construct in their minds the characteristics of a good response.
5. Look ahead at the questions to be answered so as not to become bogged down on one question, not allowing time to respond to all of the questions. (pp. 44–45)

The second category of classroom-embedded assessment is extended-time assessment. This category allows the student a longer period of time for completing the assessment measure and allows the teacher more time for collecting data for student evaluation. Extended-time assessment may be student driven or teacher driven.

Student-driven assessments are products students create over an extended time frame. They include performance assessments or products, oral reports, self-assessments, and portfolios.

A popular form of student-driven assessment is performance or product based. These may be developed by an individual student or by a group. Jacobs (1997), in her work on curriculum mapping, matched learner developmental characteristics and assessment genres by grade level (see Figure 8.5).

Figure 8.5 Matching learners and assessment genres.

K–2 Developmental Characteristics

Cognitive level is concrete operations; sensory-motor modalities dominate; egocentric; parallel play still dominates with the beginning signs of social interaction with other peers; strong need for primary affiliation with a key adult at school and parental surrogates; willingness to experiment and take risks; verbal skills generally more pronounced in girls; spatial-motor generally more pronounced in boys; evident disparities between various areas of development as in fine motor/gross motor differences; uneven development in speaking skills; reading and writing emerges at this level with the learner's fascination with sound–symbol relations.

Examples of K–2 Genres

Captions	Story boards
Labels	Story lines
Simple research	Graphs/charts
Maps	Joke telling
Interview with a key question	Observational drawing

Grades 3–5 Developmental Characteristics

Cognitive operations are moving through concrete functions with early signs of simple abstract thinking; students are able to combine several concepts and

Continued

Figure 8.5 (Continued)

perceive cause-and-effect relationships; fascination with the world; excellent "reporters" and seekers of interesting information; social skills related strongly to peers and to teachers; enjoy large group projects; social concern for others emerging; physical stability and agility.

Examples of Grade 3–5 Genres

Simple research report	Extended research report
Note cards	Interview: questions series
Short stories	Photo essay with text
Artifact analysis	Comparative observations
Newspaper articles	

Grades 6–8 Developmental Characteristics

Labile period of development; surge into formal operations; quest for personal identity; fascination with issues of fairness, justice, and trust; pronounced surges in physical development; uneven development among peers; self-consciousness about physical presence; concern for others conflicting with concern for self.

Examples of Grade 6–8 Genres

Persuasive essays	Descriptive essays
Analytical essays	Personal essays
Hypothesis testing	Issue-based forums
Blueprints and modeling	Original play writing
Museum text/captions	Four note-taking forms

Grades 9–10 and 11–12 Developmental Characteristics

Significant differences among 9th and 12th graders progressing from mid-adolescent concerns to pre-adult education; formal operations involving abstract concepts; projections; social life focused on smaller groupings and pairings; sexuality is an issue; physical maturity rapidly paces; focus on future and next steps.

Examples of Grades 9–10 and 11–12 Genres

Position papers	Legal briefs
Business plans	Anthologies
Choreography	Game book
Film and literary criticism	Senior project and defense
Work study analysis	Interview simulations
Case studies	Original musical
Compositions	

Note: From *Mapping the Big Picture: Integrating Curriculum and Assessment K–12* (pp. 36–37) by H. H. Jacobs. Copyright © 1997 by the Association for Supervision and Curriculum Development. Reprinted by permission. The Association for Supervision and Curriculum Development is a worldwide community of educators advocating sound policies and sharing best practices to achieve the success of each learner. To learn more, visit ASDC at www.ascd.org.

Types of student products or performances are numerous. Some of the types of products or performances include written work, visual presentations, hands-on experiences, oral presentations, dramatizations and performances, conversations and conferences, and reflections.

Student self-assessment, according to Marzano (2000), is well suited to the grading aspects of informational topics, process topics, thinking and reasoning, communication, and nonachievement factors (p. 87). "Although the most underused form of classroom assessment, student self-assessment has the most flexibility and power as a combined assessment and learning tool" (p. 102).

Portfolios have been in existence for a long time and are used by such professionals as artists, architects, and photographers. In education, portfolios can do the following:

- Engage students in learning content.
- Help students learn the skills of reflection and self-evaluation.
- Document student learning in areas that do not lend themselves to traditional assessment.
- Facilitate communication with parents. (Danielson & Abrutyn, 1997)

Portfolios may be "used as an assessment framework. Portfolios are systematic collections by students and teachers that serve as the basis to examine 'effort, in improvement, processes, and achievement as well as to meet the accountability demands usually achieved by more formal testing procedures'" (Johns, as cited in Danielson & Abrutyn, 1997, p. vi). Examples of assessment portfolios are listed in Figure 8.6.

Extended-time assessment measures that are teacher driven include observations, interviews, anecdotal records, assignments, homework, multiple intelligences assessment, and authentic assessment measures. Teacher observations and interviews are closely related. According to Marzano (2000), "one of the most straightforward ways to collect classroom assessment data is through informal observations of students" (p. 99). Educators need to be aware of the skills they are observing. Marzano continued, "teacher observation is probably the perfect assessment tool for the non-achievement factors—effort, behavior, and attendance" (p. 99). One type of observation is the interview, in which teachers probe students for information learned.

Anecdotal records are notes teachers keep on an ongoing basis regarding a student's work. These brief notes record the student's work progress and skill development, and where the student may need to be retaught.

Assignments and homework are also types of teacher-driven assessments. Like other response assessments, assignments and homework provide feedback on student learning and may or may not be given a grade.

Authentic assessment requires realistic demands in a real-life setting. It is sometimes used interchangeably with performance assessment, which requires a student to use the knowledge learned. Educators using authentic or performance assessment are able to provide multiple opportunities for students to perform and show work mastery.

Figure 8.6 Examples of assessment portfolios.

Reading • Audiotape or oral reading of selected passages • Original story grammar map • Transcript of story retelling • Log of books read with personal reactions, summaries, vocabulary • Representative assignments; responses to pre/post reading questions • Favorite performance • Journal entries, including self-evaluation **Science** • Representative work samples • Student-selected best performance • Report from hands-on investigation • Notes on science fair project • Journal entries, including self-evaluation	**Writing** • Scrapbook of representative writing samples • Selected prewriting activities • Illustration/diagrams for one piece • Log/journal of writing ideas, vocabulary, schematic maps, compositions, evaluations • Conference notes, observation narratives • Student-selected best performance • Self-evaluation checklists and teacher checklists **Social Studies** • Representative work samples • Student-selected best performance • Design of travel brochure, packet, or itinerary of trip • Notes on history fair project • Journal entries, including self-evaluation	**Mathematics** • Reports of mathematical investigations • Representative assignments • Teacher conference notes • Descriptions and diagrams of problem-solving processes • Video, audio, or computer-generated examples of work • Best performance • Journal entries including self-evaluation **Arts** • Best performance • Favorite performance • First, middle, and final renderings of projects • Tape of performance • Journal entries, including self-evaluation **Generic** • Learning progress record • Report cards • Personal journal • Tests • Significant daily assignments • Anecdotal observations • Photographs • Awards • Personal goals

Note: From "What Makes a Portfolio a Portfolio?" by F. L. Paulson, P. R. Paulson, and C. A. Meyer, *Educational Leadership,* 48(5), 60–63. Copyright © 1991 by the Association for Supervision and Curriculum Development. Adapted by permission. The Association for Supervision and Curriculum Development is a worldwide community of educators advocating sound policies and sharing best practices to achieve the success of each learner. To learn more, visit ASDC at www.ascd.org.

Frequently, authentic assessments, or performance tasks, are confused with essay questions. According to Marzano (2000),

> Essay items that require the application of knowledge, then, are types of performance tasks. However, not all performance tasks are essays. Some performance tasks do not require written responses, whereas all essays do. For example, a performance task requiring students to apply their knowledge and skill in playing the violin would not require the student to write (or say) anything.
>
> Like essay items, one of the most powerful aspects of performance tasks is that they can be used to assess a variety of forms of knowledge. (p. 97)

Examples of authentic assessment are given in Figure 8.7.

Howard Gardner's eight multiple intelligences provide educators yet another way to assess students. Table 8.4 presents each of the eight dispositions or intelligences and lists what a child with each intelligence may be sensitive

Figure 8.7 Examples of authentic assessment.

Reading • Actual or audio/videotape of reading to peer • Log and critiques of books read • Book review • Book jacket design **Science** • Scientific experiment to prove theory • Original investigation and a report of findings • Journal of observations of moons, stars • Solutions to local environment problems **Oral expression** • Transmission of message to several classes • Phone call to request information • Debate about current issues • Persuasive speech	**Social Studies** • Map of school or community • Design of museum exhibit on topic of interest • Advertising campaign for political candidate • Identification of social problem for co-op group **Written expression** • Student interview • Article for school paper • Written resume and job application • Invitation to party • Letter to editor **Arts** • Design and decoration of bulletin board • Submission of art to contest • Artwork design for public building • Performance in a play	**Mathematics** • Solving real-life problems using math knowledge • Solving a puzzle using logic and reasoning • Monitoring a savings account • Personal budget **Generic** • Reflective journal of learning progress • Competition for "grant" money • Planning and teaching a lesson to peer • Laser disc storage of assessment information

Note: From "Performance Assessment and Special Education: Practices and Prospects" by J. A. Poteet, J. S. Choate, and S. C. Steward, 1993, *Focus on Exceptional Children, 26*(1), 7. Adapted with permission.

Table 8.4 Intelligences as dispositions.

Disposition/Intelligence	Sensitivity to:	Inclination for:	Ability to:
Verbal-lingustic Intelligence	The sounds, meanings, structures, and styles of language	Speaking, writing, listening, reading	Speak effectively (teacher, religious leader, politician) or write effectively (poet, journalist, novelist, copywriter, editor)
Logical-mathematical Intelligence	Patterns, numbers, and numerical data, causes and effects, objective and quantitative reasoning	Findings patterns, making calculations, forming and testing hypotheses, using the scientific method, deductive and inductive reasoning	Work effectively with numbers (accountant, statistician, economist) and reason effectively (engineer, scientist, computer programmer)
Spatial Intelligence	Colors, shapes, visual puzzles, symmetry, lines, images	Repressenting ideas visually, creating mental images, noticing visual details, drawing and sketching	Create visually (artist, photographer, engineer, decorator) and visualize accurately (tour guide, scout, ranger)
Bodily-kinesthetic Intelligence	Touch, movement, physical self, athleticism	Activities requiring strength, speed, flexibility, hand-eye coordination, and balance	Use the hands to fix or create (mechanic, surgeon, carpenter, sculptor, mason) and use the body expressively (dancer, athlete, actor)

to, how the child may be inclined, and what the child's abilities are. Lazear (1998) presented an assessment menu for each of the eight intelligences (see Table 8.5).

Test design. Test design is the third aspect of test construction that can be easily adapted. Adaptations in test design include the following:

1. Use test items that reflect the techniques used in teaching. For example, if the students were taught only to recall facts, avoid essay questions.
2. Type or print legibly. Use large type when available. If you prepare the test in longhand, be sure to list items clearly, concisely, and neatly.
3. Prepare a study guide that matches the design of the test.
4. Adjust the readability level of the test to meet the students' needs.
5. Prepare the test in short sections that you can administer individually if necessary.
6. Place one type of question on each page. For example, use one page for multiple-choice questions and another for essay questions.
7. After consulting students privately about personal testing needs, adapt the test to meet those needs.

Musical Intelligence	Tone, beat, tempo, melody, pitch, sound	Listening, singing, playing an instrument	Create music (songwriter composer, musician, conductor) and analyze music (music critic)
Interpersonal Intelligence	Body language, moods, voice, feelings	Noticing and responding to other people's feelings and personalities	Work with people (administrators, managers, consultants, teachers) and help people identify and overcome problems (therapists, psychologists)
Intrapersonal Intelligence	One's own strengths, weaknesses, goals, and desires	Setting goals, assessing personal abilities and liabilities, monitoring one's own thinking	Mediate, reflect, exhibit self-discipline, maintain composure, and get the most out of oneself
Naturalist Intelligence	Natural objects, plants, animals, naturally occurring patterns, ecological issues	Identifying and classifying living things and natural objects	Analyze ecological and natual situations and data (ecologists and rangers), learn from living things (zoologists, botanists, veterinarians) and work in natural setting (hunters, scouts)

Note: From *So Each May Learn: Integrating Learning Styles and Multiple Intelligences* (p. 11), by H. F. Silver, R. W. Strong, and M. J. Perini, 2000, Alexandria, VA: Association for Supervision and Curriculum Development. ©2000 by Silver Strong & Associates, L.L.C. Reprinted with permission. To purchase this title, please call 800-962-4432 or visit www.ThoughtfulEd.com online.

8. If you use the chalkboard for a test, clear other material from the board, then print or write in large, legible letters. Avoid lengthy tests for students with copying difficulties.
9. Avoid using only oral tests and quizzes.
10. Plan to allow students with disabilities to take tests in a separate setting to overcome problems with time, reading ability, or embarrassment.
11. Clearly duplicate the test using black ink, if available.
12. Use a large sheet of dark construction paper under the test to act as a border. Provide a sheet of paper with a "window frame" cut into it to help in reading the test. This helps students with visual acuity and visual perception problems.
13. If a student has difficulty finishing on time, administer an adapted, shortened version of the test. Another option is split-halves testing, in which half the test is administered on one day and the other half on the next day.

Table 8.5 Multiple intelligences assessment menu.

Verbal-Linguistic Intelligence ***(Language arts–based assessment instruments)***	**Logical-Mathematical Intelligence** ***(Cognitive patterns–based assessment instruments)***	**Visual-Spatial Intellgence** ***(Imaginal-based assessment instruments)***	**Bodily-Kinesthetic Intelligence** ***(Performance-based assessment instruments)***
Written essays	Cognitive organizers	Murals and montages	Lab experiments
Vocabulary quizzes	Higher-order reasoning	Graphic representation and visual illustrating	Dramatization
Recall of verbal information	Pattern games	Visualization and imagination	Original and classical dance
Audiocassette recordings	Outlining	Reading, understanding, and creating maps	Charades and mimes
Poety writing	Logic and rationality exercises	Flowcharts and graphs	Impersonations
Linguistic humor	Mental menus and formulas	Sculpting and building	Human tableaux
Formal speech	Deductive reasoning	Imaginary conversations	Invention projects
Cognitive debates	Inductive reasoning	Mind mapping	Physical exercise routines and games
Listening and reporting	Calculation processes	Video recording and photography	Skill demonstrations
Learning logs and journals	Logical analysis and critique	Manipulative demonstrations	Illustrations using body language and gestures

14. If a modified test is necessary for an included student, design it to resemble the general test to avoid embarrassment.
15. Arrange tests so that questions that count the most come first. Some students generally work in order and may not finish the test.
16. If possible, use canary yellow paper with black print for the test.
17. Write the point value for each section on the test.
18. Draw a line between math problem rows to help a student finish each row and not get mixed up while moving through the problems.
19. Place a heading for each test section with directions if the directions have changed.
20. Make sure handwriting is neat and legible.
21. If typing is not possible, print the test.
22. Number all pages of the test.
23. Use a felt marker to divide sections of the test so that the student knows when to move to another set of directions.

Musical-Rhythmic Intelligence ***(Auditory-based assessment instruments)***	**Interpersonal Intelligence** ***(Relational-based asssessment instruments)***	**Intrapersonal Intelligence** ***(Psychological-based assessment instruments)***	**Naturalist Intelligence** ***(Environment-based assessment instruments)***
Creating concept songs and raps	Group "Jigsaws"	Autobiographical reporting	Hands-on labs/demonstrations
Illustrating with sound	Explaining to or teaching another	Personal application scenarios	Species/natural pattern classification
Discerning rhythmic patterns	"Think-pair-share"	Metacognitive surveys and questionnaires	Nature encounters/field trips
Composing music	"Round robin"	Higher-order questions and answers	Environmental feedback
Linking music and rhythm with concepts	Giving and receiving feedback	Concentration tests	Nature observations
Orchestrating music	Interviews, questionnaires, and people searches	Feelings, diaries, and logs	Care for plants and animals
Creating percussion patterns	Empathic processing	Personal projection	Sensory stimulation exercises
Recognizing tonal patterns and quality	Random group quizzes	Self-identification reporting	Conservation practices
Analyzing musical structure	Assess your teammates	Personal history correlation	Archetypal pattern recognition
Reproducing musical and rhythmic patterns	Test, coach, and retest	Personal priorities and goals	Natural world simulations

Note: From Lazear, D. (1988). *The rubrics way* (p. 37). Chicago, IL: Zephyr Press. Reprinted with permission.

24. Watch the complexity of sentences so that the test does not become a language test and content is lost.
25. For reading sections, put the reading selection on one page and the questions on a second page. The student can then place the reading selection and the questions side by side.

Accommodations During Test Administration. The second component of the model for adapting classroom tests (see Figure 8.1) involves the administration of the test. Many students with disabilities may need alternative modes of administration when taking the test. Adaptation of test administration relates directly to the problems that students encounter in the test situation. These include poor comprehension, modality considerations, time considerations, anxiety considerations, and response format.

Students with comprehension problems need special considerations during testing. Following are suggestions for test administration for such students:

1. Give test directions both orally and in written form. Make sure all students clearly understand.
2. Avoid long talks before the tests.
3. Allow students to tape-record responses to essay questions or the entire test.
4. Allow students to take the test in an alternative test site, usually the resource classroom.
5. Correct for content only, not for spelling or grammar.
6. Provide an example of the expected correct response.
7. Remind students to check tests for unanswered questions.
8. When the test deals with problem-solving skills, allow the use of tools, such as multiplication tables or calculators during math tests.
9. Read the test aloud for students who have difficulty reading.
10. Give a written outline for essay questions.
11. Tape-record instructions and questions for a test.
12. Use objective rather than essay tests.

Modality difficulties may require accommodations during test administration. The difficulties may occur in auditory or visual perception. Suggestions for auditory perception problems are as follows:

1. For oral spelling tests, go slowly, enunciating each syllable and sound distinctly.
2. Avoid oral tests.
3. Seat students in a quiet place for testing.
4. Allow students to take tests in an alternative test site, such as the resource classroom.
5. Place a TESTING sign on the classroom door to discourage interruptions.

Suggestions for students with visual perception problems include the following:

1. Give directions orally as well as in written form.
2. Check students discreetly to see if they are on track.
3. Give the exam orally or tape-record it.
4. Seat students away from distractions (such as windows or doors). Use a carrel or face the desk toward a wall.
5. Avoid having other students turn in papers during the test.
6. Meet visitors at the door and talk in the hallway.
7. Hang a DO NOT DISTURB—TESTING sign on the door.
8. Use an alternative test site if the student requests it.

Many students have difficulty with time constraints in testing situations. Frequently, we associate time difficulties with standardized tests. Actually, all tests are timed. Think about it. When a teacher hands out the test papers, an assumption is made that the test will be turned in by the time class is over. Technically, all tests are timed unless considerations are provided during test administrations.

For standardized tests, certain accommodations are allowed. For classroom testing, consider the following:

1. Allow enough time for students to complete the test. Inclusive students may require longer periods of time.
2. Provide breaks during lengthy tests.
3. Allow split-halves testing. Give half the test on one day and the remaining half on the second day.
4. Allow students to take the test in the resource room if necessary.
5. Allow students to complete only the odd- or even-numbered questions. Circle the appropriate questions for students who may not understand the concept of odd and even.
6. Use un-timed tests.
7. Give oral or tape-recorded tests. Students with slow writing skills can answer orally or on tape.

Test anxiety is very real for many students. Many students even become physically ill prior to a test. Sometimes the anxiety results from the embarrassment many students feel when presented with a testing situation. We always want students to do their very best. Consider the following suggestions for test administration for students experiencing test anxiety or embarrassment:

1. Avoid adding pressure to the test setting by admonishing students to "hurry and get finished" or "do your best; this counts for half of your six-weeks' grade."
2. Avoid threatening to use a test to punish students for poor behavior.
3. Give a practice test.
4. Give a retest if needed.
5. Don't threaten dire consequences for failure.
6. Grade on the percentage of items completed.
7. Have students take the regular test with the class and an adapted test in the resource room.
8. Make a modified test closely resemble the regular test to avoid embarrassing self-conscious students.
9. Avoid calling attention to inclusive students as you help them.
10. Confer with students privately to work out accommodations for testing.

Response accommodations may be required for students with fine motor problems, written expression problems, or visual or verbal deficits. In addition, students with physical and sensory disabilities require accommodations during test administration. Students with memory problems who cannot recall multiplication facts may need a calculator. Sequencing and memory issues, such as in spelling, may require a spellchecker. Some students have difficulty responding to "bubble" answer sheets. Following are suggestions for response accommodations during test administration:

1. Prepare students to respond to the test format prior to the test situations.
2. Assist students in checking the time allowed for the test. If the test is timed, response time becomes important.

3. Review with students the penalty, if any, for guessing or leaving questions unanswered.
4. Check to see that students have the necessary materials needed for the test.
5. Encourage students to check their work if time is left over.
6. Review tips for taking selected test items or responses prior to test day.
7. Provide necessary accommodations for students with physical and sensory disabilities.
8. Provide a ruler for students who have difficulty answering on a "bubble" answer sheet. The ruler can be placed under the number answered and slid down after each response.
9. Have students make a mark after every five "bubble" items. When they come to the mark, they should be on number 5, then number 10, and so on. This prevents students from completing the answer sheet with items left over, which indicates that they have misaligned the questions and answers.

If marks are not allowed on answer sheets, the same procedure can be used in the test booklet.

Test Sites. Students may need an alternative test site such as a change of place for the test (setting) or a change in the test scheduling. A change in test setting may include going to the resource room to take the test. Many students with disabilities do better when the test is given with the special education teacher, who knows the student's unique strengths and weaknesses. Students with reading difficulties (slow readers and those with low vocabulary or low comprehension) can benefit from having the test read orally, having more time to complete the test, having questions clarified and new vocabulary explained, and feeling less pressure. The test may also be recorded on a tape recorder. When students are embarrassed by taking a test that is different from the one given to peers in the regular class, a different test setting is a helpful solution. Some students are easily confused by verbal or written directions and, in a different setting, have more opportunities to ask questions. This may help them feel less frustrated. Students who are distracted by the activity within the regular classroom may find that an alternative setting contains fewer distractions. For students experiencing test anxiety and frustration, different settings can reduce anxiety because they are no longer competing with peers, can work at their own pace, and have resource support. Alternative test settings may also include small groups within the classroom, a different general education classroom, and so forth.

According to Thurlow and colleagues (2003), "scheduling accommodations are changes in when testing occurs" (p. 56). Any time a student takes a test at a time other than when the test is regularly scheduled, a scheduling accommodation has been made. Reasons for a scheduling change include avoiding the effects of medication and reducing frustration. Other reasons include avoiding scheduling too many tests on one day, skipping a day between tests for preparation, reducing test anxiety, and accommodating students who do better in smaller testing sessions.

Determining the least restrictive testing environment is the responsibility of the IEP committee and is closely tied to the student's instruction and unique learning need. According to Jayanthi, Epstein, Polloway, and Bursuck (1996), nationally, educators perceived that the three most helpful testing accommodations are assisting with test directions, reading test questions or items to students, and rewording or simplifying test question wording. As with any accommodation, the educator strives to move the student from the use of an accommodation to the removal of the accommodation. For example, a student may initially need a note-taking accommodation, but eventually move to taking notes without an accommodation. The same stands for testing accommodations. Educators plan to move students from the present level of adaptations to ones that more closely approximate the testing environment of their nondisabled peers.

Student Preferences for Test Adaptations. Nelson, Jayanthi, Epstein, and Bursuck conducted a study reported in *Remedial and Special Education* (2000, pp. 41–52) in which they attempted to discover the specific testing adaptations of seventh- and eighth-grade students with high-incidence disabilities (such as learning disabilities) and general education students with low, average, high, and very high achievement. They found that adaptations most preferred by the entire sample were as follows:

- Open-note tests
- Open-book tests
- Practice questions for study
- Multiple choice instead of short answer or essay
- Use of dictionary or calculator
- A copy of the test to study
- Extra answer space

Testing adaptations that were least preferred by students in the sample were as follows:

- Teacher reading questions to students
- Tests with fewer questions than given other students
- Tests covering less material than tests given other students
- Tests written in larger print
- Oral responses instead of written ones
- Use of computer to write answers
- Individual help with directions during the test
- Learning test-taking skills

The study looked further into whether students' academic status related to their preferences for testing adaptations. Two other of the most liked adaptations were take-home tests and working in a small group. This study deserves more explanation than space allows here. However, it appears that some of the most preferred adaptations required the least amount of extra teacher time and that all groups of students acknowledged that adaptations are of benefit. Students do not want to be singled out, or made to feel "stupid" or "different" in front of their peers. Teachers need to be sensitive to this as they make adaptations.

GRADING STUDENTS IN INCLUSIVE SETTINGS

The problems inherent in evaluating students and assigning grades can become even more complex for students in inclusive settings. Here, the integration of students with disabilities into regular education classes has created a dilemma for teachers in terms of assigning grades fairly and objectively. On the one hand, questions arise about the equity of using different standards to evaluate students in the same classroom. For example, is it fair to the other students in the classroom to award the same letter grades and course credit to a student who has not met the class performance standards? On the other hand, proponents of individualized grading point out that to do otherwise places an added burden on students already at a disadvantage for competing fairly with their peers and does not provide useful information to students and parents. For example, a grade of "satisfactory" or C does not reveal what new knowledge students have gained or how they have performed relative to their individual strengths and weaknesses. Nor does it provide information on the effectiveness of instructional adaptations. Other questions arise concerning who should assign grades and which criteria and grading process they should use.

A preliminary question to answer when considering the issue of grading a student is whether alternative grading procedures are necessary for that individual. In many cases, making appropriate adaptations of the learning environment, format of content, teaching techniques, and testing procedures will enable the student with special needs to be graded according to the same methods used for other students in the classroom. When accommodations in grading procedures are needed, they should be noted on the student's IEP along with any other adaptations that are necessary. In addition to identifying the grading procedures, the IEP should specify if a grade reporting schedule other than the standard school schedule is to be used and should identify which teacher will be responsible for determining the student's grades.

GRADING AND ASSESSMENT

Grading is clearly tied to assessment, although not every assessment must receive a grade. Grading establishes criteria for success on assessment measures and also provides feedback for reteaching. Additionally, in practice, grades also serve several other functions (Jacobsen, Eggen, & Kauchak, 1989):

- Providing feedback to parents as an indicator of their children's achievement
- Providing data for grouping students

- Guiding decisions about promotion and graduation
- Providing a basis for making awards and scholarships
- Determining a student's eligibility for extracurricular activities
- Helping determine college eligibility and participation in collegiate athletics

Traditionally, the practice of assigning grades helped the administration differentiate among groups of students rather than providing useful information to students and parents. Everyone was graded on the same outcomes, and the same measures were used for each student.

Today, we still have outcomes and measures. However, education is becoming broader in focus—outcomes, and how these outcomes are reached, may vary for certain individuals.

Letter grades are still used, but more and more predictors of future success are seen as factors, not just one grade. Students who leave school to enter the workplace need feedback that more closely resembles the type they will receive on the job. It is important for educators to continue to strive to develop grading procedures that can more appropriately meet the needs of all students.

According to Marzano (2000), teachers usually consider four factors to include in grades: academic achievement, effort, behavior, and attendance. There is value in reporting student feedback on the nonachieving factors of effort, behavior, and attendance. Effort is perceived as participation in class and work completion. Behavior is defined as following rules and being able to work in teams. Attendance is divided into the areas of absenteeism and tardiness. These factors can be assessed accurately. However, the most important factor in grading is student academic achievement.

Alternative Methods of Grading

Although the development of alternative grading criteria for students with disabilities may not be an easy task, it is an extremely important adaptation that must be made if students with special needs are to have any chance of success in the general educational environment. Table 8.6 displays 10 alternative evaluation approaches, which are discussed in detail in this section.

Pass/Fail. The establishment of general criteria for passing or failing an assignment or a course is a common modification of traditional grade criteria. Because determination of acceptable work is judged according to broad-based criteria, the student in the inclusive setting has a greater chance of success in reaching the minimum course competencies. Like any measurement procedure, there are advantages and disadvantages to using a pass/fail system. Vasa (1981) identified the following advantages:

- Students feel less pressure to compete.
- Students feel less anxiety.

Research Notes for Classroom Application

Research on grading practices used with students with learning disabilities suggests the potential for such learners to receive passing grades in inclusive classrooms, but indicates that they are at increased risk over their peers without disabilities for low or failing grades (Munk & Bursuck, 2004). Grading adaptations, which individualize the grading system for struggling students, may help alleviate this problem.

In 1990, 64% of secondary students with disabilities in inclusive classrooms were graded on the same standards as their classmates without disabilities, but this has changed over the last decade (Bauer & Brown, 2005). General education teachers are generally receptive to passing students who made an effort and about half report using grading adaptations for students without disabilities. Teachers recognize the need to consider adaptations for all students in inclusive classrooms, not just those who have a diagnosed disability.

When thoughtfully and systematically implemented, grading adaptations can increase students' access to the curriculum and avoid the perception of unfairness. Several key issues should be considered when selecting specific adaptations for a student, including "the purposes of grades, options for adapting grades, the relationship of grading adaptations to district grading policies, the impact of grading adaptations on transitions to school and work, . . . and the acceptability of grading adaptations to teachers and students" (Munk & Bursuck, 2004, 2). Teachers must also be aware that effective instructional and curricular interventions may diminish the need for grading adaptations. Students may be fairly evaluated using the same standards if they are taught in a way that meets their learning needs. When this is not practical, grading adaptations can help educators meet the challenge of making grades meaningful while acknowledging student effort and improvement, especially for at-risk learners.

Sources: Bauer, A., & Brown, G. M. (2005). *Assessing learning and evaluating progress*. Retrieved January 23, 2007 from http://www.ldonline.org/article/6016.

Munk, D. D., & Bursuck, W. D. (2004, May). Personalized grading plans: A systematic approach to making the grades of included students more accurate and meaningful. *Focus on Exceptional Children, 36*(9), 1–11.

- Students need not cheat or butter up the teacher.
- Students know what the teacher expects of them and work toward a goal.
- The teacher can increase a student's achievement or aspiration level.
- The teacher can carefully examine the student's relative abilities and disabilities.
- The teacher does not have to compare students' work.

Table 8.6 Alternative approaches to evaluation.

APPROACH	EXAMPLE
1. *Traditional grading:* Letter grades or percentages are assigned.	Students earning 94% or greater of the total points available will earn an A.
2. *Pass/fail system:* Broad-based criteria are established for passing or failing.	Students who complete all assignments and pass all tests will receive a passing grade for the course.
3. *IEP grading:* Competency levels on student's IEP are translated into the school district's performance standards.	If a student's IEP requires a 90% accuracy level and the range of 86–93 equals a letter grade of B on the local scale, then the student receives a B if he or she attains target accuracy level.
4. *Mastery- or criterion-level grading:* Content is divided into subcomponents. Students earn credit when their mastery of a certain skill reaches an acceptable level.	Students who name 38 of the 50 state capitals will receive a passing grade on that unit of the social studies curriculum.
5. *Multiple grading:* The student is assessed and graded in several areas, such as ability, effort, and achievement.	Student will receive 30 points for completing the project on time, 35 points for including all of the assigned sections, and 35 points for using at least four different resources.
6. *Shared grading:* Two or more teachers determine a student's grade.	The regular education teacher will determine 60% of the student's grade, and the resource room teacher will determine 40%.
7. *Point system:* Points are assigned to activities or assignments that add up to the term grade.	The student's science grade will be based on a total of 300 points: 100 from weekly quizzes, 100 from lab work in class, 50 from homework, and 50 from class participation.
8. *Student self-comparison:* Students evaluate themselves on an individual basis.	If a student judges that he or she has completed the assignment on time, included the necessary sections, and worked independently, then the student assigns himself or herself a passing grade for this assignment.
9. *Contracting:* The student and teacher agree on specific activities required for a certain grade.	If the student comes to class regularly, volunteers information at least once during each class, and turns in all required work, then he or she will receive a C.
10. *Portfolio evaluation:* A cumulative portfolio is maintained of each student's work, demonstrating achievement in key skill areas from kindergarten to 12th grade.	Cumulative samples of the handwriting show progress from rudimentary manuscript to legible cursive style from grades 1 to 4.
11. *Rubrics:* Establishing a point scale for students to use to evaluate their work.	Establishing clear boundaries for successful performance on a specific assessment task. The rubric may be designed for the task required of the student, and all student-required tasks are not necessarily the same.

Note: From *Reaching the Hard to Teach* by J. W. Wood, 2008, Richmond, VA: Judy Wood, Inc. Reprinted with permission.

However, the pass/fail system does have disadvantages (Vasa, 1981):

- The teacher may not provide corrective feedback in weak areas.
- The passing grade does not distinguish among students of differing abilities.
- Some students do less work when freed of traditional grade pressure.
- Students close to failing feel the same pressures they do with traditional grades.
- Teachers sometimes find minimum standards arbitrary and difficult to define.

IEP Grading. This approach bases grading on the student's attainment of the goals and objectives specified in the IEP. Because the IEP must specify target accuracy levels or minimally acceptable levels of competence for specific skills or knowledge, built-in criteria for grading exist. Teachers can determine grades by translating the competency levels on a student's IEP into the school district's performance standards. If, for example, the IEP requires 80% accuracy and 80 equals a letter grade of C on the local scale, then the student receives a C.

Mastery- or Criterion-Level Grading. This approach divides content into various subcomponents, with pre- and posttest measures required for each step. Students earn credit only after their proficiency or mastery of a certain skill reaches an acceptable level. One disadvantage of this approach is that students are rewarded or passed for minimum, rather than optimum, performance.

Multiple Grading. This approach rewards the student in several areas, such as ability, effort, and achievement. Another approach to multiple grading is to separate the process and product when grading students who are working diligently to master a concept or process, such as arithmetic computation, but cannot complete the work accurately (Gloeckler & Simpson, 1988). By assigning a separate grade for each of these "major messages," teachers can maintain school and district standards of grading while acknowledging individual student progress that may not result in their reaching mastery level for a particular skill or subject area.

Shared Grading. Here, two or more teachers determine a grade—for example, when a student in a regular classroom receives assistance from the resource room teacher.

Point System. In this approach, teachers assign points to activities or assignments that add up to the term grade. Because teachers can give equal weights to activities other than tests, they are able to individualize their instruction and evaluation much more easily than with traditional grading systems.

Student Self-Comparison. Here, students evaluate themselves on a strictly individual basis on whether they have met the goals and objectives of their instructional program. Many students with disabilities and those at risk have a history of academic failure. This often results in low self-esteem and an inability to recognize their own strengths and achievements. For this reason, it is helpful to give all students opportunities to evaluate their own work, enabling them to recognize their individual progress as well as target areas for improvement. Self-evaluation can help students notice error patterns that they can later strive to avoid, a valuable skill to acquire before leaving school for the workplace. In addition, the technique can free the teacher's time for planning and instruction.

Self-comparison can be used with even the youngest students. Kindergarten and primary-level students can be asked to compare three or four of their own projects or papers done during the school week and then tell which one they like best and why. In lieu of letter grades, upper elementary students can be asked to apply one of several descriptive statements to their work (such as "terrific," "good try," and "oops!"). More in-depth evaluations can be used with middle- and secondary-level students, changing the criteria to match the type of assignment.

If a decision is made to let students evaluate their own work, the teacher must be prepared to accept the students' judgments, even if they do not correspond with the teacher's own evaluation of their work. Most often, if a discrepancy exists, it will be in the direction of students' underestimating their own merits in comparison to the teacher's evaluation.

A number-line or Likert-scale approach can be used to let students compare their evaluation of an assignment to that of the teacher. After the teacher has evaluated the assignment on the graph, students are given a chance to mark their own evaluation on the same graph, or the judgments can be made independently and compared later. The final grade on the assignment is then derived from averaging the two scores.

Contracting. In this approach, the student and teacher agree on specified activities or assignments required for a certain grade. Contracts allow teachers to individualize both grading requirements and assignments.

Contracting is a special education technique that has been successfully adopted by many regular educators. A contract is a written agreement between student and teacher about the quantity, quality, and time lines required to earn a specific grade (Hess, Miller, Reese, & Robinson 1987). A good contract also includes statements about the types of work to be completed and about how the student's grade will be determined. Often, a contract is a direct extension of the IEP, reflecting the performance outcomes for the specific objectives written in the IEP.

One distinct advantage of contracting is that a well-written contract leaves little question about what is expected of the student to earn a passing grade. Another advantage of contracting is that it helps students prepare for the expectations of the workplace: If they perform specified job tasks, meeting a certain standard within a given amount of time, they will receive a reward in the form of wages. A disadvantage is that, if the contract is not carefully written, the quality of students' work can be overshadowed by the quantity.

Portfolio Evaluation. This alternative to traditional grading is now used in many statewide testing programs. Cumulative samples of students' work based on specific educational program goals are gathered periodically. At the end of each school year, approximately four pieces of the student's work representing key skills are selected for inclusion in the student's portfolio. The teacher and the student decide which pieces they will put into the portfolio. The remaining pieces could be compiled in booklet form and given to the student's parents as a permanent record. For each key subject area, the portfolio provides evidence of a student's growth and achievement. For example, for the skill area of writing, a student's portfolio might include samples of descriptive, persuasive, and expository writing developed over the course of several years. Because portfolio evaluation compares students' current work with their work in previous years, it eliminates the need to use letter grades in comparing students with others. This makes portfolio evaluation especially useful for those students who have unique talents or strengths in particular skill areas, yet do not perform well on graded tasks (D. Wilkin, personal communication, December 17, 1990).

Rubrics. A rubric is a popular evaluating measure that is designed on a point system. For each task to be performed, clear boundaries are established. The rubric for one student may be different from the rubric for another student. For example, if a student is asked to respond to a question, provide information from the material, share his or her experience and prior knowledge, and expand on the concept, four points would be given for a complete answer. The following would be used as a rubric evaluation:

1. Student is barely able to answer the question. (1 point)
2. Student is able to formulate a complete answer and provide information from the material, but has difficulty explaining his or her related experience and prior knowledge and is unable to expand on the concept. (2 points)
3. Student is able to formulate a complete answer, provide information from the material, and explain his or her related experience and prior knowledge, but is unable to expand on the concept. (3 points)
4. Student is able to formulate a complete answer, provide information from the material, explain his or her related experience and prior knowledge, and expand on the concept. (4 points)

Marking or Grading Tests

Teachers may use the following suggestions when marking or grading tests for students with disabilities or those at risk:

1. When students make low grades, let them tell you why. Give extra points if they can tell you where they need to improve.
2. Give extra points on tests when students include information that you taught but did not cover in test questions.
3. Be careful about letting students check one another's papers. This procedure can prove to be embarrassing.
4. Let students keep a graph of their grades.
5. Return all graded papers folded to respect privacy.
6. Place the grade on the second page of the test or at the bottom of the front page.
7. Write "see me" instead of a grade on papers with low marks.
8. Allow students to turn in projects early for teacher review before the due date. This practice encourages students to complete work early and provides the reward of teacher feedback before final grading.
9. If the grade on a project is low, allow the student to redo it for a higher grade.
10. If the test is a short quiz, let the student retake it for a higher grade. Students who receive a low grade will learn that they still need to learn the material.
11. If students can justify an answer on a test, give full or partial credit.
12. If a test question is worth 3 points and a student misses 1 point, write the score as 2 instead of –1.

Providing Feedback to Students and Parents

Regardless of the criteria or procedure selected for awarding grades, the final step in grading any student's work should be to provide feedback to the student and parents. Many teachers are required to report student progress using traditional report card formats. Report cards are concerned with general expectations for the whole class. For this reason, some schools may recommend or require that a notation be made to indicate those grades for which the program content has been adjusted to meet an individual student's ability. Teachers may choose to supplement report cards with narrative reports or checklists that more accurately reveal information about the student's progress and current status, such as skills that the student has or has not mastered; the student's ability to work with others; the student's readiness for future units of instruction; and the success of adaptations that have been made in format, content, or classroom environment. This practice may be more widespread at the elementary level, where most report cards continue to be handwritten, as opposed to the middle and high school levels, where students usually receive computer-generated report statements that do not provide space for teacher narratives.

An example of a parent feedback sheet is shown in Figure 8.8. The student is given a report card at the end of each grading period with traditional grading (A, B, C, D). The sheet in Figure 8.8 is sent with the report card so that the parent knows the exact skills (according to the standards) the child has mastered, progressed toward mastering, or not mastered at grade level. This method aligns the traditional report card to the standards.

A narrative letter is another helpful means of sharing child-specific information with parents. This format enables teachers to communicate more of the qualitative aspects of a student's work than report cards or checklists can do. Used more widely in early childhood and elementary programs, narrative letters can include a description of a student's learning style and pattern of interaction with others as well as lists of books read, projects completed, or materials used. The letter may also include descriptions of specific incidents that reflect an individual student's progress (Spodek, Saracho, & Lee, 1984).

In addition to report card grades or other standard reporting formats, students should receive feedback about their classroom behavior, participation, and study habits. If the only type of feedback given to students is a quantitative reporting of a score or a letter grade, they may not be able to realize the error patterns in their work or generalize a successful approach to a problem from one situation to another. Without understanding what their grade means in terms of the way they approached a problem or assignment, the students may continue to repeat the same erroneous pattern of problem solving in future work. Another disadvantage of presenting only scores or letter grades without constructive or supportive feedback is that it trains students to focus only on the end result of an assignment—the grade—rather than on the learning process.

An issue regarding report cards in many areas is whether to indicate by the grade whether the student received interventions during the instruction. This issue runs the continuum across the country. This author believes that interventions are a natural part of curriculum and instruction, and an indication that an intervention was made is not necessary. Interventions are a natural process. Using outlines for the total class is good practice. Giving a student who cannot use the dictionary the definitions of words is okay. Remember, we must decide what we want students to learn and take the path of least resistance for teaching. If the grade given is on work that is not at grade level, however, this must be indicated to parents and future teachers.

A final consideration for educators when reporting grades is the meaning that grades take on when they are entered in a student's permanent record. Teachers in subsequent years use grades as an indication of a student's ability levels. For this reason, if grades are based on individual ability, a note to this effect should be made on the student's permanent record so that teachers will not hold unrealistic expectations for students. Six other grading alternatives appear in Figure 8.9.

Figure 8.8 Parent report card feedback sheet.

Student's Name **Grade**

Reading/Language Arts Skills

	1	2	3	4
Vowels				
Consonants				
Digraphs/Blends				
Contractions				
ABC Order				
Phonemic Awareness				
Nouns				
Verbs				
Sight Words				
Synonyms				
Antonyms				
Syn./Ant. Combination				
Prefixes & Root Words				
Suffixes & Root Words				
Story Elements				
Plurals				
Analogies				
Guide Words				
Sequence Pictures/Sentences				
Cause and Effect				
Main Idea				
Predict Outcomes				
Identify Details				
Compare/Contrast				
Classify Pictures/Words				
Fact/Opinion				
Literal Meaning				
Context Clues				
Charts & Graphs Interpretation				
Charts & Graphs Creation				
Parts of a Book				
Dictionary Skill Usage				
Reference Books				
Real Life Applications				

Evaluation Key
M=Mastery Indicates success in learning all skills which are appropriate at this time.
P=Progress Indicates success in learning most skills which are appropriate at this time.
N=Non-Mastery Indicates no success in learning skills which are appropriate at this time.
Asterisk (*) Indicates skill instruction above grade level.
Minus Sign (−) Indicates skill instruction below grade level.
Check mark (✓) Indicates skill instruction is on-going.

Math Skills

	1	2	3	4
Addition				
Subtraction				
Multiplication				
Division				

Math Skills

Perform/Apply Word Problems

	1	2	3	4
Addition				
Subtraction				
Multiplication				
Division				
Patterns/Algebraic Thinking				
Geometric Concepts				

Measurement/Standard & Non/Standard

	1	2	3	4
Measurement				
Time				
Money				
Conversions				
Temperature				
Calendar				
Data Analysis/Prediction				
Graphs				
Estimation				

Number Sense/Exptain & Explore

	1	2	3	4
Fractions				
Place Value				
<>=				
Number Sense Recognition				
Rounding				
Skip Counting				
Roman Numerals				
Ordinal Positions/Numbers				
Number Line				
Ratio				

Note: From Raymond Elementary School, Raymond, Mississippi.

Figure 8.9 You don't have to give an F if you don't want to: Alternative grading techniques.

Traditional grading poses significant problems when working with learning-disabled students:

- A low grade reinforces failure.
- Grades do not describe strengths and weaknesses.
- Grades do not reflect each student's level of functioning.

Many of these problems may be eliminated by adapting variations of traditional grading and evaluation procedures. The following alternatives suggest a variety of ways that the grading problem may be addressed.

1. Grade by achievement level
   - The student is graded as above average or below average on each level of functioning.
   - A variation may include student self-grading on a daily basis.
2. Grade by progress (the level of performance is not as important as the rate of learning)
   - Grading is based on how much learning has occurred during a given time.
3. Multiple grades (measures achievement, ability, and attitude)
   - A grade of C would mean the student has average achievement, has progressed further than expected for his or her ability, and has a good attitude with high interest.
4. Alternative grades
   - The pass/fail and satisfactory/unsatisfactory system may be useful.
   - The teacher may allow for one free grade to be substituted for any one grade during the quarter or semester.
5. Extra credit
   - Allow special projects or assignments for extra credit to improve the grade. For example, if the student makes a poor grade on a test, he or she may be allowed to do a project on the same course content for credit to supplement the test score.
6. Task mastery grading
   - The student must attain a certain level of mastery to receive a grade.
   - A contract may be set between the student and teacher before beginning the course of work.

Note: From *Reaching the Hard to Teach* by J. W. Wood, 2008, Richmond, VA: Judy Wood, Inc. Reprinted with permission.

SUMMARY

Issues surrounding assessment, evaluation, and grading are emotionally charged and continue to be issues of concern for all students. With the emphasis on national and state standards and high-stakes testing, educators are increasingly becoming concerned with curricula, instruction, and test scores. This chapter provided an overview of standards, high-stakes testing, testing types, numerous ways to embed classroom assessment, grading students, and grading and assessment.

RESOURCES

Office of Educational Research and Improvement (OERI)
U.S. Department of Education
555 New Jersey Avenue NW
Washington, DC 20208-5500
Fax: 202-219-2135

National Center on Education Outcomes University of Minnesota
350 Elliot Hall
75 East River Road
Minneapolis, MN 55455
Telephone: 612-626-1530
Fax: 612-624-0879
Web: http://education.umn.edu/nceo

National Center for Research on Evaluation, Standards, and Student Testing
CRESST UCLA
GSE & IS Building Box 951522
300 Charles E. Young Drive, N
Los Angeles, CA 90095-1522
Telephone: 310-794-9148
Fax: 310-825-3883
Web: www.cse.ucla.edu

SUGGESTED READINGS

Arllen, N. L., Cable, R. A., & Hendrickson, J. M. (1996). Accommodating students with special needs in general education classrooms. *Preventing School Failure, 41*(1), 7–13.

ASCD Infobrief, November, 2004. *What does NCLB mean to teachers?* http://www.ascd.org/cms/index.cfm?TheViewID=372

National Education Association. *Balanced assessment: The key to accountability and improved student learning* (23 pages). www.nea.org/accountability/images/balanced.pdf.

Elliot, J., & Roeber, E. (1996). *Assessment accommodations for students with disabilities.* (Videotape recording). Alexandria, VA: National Association of State Directors of Special Education.

WEBSITES

Education Trust. Discussion of ESA (Elementary and Secondary Education Act). *www2.edtrust.org/edtrust/ESEA.*

Education Commission of the States (ECS). This page provides links to other relevant resources related to NCLB, both inside ECS and from other external sources. *nclb2.ecs.org.*

National Center on Education Outcomes: Standards and High Stakes State Tests. *www.education.umn.edu/NCEO.*

REFERENCES

1997 state special education outcomes. (1997). Minneapolis: University of Minnesota, National Center on Educational Outcomes.

Danielson, C., & Abrutyn, L. (1997). *An introduction to using portfolios in the classroom.* Alexandria, VA: Association for Supervision and Curriculum Development.

Gloeckler, T., & Simpson, C. (1988). *Exceptional students in regular classrooms.* Mountain View, CA: Mayfield.

Hess, R., Miller, A., Reese, J., & Robinson, G. A. (1987). *Grading-credit-diploma: Accommodation practices for students with mild disabilities.* Des Moines: Iowa State Department of Education, Bureau of Special Education.

Jacobs, H. H. (1997). *Mapping the big picture: Integrating, curriculum and assessment K–12.* Alexandria, VA: Association for Supervision and Curriculum Development.

Jacobsen, D., Eggen, D., & Kauchak, D. (1989). *Methods for teaching.* Upper Saddle River, NJ: Merrill/Prentice Hall.

Jayanthi, M., Epstein, M. M., Polloway, E. A., & Bursuck, W. D. (1996). A national survey of general education teachers' perceptions of testing adaptations. *Journal of Special Education, 30*(1), 99–115.

Lazear, D. (1998). *The Rubrics way.* Tucson, AZ: Zephyr Press.

Lazzari, A. M., & Wood, J. W. (1994). *125 ways to be a better test taker.* East Moline, IL: LinguiSystems.

Marzano, R. J. (2000). *Transforming classroom grading.* Alexandria, VA: Association for Supervision and Curriculum Development.

Nelson, J. S., Jayanthi, J., Epstein, M. H., & Bursuck, W. D. (2000). Student preferences for adaptations in classroom testing. *Remedial and Special Education, 21*(1), 41–52.

Spodek, B., Saracho, O. N., & Lee, R. C. (1984). *Mainstreaming young children.* Belmont, CA: Wadsworth.

Thurlow, M. L., Elliott, J. L., & Ysseldyke, J. E. (2003). *Testing students with disabilities: Practical strategies for complying with district and state requirements.* Thousand Oaks, CA: Corwin.

Turnbull, R., Turnbull, A., Shank, M., & Smith, S. J. (2004). *Exceptional lives: Special education in today's schools.* Upper Saddle River, NJ: Merrill/Prentice Hall.

Vasa, S. F. (1981). Alternative procedures for grading handicapped students in the secondary schools. *Education Unlimited, 3*(1), 16–23.

Wilson, L. W. (2002). *Better instruction through assessment: What your students are trying to tell you.* Larchmont, NY: Eye on Education.

APPENDIX A INTERVENTION/TRANSITION CHECKLIST

Reaching the Hard to Teach

INTERVENTION CHECKLIST FOR
CONTENT AREA CLASSROOM

Name of Classroom/Teacher ______ Person Completing Checklist ______ Date ______

Socio-Emotional and Behavioral Environment

Please evaluate the characteristics of the classroom setting by using the following rating system:

R (required **R**arely) **S** (required **S**ome of the time) **M** (required **M**ost of the time)

Note: If a characteristic is not applicable, leave it blank. It is not necessary to use all parts of the intervention checklist for content area classroom. Use only what is pertinent to the classroom being evaluated.

Socio-Emotional and Behavioral Environment

Peer-to-Peer Social Skills	R	S	M
making new friends	o	o	o
showing respect for others	o	o	o
respecting cultural differences	o	o	o
helping others	o	o	o
expressing appreciation	o	o	o
sharing and taking turns	o	o	o
reading social environments	o	o	o
joining in	o	o	o
disagreeing in appropriate manner	o	o	o
apologizing	o	o	o
refusing to engage in gossip and rumor	o	o	o
Communication			
interpreting facial cues and body language	o	o	o
making eye contact	o	o	o
adjusting language to situational demands	o	o	o
using greetings and farewells	o	o	o
interrupting appropriately in urgent situations	o	o	o
expressing needs and wants	o	o	o
initiating conversations	o	o	o
maintaining conversations	o	o	o
joining ongoing conversations	o	o	o
ending conversations	o	o	o
talking on the telephone	o	o	o
School-Related Social Skills			
understanding student/teacher roles	o	o	o
respecting others' space	o	o	o
ignoring distractions	o	o	o
listening	o	o	o
following directions	o	o	o
requesting permission	o	o	o
requesting assistance	o	o	o
requesting clarification	o	o	o
participating in class	o	o	o
solving problems	o	o	o
accepting responsibility	o	o	o
transitioning	o	o	o
using free time wisely	o	o	o
working cooperatively in a group	o	o	o
Self-control			
adapting to changes	o	o	o
controlling anger	o	o	o
accepting disappointments	o	o	o
accepting criticism	o	o	o
accepting praise	o	o	o
coping with rejection	o	o	o
responding to threats	o	o	o
coping with embarrassment	o	o	o
asking for time-out	o	o	o
Rules and Behavior Management			
understanding rules	o	o	o
following rules	o	o	o
adhering to unstated rules	o	o	o
accepting consequences for noncompliance	o	o	o
Dress			
complying with dress code	o	o	o
presenting neat appearance	o	o	o

Physical Environment and Related Environments

R (required **R**arely) **S** (required **S**ome of the time) **M** (required **M**ost of the time)

Physical Environment

Instructional Grouping	R	S	M
working in large group activity	o	o	o
working in small group activity	o	o	o
working alone	o	o	o
working in varied grouping	o	o	o
Seating Arrangement			
working with traditional seating	o	o	o
working with circular or horseshoe seating	o	o	o
working with cubicle/carrel seating	o	o	o
working with varied seating arrangements	o	o	o
Chalkboard Use			
working from chalkboard	o	o	o
copying from chalkboard	o	o	o
Learning Center Use			
working in learning center	o	o	o
Bulletin Board Use			
working with bulletin boards	o	o	o
Sound			
working silently	o	o	o
working with minor distractions (some interaction)	o	o	o
working with many distractions (open interaction)	o	o	o
working with varied sound levels	o	o	o
Attendance			
attending daily	o	o	o
arriving on time	o	o	o
making it through the whole day	o	o	o

Related Environments

Transportation	R	S	M
walking or riding with parent/hired driver	o	o	o
riding bus	o	o	o
using assisted transportation	o	o	o
Cafeteria			
entering cafeteria unsupervised	o	o	o
following lunch ticket purchasing and use procedure	o	o	o
following lunch line procedure	o	o	o
following cafeteria rules/routine	o	o	o
finding assigned seat	o	o	o
choosing own seat	o	o	o
returning tray after eating	o	o	o
using snack machines	o	o	o
participating in after-lunch activity	o	o	o
Physical Education			
wearing uniform	o	o	o
bringing clean uniform weekly	o	o	o
changing within time limit	o	o	o
using P.E. locker combination lock	o	o	o
showering	o	o	o
following locker room rules	o	o	o
following class rules and procedures	o	o	o
understanding game rules given orally	o	o	o
notetaking	o	o	o
participating in large group activities	o	o	o
participating in small group activities	o	o	o
exhibiting sportsmanship	o	o	o
exhibiting team playing skills	o	o	o
Assemblies/School Programs			
following irregular daily schedule	o	o	o
finding assigned seat	o	o	o
choosing own seat	o	o	o
sitting quietly during program	o	o	o
Between Classes			
lockers			
finding assigned locker	o	o	o
using combination lock	o	o	o
following locker area rules	o	o	o
using locker within time limit	o	o	o
halls			
moving from class to class using written schedule	o	o	o
moving from class to class using memorized schedule	o	o	o

Related Environments

R (required **R**arely) **S** (required **S**ome of the time) **M** (required **M**ost of the time)

	R S M
following rules for hall conduct	o o o
following pay phone rules	o o o
following drinking fountain rules	o o o
getting along with other children in halls	o o o
finding correct classroom	o o o
changing buildings	o o o
staying in specified halls	o o o
getting to class on time	o o o
Restrooms	
following restroom procedures	o o o
using restroom independently	o o o
Library	
following check-out and return procedures	o o o
finding materials	o o o
working quietly	o o o
using "browsing time"	o o o
completing teacher/librarian planned activities	o o o
appreciating literature/information	o o o
Offices/Clinic	
requesting permission to go to office/clinic	o o o
going and returning promptly	o o o
understanding services provided	o o o
interacting with secretarial staff	o o o
Fire/Tornado Drills	
following drill rules/procedures	o o o
completing drill with minimal supervision	o o o
Substitute Teacher/Instructional Assistant	
understanding procedures with substitute teacher	o o o
working with substitute teacher	o o o
working with instructional assistant	o o o
Field Trips	
following rules/procedures for field trip	o o o
adapting to change in routine	o o o
behaving appropriately (bus, guides, museum, etc.)	o o o
Computer Labs	
following lab rules/procedures	o o o
completing guided activities	o o o
completing independent activities	o o o
Music/Art	
moving to class independently	o o o
following rules/procedures	o o o

	R S M
grading system used	o o o
letter/numerical grades	o o o
pass-fail	o o o
using equipment/materials	o o o
Before and After School	
behaving unsupervised outside on school grounds	o o o
behaving unsupervised inside school buildings	o o o
following procedures (passes, etc.) to enter building	o o o
staying in assigned/designated areas	o o o
In-School Suspension	
conforming to "no talking" rule	o o o
bringing class materials for each subject	o o o
reporting directly to in-school suspension room	o o o
following in-school suspension rules	o o o
completing work assigned for in-school suspension	o o o
Other Services	
tutoring program available	o o o
honors/advanced placement program available	o o o
gifted and talented program available	o o o
Title 1 program	o o o
speech and language	o o o
occupational therapy	o o o
physical therapy	o o o
orientation and mobility	o o o

AREAS SPECIFIC TO ELEMENTARY

	R S M
Before and After School Placement	
on-campus large group care provided	o o o
on-campus small group care provided	o o o
adjusting to different adults rotating among groups	o o o
Snack Break	
bringing own snacks	o o o
eating school-provided snacks (unrestricted diet)	o o o
Playground	
participating in large group play	o o o
participating in small group play	o o o
playing alone	o o o

Related Environments and Lesson-Related Environments and Lesson Plans

R (required **R**arely) **S** (required **S**ome of the time) **M** (required **M**ost of the time)

equipment
- using slide o o o
- using play escape o o o
- using monkey bars o o o
- using balance beams o o o
- using fire truck o o o
- using swings o o o
- using jumping stumps o o o

behavioral expectations
- lining up o o o
- independently playing on equipment o o o
- interacting with classmates o o o
- requesting assistance o o o
- answering questions o o o
- relating thoughts completely and sequentially o o o
- taking turns o o o
- participating in and understanding recess o o o

AREAS SPECIFIC TO SECONDARY

Study Hall
- bringing study materials and supplies o o o
- following "no talking" rule o o o
- working independently o o o
- getting passes to go to other permitted activities o o o

Extracurricular Activities
- participating in athletics o o o
- participating in band/orchestra o o o
- participating in choir o o o
- participating in pep squad o o o
- participating in dance team o o o
- participating in cheerleading o o o
- participating in academic competitions o o o
- participating in clubs o o o
- participating in drama productions o o o

Tutoring
- tutoring provided by adults o o o
- tutoring provided by peers o o o

Vocational/Technical Education
- vocational/technical education classes provided o o o

Lesson Plans

Lesson Objective(s) R S M
- understanding lesson objectives o o o

Strategies/Procedures For Lesson Cycle
- introduction o o o
- development o o o
- acquisition of new information o o o
- retention of information o o o
- transfer of information o o o
- summary o o o

Materials/Resources
- using materials/resources o o o

Evaluation
- evaluation activities o o o

Techniques

Class Structure
- structured class o o o
- student self-structure required o o o

Instructional Variables
- lecture o o o
- note taking o o o
- explanation o o o
- audio-visual presentation o o o
- discussion o o o
- asking questions o o o
- independent study o o o
- experiments o o o
- constructing o o o
- small group work o o o
- varied teaching techniques o o o

Perceptual Styles
- visually oriented instruction/work o o o
- auditorily oriented instruction/work o o o
- kinesthetically oriented instruction/work o o o

Written Expression
- completing written expression activities o o o

Collaborative Learning
- learning from collaborative activities o o o

Format of Content, Media, and Evaluation

R (required **R**arely) **S** (required **S**ome of the time) **M** (required **M**ost of the time)

Format of Content

Directions	R	S	M
oral directions	○	○	○
written directions	○	○	○
Vocabulary Study			
understanding/learning vocabulary	○	○	○
Homework			
homework listed on chalkboard	○	○	○
homework shown on overhead projector	○	○	○
homework listed on calendar/checklist	○	○	○
homework assigned orally	○	○	○
homework filed in notebook	○	○	○
independent work required	○	○	○
homework turned in	○	○	○
Notebooks			
required notebook	○	○	○
maintaining notebook independently	○	○	○
maintaining notebook with guidance and support	○	○	○
Study Guides			
acquisition outlines provided	○	○	○
summative (test) study guide provided	○	○	○
Adaptations of Assignments			
no modifications made	○	○	○
some modifications made	○	○	○
extensive modification made	○	○	○
peer tutors used	○	○	○
resource teacher used	○	○	○
Class Procedure			
oral presentations:			
reading aloud	○	○	○
presenting projects/reports orally	○	○	○
participating in panel discussions	○	○	○
completing labs:			
following safety procedures	○	○	○
performing multi-step process	○	○	○
assembling and storing equipment	○	○	○
completing lab individually	○	○	○
completing lab with partner	○	○	○
completing lab with small group	○	○	○
Academic Transition			
making transitions without guidance	○	○	○
making transitions with guidance	○	○	○

Media

Media Used:	R	S	M
overhead projector	○	○	○
audio-visual:			
films	○	○	○
VCR/DVD	○	○	○
television	○	○	○
filmstrip projector	○	○	○
slide projector	○	○	○
computer	○	○	○
tape recorder	○	○	○
Materials			
textbook	○	○	○
handouts/worksheets	○	○	○

Student Evaluation

Test Format:	R	S	M
true-false	○	○	○
small lists of matching	○	○	○
long lists of matching	○	○	○
fill-in-the-blank with word bank	○	○	○
fill-in-the-black without word bank	○	○	○
multiple choice	○	○	○
essay	○	○	○
open book	○	○	○
typed test	○	○	○
handwritten test	○	○	○
modified test	○	○	○
Test Administration			
study guide provided prior to test			
timed tests	○	○	○
oral tests	○	○	○
tests are copied from			
text/handout	○	○	○
chalkboard	○	○	○
overhead projector	○	○	○
modified test administration	○	○	○
retesting for minimum mastery	○	○	○
Projects			
completing projects	○	○	○
Standardized Tests			
taking standardized tests	○	○	○

Evaluation and Grading

R (required **R**arely) **S** (required **S**ome of the time) **M** (required **M**ost of the time)

	R S M
Curriculum-Based Assessment	R S M
exhibiting minimum mastery on CBA	o o o
Portfolio	
completing portfolio	o o o
Grading	
Grading System(s) Used:	
letter/numerical grades	o o o
checklist	o o o
contract	o o o
point system	o o o
pass-fail	o o o
portfolio	o o o
varied grading systems used	o o o

Note: Checklist from *Reaching the Hard to Teach* by J. W. Wood, 2008, Richmond, VA: Judy Wood, Inc. Reprinted with permission.

Reaching the Hard to Teach

INTERVENTION CHECKLIST FOR
STUDENT

Student ________ Person Completing Checklist ________ Date ________

Socio-Emotional and Behavioral Environment

Please evaluate the characteristics of the classroom setting by using the following rating system:

R (demonstrates **R**arely) **S** (demonstrates **S**ome of the time) **M** (demonstrates **M**ost of the time)

Note: If a characteristic is not applicable, leave it blank. It is not necessary to use all parts of the intervention checklist for content area classroom. Use only what is pertinent to the classroom being evaluated.

Socio-Emotional and Behavioral Environment

Peer-to-Peer Social Skills	R	S	M
makes new friends	○	○	○
shows respect for others	○	○	○
respects cultural differences	○	○	○
helps others	○	○	○
expresses appreciation	○	○	○
shares and takes turns	○	○	○
reads social environments	○	○	○
joins in	○	○	○
disagrees in appropriate manner	○	○	○
apologizes	○	○	○
refuses to engage in gossip and rumor	○	○	○
Communication			
interprets facial cues and body language	○	○	○
makes eye contact	○	○	○
adjusts language to situational demands	○	○	○
uses greeting and farewells	○	○	○
interrupts appropriately in urgent situations	○	○	○
expresses needs and wants	○	○	○
initates conversations	○	○	○
maintains conversations	○	○	○
joins ongoing conversations	○	○	○
ends conversations	○	○	○
talks on the telephone	○	○	○
School-Related Social Skills			
understands student/teacher: roles	○	○	○
respects others space	○	○	○
ignores distractions	○	○	○
listens	○	○	○
follows directions	○	○	○
requests permission	○	○	○
requests assistance	○	○	○
requests clarification	○	○	○

	R	S	M
participates in class	○	○	○
solves problems	○	○	○
accepts responsibility	○	○	○
transitions	○	○	○
uses free time wisely	○	○	○
works cooperatively in a group	○	○	○
Self-control			
adapts to changes	○	○	○
controls anger	○	○	○
accepts disappointments	○	○	○
accepts criticism	○	○	○
accepts praise	○	○	○
copes with rejection	○	○	○
responds appropriately to threats	○	○	○
copes with embarrassment	○	○	○
asks for time-out	○	○	○
Rules and Behavior Management			
understands rules	○	○	○
follows rules	○	○	○
adheres to unstated rules	○	○	○
accepts consequences for noncompliance	○	○	○
Dress			
complies with dress code	○	○	○
presents neat appearance	○	○	○

Physical Environment and Related Environments

R (demonstrates **R**arely) **S** (demonstrates **S**ome of the time) **M** (demonstrates **M**ost of the time)

Physical Environment

Instructional Grouping	R S M
works in large group activity	o o o
works in small group activity	o o o
works alone	o o o
works in varied grouping	o o o
Seating Arrangement	
works well in traditional seating	o o o
works well in circular or horseshoe seating	o o o
works well in cubicle/carrel seating	o o o
works with varied seating arrangements	o o o
Chalkboard Use	
works well from chalkboard	o o o
copies well from chalkboard	o o o
Learning Center Use	
works well in learning center	o o o
Bulletin Board Use	
works well with bulletin boards	o o o
Sound	
works silently	o o o
works with minor distractions (some interaction)	o o o
works with many distractions (open interaction)	o o o
works with varied sound levels	o o o
Attendance	
attends daily	o o o
arrives on time	o o o
makes it through the whole day	o o o

Related Environments

Transportation	R S M
walks or rides with parent/hired driver	o o o
rides bus	o o o
uses assisted transportation	o o o
Cafeteria	
enters cafeteria unsupervised	o o o
purchases and uses lunch ticket	o o o
follows lunch line procedure	o o o
follows cafeteria rules/routine	o o o
finds assigned seat	o o o
chooses own seat	o o o
returns tray after eating	o o o
uses snack machines	o o o
participates in after-lunch activity	o o o
Physical Education	
wears uniform	o o o
brings clean uniform weekly	o o o
changes within time limit	o o o
uses P.E. locker combination lock	o o o
showers	o o o
follows locker room rules	o o o
follows class rules and procedures	o o o
understands game rules given orally	o o o
takes adequate notes	o o o
participates in large group activities	o o o
participates in small group activities	o o o
exhibits sportsmanship	o o o
exhibits team playing skills	o o o
Assemblies/School Programs	
follows irregular daily schedule	o o o
finds assigned seat	o o o
independently chooses own seat	o o o
sits quietly during program	o o o
Between Classes	
lockers	
finds assigned locker	o o o
independently uses combination lock	o o o
follows locker area rules	o o o
uses locker within time limit	o o o
halls	
moves from class to class using written schedule	o o o
moves from class to class using memorized schedule	o o o

Related Environments

R (demonstrates **R**arely) **S** (demonstrates **S**ome of the time) **M** (demonstrates **M**ost of the time)

	R S M
follows rules for hall conduct	o o o
follows pay phone rules	o o o
follows drinking fountain rules	o o o
gets along with other children in halls	o o o
finds correct classroom	o o o
independently changes buildings	o o o
stays in specified halls	o o o
gets to class on time	o o o

Restrooms

follows restroom procedures	o o o
uses restroom independently	o o o

Library

follows check-out and return procedures	o o o
finds materials	o o o
works quietly	o o o
uses "browsing time"	o o o
completes teacher/librarian planned activities	o o o
appreciates literature/information	o o o

Offices/Clinic

requests permission to go to office/clinic	o o o
goes and returns promptly	o o o
understands services provided	o o o
interacts with secretarial staff	o o o

Fire/Tornado Drills

follows drill rules/procedures	o o o
completes drill with minimal supervision	o o o

Substitute Teacher/Instructional Assistant

understands procedures with substitute teacher	o o o
works well with substitute teacher	o o o
works well with instructional assistant	o o o

Field Trips

follows rules/procedures for field trip	o o o
adapts to change in routine	o o o
behaves appropriately (bus, guides, museum, etc)	o o o

Computer Labs

follows lab rules/procedures	o o o
completes guided activities	o o o
completes independent activities	o o o

Music/Art

moves to class independently	o o o
follows rules/procedures	o o o

	R S M
successful under the following grading system(s):	
letter/numerical grades	o o o
pass-fail	o o o
uses equipment/materials	o o o

Before and After School

behaves unsupervised outside on school grounds	o o o
behaves unsupervised inside school buildings	o o o
follows procedures (passes, etc.) to enter buildings	o o o
stays in assigned/designated areas	o o o

In-School Suspension

conforms to "no talking" rule	o o o
brings class materials for each subject	o o o
reports directly to in-school suspension room	o o o
follows in-school suspension rules	o o o
completes work assigned for in-school suspension	o o o

Other Services

benefits from tutoring	o o o
qualifies for honors/advanced placement program	o o o
qualifies for gifted and talented program	o o o
qualifies for Title 1 program	o o o
qualifies for speech and language	o o o
qualifies for occupational therapy	o o o
qualifies for physical therapy	o o o
qualifies for orientation and mobility	o o o

AREAS SPECIFIC TO ELEMENTARY

Before and After School Placement

successful in on-campus large group care	o o o
successful in on-campus small group care	o o o
adjusts to different adults rotating among groups	o o o

Snack Break

brings own snacks	o o o
eats school-provided snacks (unrestricted diet)	o o o

Playground

participates in large group play	o o o
participates in small group play	o o o
plays alone	o o o

Related Environments and Lesson Plans

R (demonstrates **R**arely) **S** (demonstrates **S**ome of the time) **M** (demonstrates **M**ost of the time)

	R S M
equipment	
safely uses slide	o o o
safely uses play escape	o o o
safely uses monkey bars	o o o
safely uses balance beams	o o o
safely uses fire truck	o o o
safely uses swings	o o o
safely uses jumping stumps	o o o
behavioral expectations	
lines up	o o o
independently plays on equipment	o o o
interacts with classmates	o o o
requests assistance	o o o
answers questions	o o o
relates thoughts completely and sequentially	o o o
takes turns	o o o
participates in and understands recess	o o o

AREAS SPECIFIC TO SECONDARY

Study Hall

brings study materials and supplies	o o o
follows "no talking" rule	o o o
works independently	o o o
gets passes to go to other permitted activities	o o o

Extracurricular Activities

participates in athletics	o o o
participates in band/orchestra	o o o
participates in choir	o o o
participates in pep squad	o o o
participates in dance team	o o o
participates in cheerleading	o o o
participates in academic competitions	o o o
participates in clubs	o o o
participates in drama productions	o o o

Tutoring

benefits from adult tutoring	o o o
benefits from peer tutoring	o o o

Vocational/Technical Education

benefits from vocational/technical education classes	o o o

Lesson Plans

Lesson Objective(s)

	R S M
understands lesson objective(s)	o o o

Strategies/Procedures For Lesson Cycle

understands introduction	o o o
understands lesson development	o o o
acquisition of new information	o o o
retains information	o o o
transfers information	o o o
understands summary	o o o

Materials/Resources

uses materials/resources	o o o

Evaluation

performs satisfactorily on evaluation activities	o o o

Techniques

Class Structure

works well with structure	o o o
student imposes self-structure	o o o

Instructional Variables

retains materials from lectures	o o o
takes adequate notes	o o o
comprehends explanations	o o o
retains audio-visual presentations	o o o
participates in class discussion	o o o
responds adequately to questioning	o o o
studies independently	o o o
performs experiments	o o o
independently builds projects	o o o
works in small groups	o o o
adapts to varied teaching techniques	o o o

Perceptual Styles

learns and performs visually	o o o
learns and performs auditorily	o o o
learns and performs kinesthetically	o o o

Written Expression

completes written expression activities	o o o

Collaborative Learning

learns from collaborative activities	o o o

Format of Content, Media, and Evaluation

R (demonstrates **R**arely) **S** (demonstrates **S**ome of the time) **M** (demonstrates **M**ost of the time)

Format of Content

Directions	R	S	M
understands and follows oral directions	o	o	o
understands and follows written directions	o	o	o

Vocabulary Study

understands/learns vocabulary	o	o	o

Homework

copies accurately from chalkboard	o	o	o
copies accurately from overhead projector	o	o	o
follows calendar/checklist	o	o	o
understands and retains oral directions	o	o	o
accurately files homework in notebook	o	o	o
completes homework independently	o	o	o
locates and turns in homework	o	o	o

Notebooks

brings required notebook to class	o	o	o
independently maintains notebook	o	o	o
maintains notebook with guidance and support	o	o	o

Study Guides

acquires information with acquisition outline	o	o	o
benefits from summative (test) study guide	o	o	o

Adaptations of Assignments

proficient without modifications	o	o	o
requires some modifications	o	o	o
requires extensive modifications	o	o	o
benefits from peer tutor	o	o	o
requires assistance of resource teacher	o	o	o

Class Procedure

oral presentations:			
reads aloud	o	o	o
presents projects/reports orally	o	o	o
participates in panel discussions	o	o	o
completes labs:			
follows safety procedures	o	o	o
performs multi-step process	o	o	o
assembles and stores equipment	o	o	o
completes lab individually	o	o	o
completes lab with partner	o	o	o
completes lab with small group	o	o	o

Academic Transition

makes transitions without guidance	o	o	o
makes transitions with guidance	o	o	o

Media

Media Used:	R	S	M
overhead projector	o	o	o
audio-visual:			
films	o	o	o
VCR/DVD	o	o	o
television	o	o	o
filmstrip projector	o	o	o
slide projector	o	o	o
computer	o	o	o
tape recorder	o	o	o

Materials

reads textbook at grade level	o	o	o
understands and completes handouts/worksheets	o	o	o

Student Evaluation

Successful With Following Test Formats:

true-false	o	o	o
small lists of matching	o	o	o
long lists of matching	o	o	o
fill-in-the-blank with word bank	o	o	o
fill-in-the-blank without word bank	o	o	o
multiple choice	o	o	o
essay	o	o	o
open book	o	o	o
typed test	o	o	o
handwritten test	o	o	o
modified test	o	o	o

Test Administration

uses study guide provided prior to test	o	o	o
finishes tests within time limit	o	o	o
understands and completes oral tests	o	o	o
accurately copies tests from:			
text/handout	o	o	o
chalkboard	o	o	o
overhead projector	o	o	o
needs modified test administration	o	o	o
needs opportunity to retest for minimum mastery	o	o	o

Projects

completes projects	o	o	o

Standardized Tests

takes standardized tests	o	o	o

Evaluation and Grading

R (demonstrates **R**arely) **S** (demonstrates **S**ome of the time) **M** (demonstrates **M**ost of the time)

Curriculum-Based Assessment	R S M
exhibits minimum mastery on CBA	o o o
Portfolio	
completes portfolio	o o o
Grading	
Performs Satisfactorily Under These Grading Systems:	
letter/numerical grades	o o o
checklist	o o o
contract	o o o
point system	o o o
pass-fail	o o o
portfolio	o o o
adapts to varied grading systems	o o o

APPENDIX B STUDENT ACTIVITIES

CHAPTER 2

Using handout 2.1, consisting of the various roles people might have when teaching a student with a disability (parent, special education teacher, general education teacher, support personnel, paraeducator, and/or intervention team member), brainstorm various responsibilities each person might have in the collaborative process of educating a student with a disability.

CHAPTER 3

Have students work with a partner. Students should bring his or her own copy of a blank Intervention/Transition Checklist (Appendix A). Have one student compete the teacher version and the other student complete the student version. Both can complete the checklist based on their own characteristics or experiences in class. Students should then compare the lists to identify mismatches.

CHAPTER 4

Have students take about 2 minutes at the beginning of this chapter to visualize what their classroom will be like. Ask them to envision what students are doing. After visualizing all of these things, ask the students to write what they saw in a list format. Finally, ask student to compare this list to the description of a risk-free environment and write a brief paper.

CHAPTER 5

Have students bring to class 2 or 3 standards from the state curriculum framework. They may find these frameworks on most state departments of education websites. Ask students to choose a skill or concept from these standards and write an instructional objective to teach the skill or concept.

CHAPTER 6

Have students work with a partner to complete this activity. After studying the four teaching modes, have students choose a skill or concept they would like to teach. Have them develop lesson plans that include the four teaching modes. It's possible to teach in two or more modes in the same lesson. However, if they can't logically incorporate all four modes into one lesson plan, they need to develop enough lesson plans to teach to all four modes. The point of the activity is to illustrate to students that as we teach, we alternate between or among the four modes.

CHAPTER 7

Have students review worksheets that they find on line or in the teacher's manuals for textbooks. Have students correct the work sheets according to the guidelines for directions and worksheet construction.

CHAPTER 8

Have students research state-required assessments and alternate assessments for the state in which they reside or plan to teach. Students may share their findings in class or submit to the professor.

Handout 2.1 Various roles and responsibilities.

TEAM MEMBER/ROLE	RESPONSIBILITIES
Parent	
Special education teacher	
General education teacher	
Support personnel (may be more than one)	
Paraeducator	
Intervention team member	

Glossary

A

Acquisition Original learning; learning a new skill, idea, or concept.

Alternative Assessment A state test for students with selected disabilities. An alternative test to the regular state test. The test is established by each state.

B

Benchmarks Standards grouped by scope and sequence; what needs to be taught in each grade; and what within the grade level will be taught first, second, etc.

C

Classroom-Embedded Assessment Ongoing assessment completed by the classroom teacher. These include projects, observations, interviews, etc.

Cognitive Style "Each of us develops a typical approach in our use of our cognitive characteristics to perceive, to think, and to remember. This approach constitutes our cognitive learning style" (Fuhrman, 1980, p. 2).

Collaboration How people work together, not what they do.

Communication The verbal and nonverbal expressions a person makes. Also, the exchange of ideas, information, and suggestions.

Co-Teaching A model for integrating students with disabilities into general education classrooms. The special educator participates in instruction.

F

Figure-Ground Hearing an important word and selecting it from a background of other words.

Formative Study Guide Organizes information in short, distributive segments and focuses on specific details of information covered.

G

Generalization (or Transfer) Taking a learned skill, idea, or concept and using it in another location.

H

High Stakes State tests have high stakes for educators, students, and parents because they affect pass/fail rates, graduation rates, and funding.

I

Indicators Established to measure outcomes. They act as a stop sign to show when a student exhibits the indicated behavior or desired behavior.

Instruction A continuous process of presenting information, adapting information, representing information, and testing for concept mastery.

Interventions Trying what we have not tried.

Intervention/Transition Checklist A helpful and practical instrument for identifying where adaptations or interventions in the learning environment may be needed.

L

Learning Styles Students' individual approaches to learning.

M

Mismatch A point where the child cannot succeed because the teacher has expectations that are not compatible with the student's abilities.

P

Preplanned Interventions Interventions preplanned by the educator during lesson plan development.

R

Retention Remembering a skill, idea, or concept already learned.

Risk-Free Environment An environment in which students are not afraid to take chances; a safe place for students in which mistakes are seen as stepping-stones to success.

S

SAALE Model A systematic approach for adapting the learning environment for students at risk. A process for differentiating instruction and assessing for inclusion.

School Improvement Schools strive to improve all aspects of their systems.

Spontaneous Interventions Interventions implemented by an educator when a student's needs for alternative instruction become evident during instruction implementation.

Standards Broad concept established by states of what students should know.

Statewide Assessment State tests developed to determine whether students meet state requirements.

Summative Study Guide A guide designed to provide general information about notes to be quizzed, which lays the foundation for organizing the study effort.

T

Teaching Techniques Methods of imparting knowledge, skills, or concepts to learners; how teachers teach and what types of strategies they employ depend greatly on previous training, models observed, areas of interest, value judgments, and common sense.

INDEX

Note: Locators in italics indicate tables and figures.